Youth Work

Youth Work

Global Futures

Edited by

Graham Bright and Carole Pugh

BRILL

SENSE

LEIDEN | BOSTON

All chapters in this book have undergone peer review.

Library of Congress Cataloging-in-Publication Data

Names: Bright, Graham (Lecturer in Education), editor. | Pugh, Carole, 1976-
    editor.
Title: Youth work : global futures / edited by Graham Bright and Carole Pugh.
Description: Boston : Brill Sense, [2019] | Includes bibliographical
    references and index. |
Identifiers: LCCN 2019003773 (print) | LCCN 2019006507 (ebook) | ISBN
    9789004396555 (E-book) | ISBN 9789004396531 (pbk. : alk. paper) | ISBN
    9789004396548 (hbk : alk. paper)
Subjects: LCSH: Youth workers--Great Britain. | Youth workers. |
    Communities--Great Britain. | Communities.
Classification: LCC HV1441.G7 (ebook) | LCC HV1441.G7 Y66 2019 (print) | DDC
    362.7083--dc23
LC record available at https://lccn.loc.gov/2019003773

Typeface for the Latin, Greek, and Cyrillic scripts: "Brill". See and download: brill.com/brill-typeface.

ISBN 978-90-04-39653-1 (paperback)
ISBN 978-90-04-39654-8 (hardback)
ISBN 978-90-04-39655-5 (e-book)

Contents

Notes on Contributors

Michael Baizerman

has been active since 1972 co-developing and teaching in the undergraduate Youth Studies Program and graduate Youth Development Leadership Programs in School of Social Work, University of Minnesota, USA. Taught classes include the Everyday Lives of Youth, including courses on Hmong and on Somali young people, practical research with and about youth, youth policy, and youth worlds. He has a twenty year working relationship with youth civic engagement work in Northern Ireland and has published extensively on the topic, and has consulted on civic youth work and youth civic engagement also in Laos, South Korea and Nepal.

Janet Batsleer

works as a Principal Lecturer at Manchester Metropolitan University, where she is a Reader in Education and a specialist in the field of Youth and Community Work. She has written widely on feminist anti-oppressive approaches to a practice of youth work as informal education, which is open, collaborative, improvisatory and full of joy.

Rod Baxter

has been a youth worker in Aotearoa, New Zealand since that time when everyone was panicking about the Y2K bug. He is qualified in youth work and supervision and now teaches students in both programmes. Rod served rowdy and talented young people in an inner city youth centre for sixteen years, facilitating mentoring camps, painting street art murals and enabling participatory leadership groups. Rod co-founded the peak body Ara Taiohi and co-created Korowai Tupu – the youth work professional association. Rod lives in the canopy of trees with kākā, tūī and kereru at Te Whare Manaaki o Ngaio.

Graham Bright

is Senior Lecturer in Childhood and Youth Studies and Youth and Community Work at York St John University, UK. His PhD with Durham University explores youth workers' life and practice narratives. Graham is editor of *Youth Work: Histories, Policy and Contexts* (Palgrave, 2015). His practice continues to support work in the voluntary and faith sectors.

Ilona Buchroth

is Senior Lecturer in Community and Youth Work at the University of Sunderland. Prior to this, she worked as a community education service manager, youth and community development worker, adult education tutor and teacher. She has a longstanding and active involvement in the voluntary sector. Her primary research interests focus on grass-roots responses to social justice issues and the impact of neoliberalism on the role and voice of voluntary engagement.

Annette Coburn

is Senior Lecturer in Community Education at the University of the West of Scotland. Her teaching and research interests are driven by 23 years as a community and youth work practitioner and 15 years in Higher Education, where her doctoral research informed understanding of how young people learn about equality in youth work. She is committed to helping create a vision of more socially just society, where everyone is able to make a good life.

Dan Connolly

managed projects in the Voluntary and Community Sector for 25 years, working alongside young people from across North East England in a range of contexts including rural and environmental youth work, outdoor education and children and young people's participation. Dan became a full-time lecturer at Sunderland University in 2014, having taught on the Community and Youth Work MA programme at Durham University as a Visiting Lecturer for several years. Dan is currently undertaking research towards a PhD focussing on children and young people's rights.

Trudi Cooper

was a youth worker for ten years in the UK, before becoming a youth and community work lecturer. Since 1991 she has led the Youth Work degree programme at Edith Cowan University, in Perth, Australia, and is director of the Social Program Innovation Research and Evaluation (SPIRE) group. Trudi led a national team funded by the Office of Learning and Teaching to renew the youth work curriculum for Australian higher education. She received local and national awards for her outstanding contribution to learning and teaching, and in 2016 became an Australian Learning and Teaching Fellow.

Filip Coussée

is a researcher at Ghent University and coordinator of a local centre for youth care. His focus is on social pedagogy as a perspective on social work and youth and community work. He has studied the history of youth work in Europe and its connections to other social professions.

Bernard Davies

is a qualified youth worker who has practised in open access youth work settings, taught on qualifying youth work, teaching and social work courses and is active in *In Defence of Youth Work*. His publications include a three-volume history of the Youth Service in England and *Youth Work: A Manifesto for Our Times – Revisited*.

Steve Drowley

has been a Youth and Community Work professional since 1980. A youth worker in Brixton around the time of the 'riots', he worked in Community Education in Devon for 12 years before becoming Principal Youth Officer. A stint at the National Youth Agency preceded his appointment as Programme Director at Cardiff Metropolitan University in 2007. Now a freelance consultant and part-time lecturer he represents Wales on TAG/PALYCW and is Vice-Chair of ETS Wales. He has written on youth work models for the Welsh Government, and most recently a review of the Strategy for Youth Work in Wales.

Dana Fusco

is a Professor of Youth Studies and Education at the City University of New York, York College. She has written and edited three books on youth work and dozens of referenced articles, all with an eye towards articulating and advancing youth work as a field and an academic discipline. Having begun her career as a youth worker herself, Dana is deeply committed to co-creating spaces with young people that support their agency to curate their lives, their communities and the world.

Tony Jeffs

recently retired from the Department of Applied Social Sciences Durham University. He still teaches intermittently at Durham and the University of Bolton. In addition, he is a member of the Editorial Board of the online open-access journal *Youth and Policy*.

Karen McCarthy

is a founder of, and long term volunteer with, the Lesbian Immigration Support Group, Manchester. She is Senior Lecturer in Youth and Community Work at Manchester Metropolitan University. Her previous professional experience includes over 20 years as a community development worker working with a wide range of communities on a variety of issues. Karen's MA dissertation focussed on the lived experience of lesbian asylum seekers of their sexuality in their home countries and in the UK.

Jane Melvin

is Principal Lecturer and Programme Leader for the Undergraduate Work-based Learning Programme at the University of Brighton, which includes a BA (Hons) Youth Work. She is currently a director of the Professional Association of Lecturers in Youth and Community Work (TAG PALYCW), and a founder director of the Commonwealth Alliance of Youth Work Associations (CAYWA). Her research interests centres on the use of digital technologies as a vehicle for engaging young people in informal and experiential learning contexts, and her recent doctoral research explored ideas relating to 'digital tools, space and place' and their compatibility with youth work practice.

Carole Pugh

is Senior Lecturer in Youth and Community Work at York St John University, UK. Prior to this she worked as a Youth Worker in Local Authority contexts. Her PhD at Huddersfield University explores youth work's capacity to support the political engagement of young people.

Alastair Scott-McKinley

lectures in Community Youth Work at Ulster University in Northern Ireland. He has written on curriculum use in youth work and community relations practice. He is currently researching epistemic culture amongst youth work professionals. As a practitioner, he has experience in a range of youth work settings, including youth justice, political education, community relations work, centre-based youth work and curriculum training.

Tony Taylor

has had a career in youth work that spans five decades, witnessing him journey from part-time youth worker to Chief Youth Officer within the local state sector, and from university lecturer to the volunteer coordinator of *In Defence of Youth Work*. He has written extensively, drawing on his experience as a practitioner and trade union activist. Particular areas of interest are anti-sexist work with young men, the relation of youth work to class and democracy, as well as the psychology of youth work. Most recently he has focused on the insidious impact of neoliberal ideology upon the improvised and provisional world of open access, young people-centred, process-led practice.

Naomi Thompson

is Lecturer in youth and community work at Goldsmiths, University of London. Her research specialisms include young people, youth work, religion and inclusion. Her recent book *Young People and Church since 1900: Engagement and Exclusion* was published by Routledge in 2018. She edits for the open access journal *Youth & Policy.*

Howard Williamson

is Professor of European Youth Policy at the University of South Wales in the United Kingdom. He is a nationally qualified youth worker and ran a youth centre for 25 years in parallel with his academic research that spanned issues such as youth crime, youth unemployment, vocational training, enterprise and entrepreneurship, substance misuse, homelessness, school curricula and youth work. He has advised many levels of governance on youth policy issues, from the Welsh and UK governments, the European Commission, the Council of Europe and the United Nations.

Stuart Wroe

is Lecturer in Youth and Community Development at the University of Cumbria, specialising in global learning. Stuart is experienced in working with some of the most marginalised young women and men globally. He is currently undertaking a PhD at the University of Cumbria: Youth Work, Radicalisation and Islam which engages Participatory Action Research to explore the formation of empathic spaces for young Muslim people.

Introduction

Graham Bright and Carole Pugh

This book was conceived following our engagement with a number of UK conferences on the future of youth work, held as statutory services in England were being decimated. Austerity measures, competition, targets, targeting and neoliberal governmentality have combined to produce an environment where concerns about the erosion of 'professional' values and informal educational practices with young people had reached a crisis point. The conditions in which youth work was trying to operate seemed unable to provide the spaces, resources and freedom to work with young people in a holistic, critical, honest and person-centred way. However, despite this sense of desolation, a palpably passionate belief in, and commitment to, youth work's values and approaches remained amongst youth workers and young people. We were each challenged by the need to move beyond critique towards imagining different professional futures, which remained rooted in the profession's historical values, whilst critically responding to the actualities of present conditions.

Whilst recognising that the context in England is specific, many of these concerns about the destructive effects of neoliberalism on practice resonate more widely. However, because globally, youth work has developed in different political and cultural environments, practitioners and managers are finding different ways to resist and respond with resilience, creativity and integrity. For us, these insights have been the joy of this project. Youth work represents a diverse set of practices that are underpinned by shared values and a commitment to young people, informal education and social justice. Our contributors have reflected this diversity, and drawn on the patchwork of national and regional practices, as mediated by differing organisational contexts and young people's situated experiences, to produce a rich picture of global practice. This provides both depth and perspective from which to gain new insights regarding possibilities for future practices, which imagine fairer and more participative societies.

Asking people to futurize the unknown is, in many ways, an impossible task. These chapters represent perceptual snapshots, which are inherently linked to their time of writing between the middle of 2016 and 2018. This book is not concerned with prediction, but rather with exploring possibilities in different contexts, and thus promoting learning and reflection which seeks to shed light on potential directions. In asking colleagues to imagine futures, each appear to have instinctively drawn on the past as a means of providing a framework for discursive imaginaries. Looking back enables stocktaking, but historical examination must avoid nostalgic naval gazing that hankers sentimentally for an ideal past, which may not even have existed. Through critical contextual examination of youth work's historical development, contributors plot foundations, identify strengths and diversity, and map tensions and weaknesses. This enables the identification of sites and trajectories that are ripe for further exploration. These may be places we have been before, but which can be approached from different angles, or where new perspectives or technologies can enable us to draw on untapped resources. Current conditions afford us the opportunity to re-view, re-explore and re-imagine the significance of practice traditions, and to find the best places to set-off from in pursuing different futures. Each chapter offers a distinct approach to this challenge; some are more conceptually orientated, whereas others offer a more pragmatic re-envisioning of policy and practice. Our approach in editing this book has been to allow each of these chapters to speak for themselves. We trust that this has enabled nuances of substance and style to be expressed. We would like to thank each of our colleagues for their willingness to undertake this task, for their hopefulness and integrity, and for daring to 'shake the tree', in imagining possible futures.

In Chapter 1, Bernard Davies and Tony Taylor reflect on key tensions in the past 150 years of UK youth work. They explore key debates in youth work's enacted functions: education versus protection, voluntary versus compulsory participation, individual versus collective approaches and social conformity versus social change. They critique the impact of political and policy changes, and argue that consideration of these debates, and youth work's capacity to be volatile, voluntary, creative and collective in its promotion of social justice, can serve as fulcrum from which critical reflection can continue to guide the development of future practice.

Chapter 2 extends these discussions, reviewing the contrasting development of devolved youth work policy across England, Scotland, Northern Ireland and Wales. Tony Jeffs highlights the impact of social, cultural and technological changes on young people and communities in England, and argues that it may be time to develop new forms of dialogical and informal educational practice, which seek to establish deeper and more meaningful attachments and bonds across generational boundaries. Annette Coburn considers the radical socialist and emancipatory foundations of Scottish youth work which have enabled a vibrant youth work sector to survive. She explores the potential offered in developing an international community of youth work practice centred on the political nature of a praxis that reaches across professional and geographical boundaries in search of equality and social justice. Alastair Scott-McKinley considers the development of youth work in Northern Ireland, which, since the 1970s, has followed a different course from the rest of the UK – firstly, in response to the impact of the sectarian 'Troubles', and secondly, because of the influence of devolved government. However, in common with other UK jurisdictions, increased managerialism and targeting inhibits youth workers' ability to respond flexibly to young people. While the future of youth work in Northern Ireland seems secure, questions arise about its ability to thrive in in an increasingly alien policy and organisational environment. In the final part of the chapter, Steve Drowley provides a contrasting account of development of youth work in Wales. The Welsh government indicated their intention to secure a universal entitlement to educational, employment and community opportunities for all 11–25 year olds. Although some policies have prioritised targeted work, partnerships between maintained and voluntary services have secured a commitment to open-access services. The compulsory registration of all full-time professional youth workers has also bolstered the profession, and while a clear policy direction is still to emerge, there are grounds to view the future with cautious optimism.

In Chapter 3, we adopt a more conceptual approach. Drawing on cartography, Foucault and Freire, we seek to plot the territory that youth work finds itself in, considering the route it has taken to get here, and the impact that neoliberal landscaping has had on practice environments. Adopting a utopian analysis, we contemplate alternative journeys and destinations, which may support the exploration of new routes.

Chapter 4 sees Howard Williamson and Filip Coussée outline the diversity of youth work practice across Europe, which contains many tensions and dilemmas, but from which a common description of practice emerges. They argue that youth workers must engage in critical social and political analysis, and struggle with the inherent paradoxes and tensions in their work. Adopting a historical analysis, they argue that future practice needs to be to re-socialised and focussed on the ability of youth work to create free spaces where young people can explore and express their identity and autonomy, and build bridges between these and participation in economic and civic life.

While there are a range of different youth programmes, the term 'youth work' is not present in American practice discourse. In Chapter 5, Dana Fusco and Michael Baizerman argue that considering the possible and multiple futures of youth work, also involves actively working to create these. They emphasise the importance of centring future work on the realities of young people's social, cultural and economic experiences. This, they posit, relies on youth organisations working together to challenge pathologising and deficit perspectives regarding young people and exploring the possibilities of applying a 'youth work stance' in different organisational contexts.

In Australia and New Zealand, the impact of contemporary neoliberal policies have been shaped by colonial and postcolonial histories. The development of youth work also reflects cultural connections to Pacific and

South and East Asian counties, and the differing relationship with the First People in each country. In Chapter 6, Trudi Cooper and Rod Baxter examine the current opportunities and threats facing youth work, and draw on analysis of differing structures and approaches to explore possible ways forward.

Stuart Wroe commences Chapter 7 with a discursive critique of the language that underpins assumptions about the 'developing world'. He utilises critical perspectives to frame discussion regarding young people's active participation, and draws on empirical research with a leading member of the Afrika Youth Movement (AYM) in developing a rich understanding of the power and potential of community, and, youth engagement. Wroe challenges us to reimagine, and draw upon the possibilities of, a critical pedagogy that thinks and acts globally *and* locally in collectivising for change.

In Chapter 8, Ilona Buchroth and Dan Connolly consider the impact of neoliberalism and austerity on the character and practices of voluntary sector (NGO) youth work organisations. Drawing on empirical data from the North-East of England, they contend that the collectivity and position of voluntary sector organisations remains key to developing critically resistant, participative and locally-accountable practices which can continue to demonstrate and articulate the *true* value of youth work.

In Chapter 9, Naomi Thompson explores the possibilities that current conditions present for the development of partnerships between faith-based and 'secular' youth work organisations in building capacity in the civil sphere. The chapter argues that these partnerships hold significant collaborative potential to resist assumptive right-wing ideologies and bolster socio-democratic ideals in promoting the common good.

In Chapter 10, Jane Melvin draws on her doctoral research to contend the power and potential of online engagement as complementary to face-to-face youth work practice. Melvin highlights the pedagogical possibilities of online practices, and argues that youth workers should address digital exclusion and promote digital citizenship. The chapter argues that this re-imagination and hybridisation of youth work pedagogy presents particular spatial, ethical and professional challenges and opportunities that need to be addressed *and* embraced.

In Chapter 11, Janet Batsleer and Karen McCarthy draw on feminist ideas to offer a reimagining of the value of community in neoliberal times. They note how women have sustained communities of belonging, often at personal cost. Citing practice with lesbian and bi-sexual asylum seekers and refugees, and practice-based research with young women from disadvantaged communities regarding mental health issues, they challenge readers to build communities of respectful inclusivity, which resist the dividing forces of hatred, pathologization and oppression. The chapter highlights ways in which informal educational pedagogies can be engaged to enable people to name, connect, resist and re-imagine.

In the concluding chapter, we build on our work in Chapter 3, to develop conceptual thinking regarding possible future directions for youth work practice. We utilise Deleuze and Guattari's rhizome analytic as a means of promoting discussion regarding the multiplicity of possibilities that exist beyond the known. We link these ideas of becoming to the liminality and possibility of border praxes, contending that youth and community work has always been engaged processes of inbetweenness and becoming. We argue that its future, as a creative and critical movement also lies here.

We hope that this collection prompts reflection, discussion *and* action. It is not intended as a map, or blueprint, from which future journeys should be navigated, but rather as a resource that inspires (re)new(ed) expeditions.

CHAPTER 1

On Critical Beginnings: How We Got to Where We Are

Bernard Davies and Tony Taylor

Framing Our Narrative and Analysis

In attempting to make sense of a hundred and fifty years of youth work in the UK our narrative poses four interrelated questions.
- Should youth work be educative or protective/preventative?
- Should practice be rooted in a voluntary relationship, free from compulsion or can youth work be imposed?
- Should the practice be individual or collective in its emphasis or intent?
- Should youth work be a vehicle of social conformity or social change?

To list these oft-repeated dilemmas is hardly to break new ground. Yet they remain contested, retaining all their pertinence in the present neoliberal period, within which practice leans significantly to the preventative, the targeted and individualised conformity. Indeed, for our perspective is patently not neutral, we oppose this instrumental tendency, sharing a career-long commitment to a holistic, 'open-access' youth work, which has been severely mauled in recent decades. Thus, we are both activists within In Defence of Youth Work (IDYW), whose Open Letter (2009) set out eight cornerstones of practice, mirrored in Bernards revised 'Manifesto for our Times' republished in 2015 (Davies, 2015). Our passionate resistance, dismissed in the managerial milieu of Youth Sector CEO's as naive, but favoured by such as Pimlott (2015) and de St Croix (2016), is captured in IDYW's characterisation of youth work as 'volatile and voluntary, creative and collective – an association and conversation without guarantees'.

We will engage with our questions by focusing on four periods of policy and practice, grounding these in their specific social and political circumstances.
- Youth Work's philanthropic creation and consolidation in the late nineteenth and early twentieth centuries.
- Youth Work's Albemarle-inspired social-democratic, professional revival (1960s).
- Youth Work's social movement-inspired politicisation (1980s).
- Youth Work's neoliberal loss of identity in the twenty first century.

© KONINKLIJKE BRILL NV, LEIDEN, 2019 | DOI:10.1163/9789004396555_001

Nineteenth Century Origins: 'Youth Leadership' and the 'Adolescent'

Engaging Young People by Choice

Embedded within the 'youth leadership' which emerged in the UK in the mid- to late-nineteenth century was a challenging reality: the young people these 'pioneers' wanted to work with were *choosing* whether to take up their offer – or not.

In 1890 an early girls' club leader, Maude Stanley, thus acknowledged that 'It is no use asking girls to whom one is unknown; they will not come ...' (Stanley, 1890: 57) while nearly a half century later Basil Henriques, who had been running boys' clubs in London's east end since 1914, was still commenting that:

> ... it is more difficult to be a club leader than a schoolmaster. Both are educationalists. With the one, the pupils come compulsorily, with the other voluntarily – a vital difference – ... a certain leakage (of members) is to be expected. (Henriques, 1933: 67/90)

Indeed, not all were convinced that this approach was effective. Enquiring into 'boy life and labour' in Birmingham in 1913, Arnold Freeman pointed to what he called 'the tragedy of the Club movement' – that:

> Insofar as it fails to provide amusement (the club) will not attract boys; while in so far as it provides amusement, it is not assisting, except incidentally, the moral and mental unfoldment of the boy. (Freeman, 1913: 128–129)

By the early 1950s, Henriques was expressing similar doubts when – with a focus clearly on youth work as prevention – he suggested that the 'so-called unclubbable boys are beyond the scope of the ordinary boys' club' (Henriques, 1951: 295).

Nonetheless, the country-wide networks of youth clubs, Scout and Guide troops and Girls' and Boys' Brigades established by the early decades of the twentieth century were all based on this core assumption: that, albeit within different methodologies, young people's initial engagement and continuing participation would always be voluntary.

'Education' through 'Recreation'

For these early youth workers, however, this challenge had to be faced. Their target group – the newly identified 'adolescents' – were seen as needing 'guidance' on their risky developmental journey to adult 'maturity', not least because many were being reached by neither of the existing 'disciplining' regimes of schooling and work. For Lily Montagu, founder in 1893 of the West Central Jewish Girls Club:

> ... as soon as the discipline of school is removed and the process of wage-earning begins, girls are most seriously in need of training and protection. (Montagu, 1904: 246)

Such 'protective' measures were regarded as particularly necessary during the young's unsupervised leisure to divert them – boys no less than girls – from the corrupting attractions of the 'drink-shops', the 'low' music halls and 'the street's ... one main amusement', gambling (Russell & Rigby, 1908: 10–11).

Given young people's voluntary attendance, two of the early boys' club innovators, Lillian Rigby and Charles Russell, made their 'first object ... Recreation ...' – described as 'the compelling force which brings members to the clubs'. They nonetheless remained uncompromising on:

> ... the second object (which) we may call Education, taking the word not in its narrower sense, but as comprising the whole physical, moral and mental training of the lads. (Russell & Rigby, 1908: 19)

Montagu (1904: 234) even added a strikingly early feminist gloss – to teach girls:

> ... that they do not exist as mere supplements to men, but that they possess the dignity of human beings with infinite possibilities and definite responsibilities.

Individual or Collective?

Most of these early workers, too, sought to 'organise' young people's 'natural instinct for association' (Henriques, 1933: 8) and ensure 'opportunities ... for members to get to know one another well'. (Montagu, 1954: 75). These aspirations also contained commitments to what today in the UK would be called 'participation' or 'young people's voice':

> A few boys' clubs place great reliance on the principle of self-government by the members. (Russell & Rigby, 1908: 85)

> Gradually (the girl) herself is required to take a share of (her club's) management. (Montagu, 1904: 248–249)

However, these collective tendencies often focussed more on methods, with the work's desired longer-term outcomes ultimately shaped by the dominant individualistic values of the time. As Henriques explained in 1951, one reason why a boy 'has to be trained as a member of a group is to learn how to fit into the group ... to learn tolerance, loyalty and unselfishness in the group' (Henriques, 1951: 5).

Capturing this personalised concern particularly succinctly was the commitment to 'character development' which, for William Smith, founder of the Boys' Brigade in 1883, meant:

> ... the promotion of habits of obedience, reverence, discipline, self-respect and all that tends towards true Christian manliness. (Birch, 1959: 22)

Setting some firm individualistic boundaries to her feminist vision, Montagu also sought '... to see in girls ... the greatest capacity for self-restraint and for the highest joys of self-sacrifice' (1904: 234–235).

Beyond the Personal to the Political

These individual developmental and 'child-saving' purposes, however, often had a sharp political edge. At a time when the 'lower orders' were again showing signs of unrest and a church minister was warning in 1880 that 'If we in the Church of England do not deal with the masses, the masses will deal with us' (Inglis, 2013: 34), the new providers of 'youth leadership' were very clear that the 'training' and 'education' they were offering must have more than just personalised intentions.

Montagu (1904: 244) recognised that 'the economic conditions ... at the root of our social demoralisation ... cannot be speedily eradicated' while Stanley (1890: 63), with rather condescending restraint, declared:

> We have not wished to take our girls out of their class, but we have wished to see them ennoble the class to which they belong.

Nonetheless, for Russell and Rigby the need for 'societal' – that is ruling class – gains from their 'humanising' work was often unqualified:

> ... it was not until ... the ruffianism of youths had reached such a pitch as to become an absolute danger to the community that ... men who had the welfare of their city and country at heart ... cast around for some means of checking so alarming a development. (Russell & Rigby, 1908: 9)

By the 1950s, Henriques (1951: 5) believed that one of the reasons youth workers needed to work with young people in their groups was to enable them to practise 'virtues' which would eventually benefit 'the State'.

Social Democratic Youth Work: The Albemarle Report and Beyond

The State Intervenes: From 'Moral Exhortation' ...

Though the terminology and balance between them changed over time, 'education' and 'protection' – commitments both to liberating young people's potential and diverting them from socially risky behaviour – remained deeply rooted within the youth work philosophy. The firmly entrenched voluntary youth organisations remained committed to these complexly inter-related purposes. As the post-war social democratic ideology took hold, by the 1950s the state, too, was indicating interest in them. In 1951, the Permanent Secretary to the Ministry of Education, Sir John Maud, proposed a definition of youth work which quickly became its oft-repeated mantra. This again focused on 'individual young people' and on how 'leisure time opportunities' could help them '... discover and develop their personal resources of body, mind and spirit' as well as 'live the life of a mature, creative and responsible member of society' (Ashbridge Conference, 1951: 13).

By the time the state acted directly on these ideas, some of the 'traditional' youth organisations' taken-for-granted values were under severe challenge, not least from young people themselves. Here, the catalyst for youth work was the Albemarle Report on the local authority Youth Service in England and Wales (Ministry of Education, 1960). Starting from a recognition that 'teenagers' were much less deferential than their predecessors, the Committee insisted it was time to move on from the 'moral exhortation' which had historically characterised youth leadership (para. 145).

More positively, in locating itself in the 'education versus protection/prevention' debate, the Committee went beyond the concerns which had prompted the government to set it up – in particular, the imminent ending of national military service for young men and rising levels of delinquency:

> ... a Youth Service may be of value to the great majority who will never enter a juvenile or adult court. The Service is not negative, a means of 'keeping them off the street' or 'out of trouble'. (para. 129)

Even more boldly, it stated its aim was not '... to remove tension so as to reach towards some hypothetical condition of 'adjustment' to individual or social life' (para. 135). It was even dubious about youth work's historic offer as a 'training in citizenship', about which, it said, many of the young were highly suspicious. With a significant nod to the importance of *how* the work was done it even suggested that:

... the beginnings of 'citizenship' can be seen as much in the subtlety and tact of social relations in a good youth club, even in a tough area, as in straightforward discussions of good citizenship'. (para. 144)

... to 'Social Education'

Seeing 'voluntary attendance (as) important because it introduces adult free-dom and choice' (para. 34), the Committee, in passing, suggested a term to describe youth work's purpose – 'social education' (para. 132) – which subse-quently gained wide currency. Alongside ensuring opportunities for 'training' and 'challenge', it said, 'the (Youth) Service should seek first to provide places for association in which young people may maintain and develop ... their sense of fellowship' – not least because 'association in itself ... may be immensely educational, according to the imagination of the leadership' (paras. 135, 136). Far from assuming that young people were in need of being protected, it also defined them as 'the fourth partner' in Youth Service provision, able to fur-ther their development through what it called 'self-programming' groups (paras. 173, 174).

However, the Report's endorsement of engaging young people in and through their groups stopped short of making collective *outcomes* a priority goal. Indeed, its thinking and overall approach were largely uncritically under-pinned by the social democratic ideology which had been shaping the UK's wider welfare policies at least since 1945. It thus continued to urge youth work-ers to 'help many more young people find *their own way* better, personally and socially' (emphasis added) (para. 138), and endorsed the Maud definition out-lined earlier with its offer of new opportunities to 'individual young people' as 'comprehensively' expressing the Service's educational purpose (para. 134). And, although the Committee supported 'partnership' between statutory bod-ies and the voluntary youth organisations which were still significant actors in the field, in recommending that local authorities become much more proac-tive in funding and supporting youth provision, it prompted significant shifts in the balance of influence, and indeed, control towards the state. Until the post-2010 'austerity' cuts, this particularly extended the role of local authorities whose structures and procedures over time became increasingly bureaucratic and professionalised.

The Albemarle Legacy

Many of the Albemarle Committee's more ambitious aspirations for deeper organisational and cultural changes in the Service's operations thus never materialised – particularly its advocacy of a more genuinely participative role for young people in decision-making and direct provision. In 1975, John Ewen, the Director of the National Youth Bureau, was thus still echoing the long-standing dilemma of a Youth Service that:

> ... is not sure where it sits on that spectrum between an emphasis on indi-vidual development and an emphasis on equipping young people with the skills and attitudes which enable them to conform to certain rules of acceptable social conduct .... (Ewen, 1975: 3)

Nonetheless, Albemarle opened up space within youth work for practice which, far from being concerned with 'child-saving' – with 'prevention' – was not only broadly educational but, for a state provision, radical and indeed 'political'. Youth and Community Work in the 70's, a report published in 1969 by the Youth Service Development Council (YSDC), the government advisory body recommended by Albemarle, not only confirmed that 'the primary goal of youth work is the social education of young people' (DES, 1969: 152), but in seeking to prepare them for the 'active society', echoed Albemarle's rejection of a search for 'some hypothetical condition of 'adjustment':

> ... it is no part of our aim to achieve a comfortable integration of the youth and adult populations, nor to attempt to 'socialise' the young so that they are reconciled with the status quo, and capitulate to its values. (para. 197)

Indications of the coming shift from these social democratic to neoliberal ideas emerged quickly however. Following two years of near silence, Educa-tion Secretary Margaret Thatcher rejected the report's proposal to 'change the nature of the service ... radically'. She was particularly unimpressed by its suggestions that youth work adopt community development approaches. And though many local authorities added 'community' to their Services' title, this often seemed to be a merely rhetorical gesture which only exceptionally prompted the more 'political' forms of young people's collective activities which the report had advocated.

From Social Democracy to Neoliberalism: The Politicised Years

The challenging words of the YSDC report reflected indirectly, at least, the anti-establishment political ferment of the 1960s and the growing impact of the social movements, particularly those organised around gender, race and sexuality, even hinting perhaps at the class conflict to come. Yet social turmoil seemed to be passing youth work by. On the ground the voluntary sector's deep-rooted, character-building tradition was not without adherents within the burgeoning state provision. Many practitioners remained distinctly unimpressed by the, oft-derided as trendy, non-directive and non-judgemental approaches promoted by the National College for the Training of Youth Leaders, one of the key products of Albemarle (Ewen, 1972). Hence the tensions between tradition and trendiness, discipline and permissiveness were experienced as a profound clash of cultures and styles. This chasm was symbolised by endless debates within staff meetings about young people's behaviour and whether the sin of swearing merited expulsion from the club. Nevertheless, both sides, and those caught in the middle, remained committed in principle to the voluntary relationship with the overwhelming emphasis still one of enabling young individuals make the most of the opportunities allegedly available to them. And though a research project into the Youth Service published in 1976 cautioned that 'the enthusiasm of *Youth and Community Work in the 70's* for innovative work ... is not greatly in evidence' (Eggleston, 1976: 65), this conclusion did not take into account the rare space within public services which these two 1960s reports were, briefly, to open for more radical and indeed 'political' forms of emancipatory practice.

A significant barrier to a greater agreement about purpose and method was the relationship between the new vanguard of full-time professionals and the growing number of part-time workers needed in the expanded Service. Whilst not all the National College's graduates were signed up to its philosophy, full-time staff sought to stress the educational, part-time staff the recreational and preventative – 'keeping them off the streets'. Thus the development of part-time youth worker training, though by and large conformist in its assumptions and outlook, became a priority for winning these doubters to the educational cause.

It was well into the 1970s before the notion of social education as advocated by Davies and Gibson (1967) took a real hold. Their repudiation of the dominant idea of adolescence as an incremental series of steps towards adult maturity and their emphasis on cooperation and the common good challenged the individualistic and apolitical assumptions of the bulk of practice. Indeed Bernard himself wrote a searching self-critical piece acknowledging that his youth work presence in a northern industrial town had ignored the stifling significance of structures and institutions in young people's lives:

> Youth work, like any form of people-work (or indeed any form of work?) is thus inescapably a political act through which a political commitment to freedom, equality and justice is constantly expressed. (Davies, 1976: 17)

In tune with this conclusion, the concept of social education, even as its usage grew, came under fire from activists entering the profession out of the late 1970s social movements. From within these vibrant, if short-lived settings, workers sought to politicise social education, expressed through the rise of autonomous work with young women, black youth, gay and lesbian, and disabled young people. Hence an edition of the Inner London Education Authority's 'Schooling and Culture' carried articles by ourselves, entitled, 'Stuttering Steps in Political Education' (Ratcliffe & Taylor, 1981) and 'Social and Political Education: In Search of Integration', within which Bernard argued passionately for 'the politicisation of social education and the humanisation of political education' (Davies, 1981: 36).

Contradictorily, though, following the Conservatives' 1979 General Election victory, even a tame form of social education seemed too much for Thatcherism. As the new government pieced together an increasingly coherent national youth policy, focused on schooling, employment, welfare and justice, it spurned youth work. Distrusting what it saw as a refuge of permissiveness, it shelved the 1982 Thompson Report which had failed to jettison youth work's commitment to the whole young person. Targeting the young unemployed, the Tories sought to bypass or colonise youth work and the Youth Service via the ever-expanding Manpower Services Commission and its proliferation of Youth Training Schemes. Within which social instruction trumped social education, its instrumental emphasis on skills seen as more worldly than a focus on self-awareness. For the time being, this neoliberal offensive was eloquently criticised (Davies, 1986) and resisted, particularly through the Community and Youth Workers Union's (CYWU) defence of the social-democratic ideological underpinning of professional practice.

Yet it would be misleading to suggest a uniformity of agreement about the nature of practice across youth work's undulating terrain. Within the professional ranks there was a fierce battle between the Community and Youth Service Association's apolitical adherents to an individualistic focus and the recently arrived, collectively-inclined political activists, who caucused to transform the organisation into the CYWU, explicitly committed to youth work as an agency of social change (Taylor, 2012). This tension was highlighted in a major piece of research into the state of part-time youth worker training (Butters & Newell, 1978). The authors claimed that the traditional character-building model had been superseded by the social education repertoire (SER) – a mix of personal awareness, community development and institutional reform. However, in their view, the SER itself had to be overthrown by a radical paradigm, within which young people were transformed into a vanguard leading the struggle against oppression. The analysis was incisive, yet skewed. However, its use in the National Youth Bureau's Enfranchisement project (1985) illuminated the contested nature of youth work practice. The emerging incongruity was that, although a radical interpretation of youth work was becoming the dominant voice at a rhetorical level and had supported imaginative pockets of practice, a conventional view of work with young people was still hugely significant. To take but two examples of the clash experienced directly by Tony as a youth officer, in Wigan the struggle to cement Girls' Work as central to the Service split the workforce, whilst in Leicester a tense relationship developed between independent Black projects born out of the community and staffed by local, unqualified workers, and a Community Education Service perceived as institutionally racist.

Hence youth work training was in turmoil, reflecting a feeling that its perspective was white, male and behind the times. By the mid-1980s, an infusion of women and black lecturers had begun to alter the training agencies' outlook. Indeed, by the end of the decade, an anti-oppressive and anti-discriminatory (AOP/ADP) analysis of practice had achieved a contradictory hegemony, reflected in the determination of Jeffs and Smith (1987) to puncture youth work's anti-theoreticism; in Val Carpenter's (1986) avowal of independent Girls' Work, together with the seminal exploration of the experience of black youth by Gus John (1981). Faced with this convulsion, youth work theory and training, both full and part-time, had to run to catch up with the prefigurative, oppositional work emerging on the ground, seeking to marry its liberalism with its rising radicalism.

However, as the decade drew to a close, youth work's radical insurgents, in common with the left as a whole, were in retreat. The miners' defeat in 1985 had devastated the labour movement. The maverick 'socialist-feminist' councils such as Sheffield and Derbyshire, losing both confidence and finance, abandoned being refuges of progressive politics, especially as the Labour Party itself began reinventing itself as a party of the centre (Taylor, 2008). Facing similar pressures, the social movements were abandoning their autonomy, taking the grants and seeing their leaders recuperated by the state (Shukra, 1998).

As we take stock of this period, the first contradiction concerns how for a time a radicalised social-democratic youth work made headway, swimming against a neoliberal tide already threatening to engulf the very idea of public services; the second, the suspicion that this resistance in practice was confined to a scattering of local authorities. The third most striking anomaly was that increasingly a prescriptive right-wing agenda nationally, began to be mirrored by an imposed left-wing agenda locally. The insistence was still that youth work was educative at heart, but the radical praxis, which had sought to supersede the failings of social education shorn of politics, forgot its roots in diversity and critical tolerance, taking on an authoritarian character. Failing to win hearts and minds, some of its advocates began to insist that their agenda be met or else, undermining their ability subsequently to criticise the imposition of outcomes of a different kind.

Neoliberalism Turns the Screw – Predictable and Prescribed

As the neoliberal introduction of the discourse of the market continued apace, the Conservative government remained equivocal about youth work. Turning a little of its attention to this uncertainty, it called a series of ministerial conferences, the first in 1991 in Birmingham. The Tories hoped to persuade the disparate elements within youth work to agree a core curriculum, against which performance could be measured. In perhaps its last moment of collective solidarity, an alliance of the voluntary and state sectors, remembering its rich and pluralist history, repelled the government's intrusion. From this moment on and particularly after major cuts to youth services, successive governments, sought to smuggle their ideology into practice by channelling any new state funding for work with young people through specific, time-limited initiatives such as the Single Regeneration Budget. To compete for this finance, politicians, bureaucrats and youth work managers had to agree to achieve predetermined targets and outcomes. Although the monitoring of this strategy was still sloppy, youth work was manoeuvred in the direction of a preventative and welfare model, with the tradition of social and informal education surviving often only at the level of soothing platitudes.

Yet contradiction did not disappear entirely. Within the training agencies, though the anti-discriminatory commitment of the 1980s clung on, its dominance was showing signs of stress. Some within the institutions felt that the litany of anti-sexist and anti-racist practice was becoming institutionalised. Inexorably, though, the employer was to move to the centre of the validation process, riding on the back of the National Occupation Standards framework which relied on the notion of agreed competencies and outcomes to establish a comprehensive standard for qualification. Teaching to predetermined outcomes began to instrumentalise the relationship between lecturer and student with the latter becoming 'customers' and the process of learning redefined as 'knowledge transfer'. As the youth work landscape fractured and the workforce fragmented, it proved evermore difficult to find placements where informal education was the guiding philosophy. The rehearsed rationalisation became that, wherever placed, the student carried with her youth work's values and skills.

Meanwhile in practice a tightrope was walked. The devastating cuts of 1992–1993 were paving the way for a step-by-step change. Within the field, many began to make their pact with so-called 'new managerialism' and its insistence that youth work had no option but to embrace metrics. Others sought to duck and dive in defence of a pluralist tradition. In Wigan, calling the bluff on the increasing calls for a corporate approach, a new structure underpinning services for young people was proposed, bringing together all departments of the council – education, social services, leisure, housing along with other interested parties such as the police and the Council for Voluntary Youth Work. Within this collective of concern, the Youth Service preserved its distinctive identity and autonomy, being identified as the soul and conscience of the enterprise. This initiative was not to survive as increasingly youth work was moved from the core to the periphery.

After 1997, once in power, New Labour slowly inflicted an instrumental agenda upon youth work, utterly in keeping with a neoliberal desire to generate individualised conformity and with the renouncing of any alternative future vision. As Jeffs and Smith note, a decade of governmental documents such as 'Every Child Matters' (DES, 2003) and 'Transforming Youth Work' (DfES, 2002) were 'simply prospectuses for the delivery of already agreed priorities and outcomes' (Jeffs & Smith, 2008: 280). With the strategy of integrated youth services, youth work as a distinctive site of practice came under increasing threat. New Labour all but deleted the term "youth work" from their authoritarian discourse, replacing it with the patronising and simplistic notion of "positive activities". Youth work's incorporation into multi-disciplinary teams dominated by child-protection concerns weakened its educational commitment as did policies developed ever more systematically to prioritise 'early intervention' and the 'targeting' of young people 'at risk'. Increasingly, youth workers were saddled with caseloads of referred young people, causing many to describe their practice as 'social work-lite'. Implicitly or explicitly informal youth work was judged to be antagonistic to this instrumental project, and voluntary engagement with young people defined as inherently out of control.

The election of a Coalition government, followed by a Conservative administration in full control, changed little or nothing ideologically. Conspicuous by its absence at a theoretical level was any serious debate about what ideas might be supporting the shift from the educational to the preventative or from improvised informal education to structured non-formal programmes. Managers, revelling in their pragmatism, had simply obliged workers to accept a prescribed approach to their engagement with young people. To their relief organisational and theoretical nourishment was on the horizon – outcomes-based management and 'youth development'.

The Centre for Youth Impact (CYI), the driving force behind the promotion of outcomes-led-and-fed youth work, grew out of the market-obsessed Catalyst consortium, headed by the now defunct NCVYS, supported by the National Youth Agency (NYA) and the Young Foundation (YF). The CYI's Director was co-author of the thoroughly neoliberal 'Framework of Outcomes for Work with Young People' (McNeil et al., 2012). The YF made plain its aim at the document's outset to manufacture the 'emotionally resilient' young individual who, through the planned interventions of youth workers, would shrug off all politically created adversity. The idea that young people might be encouraged collectively to question their circumstances was utterly absent from the script. The adolescent of YF's dreams, normative in behaviour and attitude, attuned to the needs of the prevailing order, was neoliberalism's 'empowered' model citizen. In parallel, YF offered management the prospect of the model youth worker, planning meticulously scientifically predetermined programme of social integration.

Noting youth development's growing influence, Jeffs and Smith illustrated its congruence with the increasing emphasis on 'managing transitions' and the need to address through positive activities and pre-determined programmes young people 'at risk' of falling behind. They suggested that the youth development approach favoured formation rather than education, being 'less open-ended and more oriented to delivering a message' (Jeffs & Smith, 2008: 288) or, as would come plain, the delivery of an approved, resilient type of young person. It took another decade before Stuart and Maynard (2015) clarified the character of youth development, rooting it in non-formal education as a structured and planned intervention into young people's lives with identified and intended measurable outcomes. Claiming this approach was robust and rigorous, they compared it favourably with youth work, which was demeaned as no more than unintentional learning, having little need for an educator or preparation.

In common with much of the rebranded Third Sector, leading voluntary youth organisations such as the NYA, NCVYS and UK Youth compromised their independence by acting, largely uncritically, as agents for delivering government programmes such as the National Citizen Service. This unremarkable three week programme of team-building and volunteering kicked off by a residential outdoor activities experience ran up a budget of £140M in catering for 58,000 young people compared with the up to a million young people who had been sampling or making regular use of local Youth Service provision (NCVYS, 2015). As part of this process of recuperation by the State, and fearful for their futures, these organisations were prominent in redefining youth work as more or less any form of practice with young people for which funding could be achieved, be it youth justice, youth social work or pastoral care in schools. Rather than youth work, they preferred to talk about the corporate youth sector.

Such a watering down of youth work's distinctiveness has been opposed by a revived faith-based practice, critical of neoliberalism's amorality. For Bright and Bailey this resistance is reflected in the task of developing 'a social ethic, which transcends the rigid and performative prescriptions of contemporary social and policy frameworks and which re-elevates the humanity of relationships and relatedness'. Tellingly they are critical of the danger under neoliberalism of ethical concerns being divorced from politics, ending up as rigid rule books rather than flexible frameworks for practice (2015: 157). Nor should we overlook the emergence of local independent youth projects initiated often by redundant youth workers drawing upon a variety of funding streams via social enterprises whilst seeking to maintain their autonomy.

A decade on from our Open Letter, neoliberal capitalism is once again in deep crisis. It remains though nothing if not resilient. Its era of hegemony has undermined insidiously the nature of both pluralist and radical youth work.

– Youth work as purposeful, improvisatory, timeless dialogue starting from young people's agendas has given way to structured, time-limited programmes informed by the state's agenda. The informal has been formalised. The purpose of the work is expressed increasingly in preventative terms.

– The voluntary principle, which bound together youth work organisations of very different persuasions, has been eroded from without by neoliberal social and educational policy pushing youth workers and youth work organisations into situations where young people are not present of their own choosing. From within, this major transformation has led to managers and academics arguing that youth work can take place in settings where the relationship is compulsory, for example within Youth Offending Teams. Using the example of youth work in schools, claiming to follow Giroux (2005), Coburn and Gormally (2015) argue for a border pedagogy which helps youth workers to reconceptualise their practice, to cross boundaries and forge 'new ways of knowing'. Given that youth work graduates end up more and more in formal institutions, their argument is understandable if problematic, offering a seductive rationalisation for youth workers' required presence in other agencies.

– Notwithstanding the pressure to address young people's participation at a national level through mechanisms such as the Youth Parliament, the overwhelming emphasis is on the need for young individuals to get their act together. Even such pioneering initiatives as Young Minds (2017) see young people's mental health as primarily an individual rather than a social and political issue. Revealing, too, is the latest theory being embraced within youth work, namely neuroscience's notion of the teen brain as an explanation for young people's behaviour. It is well suited to the neoliberal imperative to separate the personal from the political (Sercombe, 2010).

– As for the classic question – 'Is youth work an agency of social control or social change?', neoliberalism is unhesitating in demanding it be the former. It has little patience with the proposal that it ought to be a contested ideological space. Indeed its policy has been to bring order to an unruly corner of civic society. Thus neoliberalism in the guise of the Tory administration in power, as we write, can live with the CEOs of leading youth organisations, with think-tanks and entrepreneurial academics invoking social equality, justice and empowerment in their pronouncements about work with young people, so long as these youth sector 'spokespersons' collude uncritically, often enthusiastically, with whatever the government proposes.

Our conclusion to this sweeping historical overview is simple, yet profound. In our view youth work is not to be understood as possessing a corporate set of values and skills, unbeknown to other professionals or volunteers, or indeed the rest of humankind. Rather history calls on us to cherish and defend youth work as a contradictory but still distinctive setting and practice, wherein we meet with young people outside of either the iron fist or the velvet glove of the powerful.

References

Ashbridge Conference Report. (1951). *Youth service tomorrow*. London: King George's Jubilee Trust.

Birch, A. E. (1959). *The story of the boys' brigade*. London: Frederick Muller Limited.

Bright, G., & Bailey, D. (2015). Youth work and the Church, chapter 8. In G. Bright (Ed.), *Youth work: Histories, policy and contexts*. London: Palgrave Macmillan.

Butters, S. (1978). *Realities of training*. Leicester: NYB.

Carpenter, V. (1986). *Coming in from the margins*. Leicester: National Association of Youth Clubs.

Coburn, A., & Gormally, S. (2015). Youth work in schools, chapter 11. In G. Bright (Ed.), *Youth work: Histories, policy and contexts*. London: Palgrave Macmillan.

Davies, B. (1976). *Part-time youth work in an industrial community*. Leicester: National Youth Agency.

Davies, B. (1981). Social education and political education: In search of integration. *Schooling and Culture, 9*, 9.

Davies, B. (1986). *Threatening youth*. Buckingham: Open University Press.

Davies, B. (2015). Youth work: A manifesto for our times – revisited. *Youth and Policy, 115*, 96–117.

Davies, B., & Gibson, A. (1967). *The social education of the adolescent.* London: University of London Press.

DES. (1969). *Youth and community work in the 70s.* London: HMSO.

de St Croix, T. (2016). *Grassroots youth work: Policy, passion and resistance in practice.* Bristol: Policy Press.

DfES (Department for Education and Skills). (2002). *Transforming youth work: Resourcing excellent youth services.* London: DfES/Connexions.

DfES (Department for Education and Skills). (2003). *Every child matters.* London: HMSO.

Eggleston, J. (1976). *Adolescence and community: The youth service in Britain.* London: Edward Arnold.

Ewen, J. (1972). *Towards a youth policy.* Leicester: MBS.

Ewen, J. (1975). *A positive future for the youth service.* Leicester: National Youth Bureau.

Freeman, A. (1913). *Boy life and labour.* London: P. S. King and Son.

Giroux, H. (2005). *Border crossings.* Oxon: Routledge.

Henriques, B. (1933). *Club leadership.* London: Oxford University Press.

Henriques, B. (1951). *Club leadership today.* London: Oxford University Press.

IDYW. (2009). *Open letter.* Retrieved from https://indefenceofyouthwork.com/the-in-defence-of-youth-work-letter-2/

Inglis, K. (2013). *Churches and the working class in Victorian England.* London: Routledge.

Jeffs, A., & Smith, M. (Eds.). (1987). *Youth work.* London: Palgrave Macmillan.

Jeffs, T., & Smith, M. (2008). Valuing youth work. *Youth & Policy, 100*, 277–301.

Jeffs, T., & Spence, J. (2008). Farewell to all that? The uncertain future of youth and community work education. *Youth and Policy, 97*(8), 135–166.

John, G. (1981). *In the service of Black youth: The political culture of youth and community work with Black people in English cities.* Leicester: National Association of Youth Clubs.

Leigh, M., & Smart, A. (1985). *Interpretation and change.* Leicester: National Youth Bureau.

McNeil, B., Reeder, N., & Rich, J. (2012). *A framework of outcomes for young people.* London: Young Foundation.

Ministry of Education. (1960). *The youth service in England and Wales.* London: HMSO.

Montagu, L. (1904). The girl in the background. In E. J. Urwick (Ed.), *Studies of the boy life in our cities.* London: J. M. Dent and Company.

Montagu, L. (1954). *My club and I: The story of West Central Jewish club.* London: Neville Spearman Ltd/Herbert Joseph Ltd.

NCVYS. (2013). *Youth report 2013*. Retrieved from http://www.ncvys.org.uk/sites/default/files/Youth%20Report%202013v2.pdf

Norris. A. H. (1932). Preface. In C. E. B. Russell & L. M. Russell (Eds.), *Lads' clubs: Their history, organisation and management*. London: A. & C. Black.

Pimlott, N. (2015). *Embracing the passion: Christian youth work and politics*. London: SCM Press.

Ratcliffe, R., & Taylor, T. (1981). Stuttering steps in political education. *Schooling and Culture*, p. 9.

Russell, C., & Rigby, L. (1908). *Working lads clubs*. London: Macmillan and Co.

Schill, P. H. (1935). *The history of the Ardwick Lads' and men's club*. Manchester: J. Ellis Benson Ltd.

Sercombe, H. (2010). The 'teen brain' research: Critical perspectives. *Youth and Policy, 105*, 71–80.

Shukra, K. (1998). *The changing pattern of Black politics in Britain*. London: Pluto.

Stanley, M. (1890). *Clubs for working girls, reproduced*. In F. Booton (Ed.), *Studies in social education, Vol. 1, 1860–1890*. Hove: Benfield Press.

Stuart, K., & Maynard, L. (2015). Non-formal youth development and its impact on young people's lives: Case study – Brathay trust, UK. *Italian Journal of Sociology of Education, 7*(1), 231–262.

Taylor, T. (2012). From CYSA to CYWU: A radical journey subverted. In R. Gilchrist et al. (Eds.), *Reflecting on the past*. Lyme Regis: Russell House Publishing.

Young Minds. (2017). *Young Minds*. Retrieved from https://youngminds.org.uk/

CHAPTER 2

Contrasting Futures? Exploring Youth Work across the UK

Tony Jeffs, Annette Coburn, Alastair Scott-McKinley and Steve Drowley

An English Perspective

Foundations

Neither central nor local government took much interest in 'club work' prior to 1937. Each, since boys' and girls' clubs and uniformed organisations emerged in the 1860s, viewed this as an endeavour best left to voluntary organisations, irrespective of whether they were religious or secular. This stance was reflected in the decision of the leading UK youth organisations in 1936 to set aside their differences and establish a National Council for Voluntary Organisations (subsequently National Council for Voluntary Youth Services) in part to co-ordinate opposition to incursions by central government. This opposition was primarily driven by fears that what was occurring elsewhere in Europe, where authoritarian governments of differing hues had closed-down the voluntary youth sector and replaced it with state controlled provision, might be replicated here. Justifiably, these developments encouraged many club workers to be suspicious of all governmental intrusions and view their clubs and national bodies as one of those small 'platoons we belong to in society' which protect our liberty from inroads by the state and its servants (Burke, 1791: 68–69).

Fears of governmental 'take-over' were not their sole concern during the 1930s. For already the proportion of 14 to 21 year olds belonging to boys' or girls' clubs and uniformed organisations was falling. Like the Sunday Schools before them, they found that once members secured an independent income, they tended to favour cinemas, dance-halls, and adult social and sporting clubs. Boys' clubs with their purpose-built premises, sports teams, gymnasia and activity base generally fared better than girls' clubs, which overwhelmingly met in borrowed premises; however, both were acutely aware by this juncture that their older clientele mostly wanted mixed provision. In 1931 the earliest book to utilize the term 'youth work', a euphemism for mixed provision, surfaced (Walkey, Wills, & Motley, 1937). Two years later, the first mixed 'youth centre', run by probably our first designated youth worker, opened in Dagenham. Its popularity plus the slow emergence of mixed clubs had, by 1938, convinced many, including the leadership of the National Organisation of Girls' Clubs that the future lay in mixed 'youth work'.

In 1937, central government, sensing war was imminent, released funding to support activities aimed at improving young people's physical fitness. This led to voluntary agencies receiving grants for staff training, the acquisition of playing fields and construction of facilities. Despite earlier opposition to state intervention, national organisations and clubs, who all operated on a shoe-string, eagerly sought these subventions. This interlude ended with the out-break of war when the government decided a national network of clubs and centres was essential to; (a) provide places where young people might social-ise after work; (b) keep them off the streets and out of trouble at a time when parental supervision was curtailed; and (c) provide informal educational experiences that fostered respect for democracy and sense of common pur-pose. Given the young person's affiliation to a club or centre was voluntary, the latter was to be achieved via conversation and dialogue; social service activi-ties; and a club ethos that encouraged members to create nascent democratic communities.

Overnight, youth work's predicament was no longer a dearth of members, but vast unmet demand. For now, in unprecedented numbers young peo-ple clamoured to join organisations or clubs that would help them become 'involved'; so much so that some founded their own self-managed clubs. The prime obstacle facing a government seeking to create a universal service was the shortage of leaders and premises. So it adopted a two-pronged strategy by first investing in the existing voluntary organisations so they might develop their current units; expand their staff training programmes; and recruit addi-tional staff. Second, it launched a nationwide youth service managed by local education authorities, who besides supporting existing voluntary provision, would set-up and manage their own network of clubs and centres initially housed in schools and community venues.

By late 1939, this strategy produced a settlement that loosely-coupled the 'statutory' and 'voluntary' sectors to form a partnership known as the 'youth service'. This settlement with minor modifications remained intact for approx-imately four decades. Predictably, given the former held the purse-strings, this was never a symmetrical partnership. Consequently, the voluntary sector became perilously reliant upon subventions from various arms of the state. Only the uniformed organisations (apart from the cadet forces) remained financially autonomous primarily by not lumbering themselves with a port-folio of salaried employees and expensive buildings. These new arrangements presaged a further noteworthy adjustment. Previously major voluntary organi-sations, although they operated via federal structures, justifiably claimed a UK wide remit. Post-1940, that assertion rapidly lost credence for the jurisdiction of the Board of Education covered neither Scotland nor Northern Ireland who enjoyed devolved responsibility for education policy. Thereafter, the administrative structures of statutory youth work in those two locales diverged from that prevailing in England and Wales. Voluntary youth organisations now accessed funding by negotiating independently with their own regional governmental department. This culminated in the break-up of many leading voluntary organisations and the emergence of three discrete 'youth services'; subsequently to be augmented by a fourth following the creation in 1999 of the Welsh Assembly.

Where Now?

In England, the settlement gradually unravelled post-1970, until, by the onset of the present century it became unrealistic to talk of a coherent 'youth service' comprising a partnership of the 'voluntary' and 'statutory' sectors. Both structural and administrative causes generated this eclipse. Amongst the former, two stand out.

First was a far-reaching re-configuration of the youth labour market from the mid 1950s onwards. Initially the youth service in England was fashioned to offer support; social and physical activities; and informal education for the 90 per cent plus who entered employment at 14. Centres and clubs were envisaged as havens where young workers might socialise with their peers after a working-day spent in the company of adults; and as an alternative to crowded homes, the street-corner and intellectually vacuous commercial venues. Officially funded to cater for 14 to 21 year olds its patrons were from the outset predominately under 18 – the age when males were conscripted (pre-1959) and females usually embarked stable relationships (Reed, 1950; Jephcott, 1948, 1954). Gradually the rationale for this age band was eroded as the school-leaving age first rose to 15 in 1947 and then by stages to the current *de facto* age of 18. Alongside this re-calibration, a contracting youth labour market encouraged heightened levels of voluntary 'staying-on' so that now over three-quarters at 18 are in full-time education as are over half at age 20 (Dept. of Education, 2017). Therefore, year-on-year, the youth service lost its original *raison d'etre*. Moreover, the educational settings where they spend most waking days possess far superior sporting and cultural facilities to those offered by youth organisations. Second, improvements in living and housing standards plus falling family size permitted teenagers to carve out their own private spaces wherein they can enjoy electronic entertainment, entertain friends and relax. Simultaneously, affluence promotes a relentless escalation in their access to a widening array of commercial leisure pursuits. Cumulatively, these trends contribute to an unremitting decline in youth service affiliations notably amongst those over 14.

Administrative and fiscal changes during the last two decades also hastened the 'settlement's' demise. First in 1999, central government sought to impose a restructuring of non-formal statutory provision via the unification of youth and careers services to create the Connexions Service. The ambition was to form a universal advice and guidance service for 13 to 19 year olds to enable individuals to successfully transition to adulthood. Delivered via individual contact, drop-in centres, outreach and detached teams, and re-branded youth centres, every teenage 'client' was theoretically allocated a dedicated Personal Adviser. Careers officers and youth workers were (re)trained, alongside a larger cohort of new, frequently poorly qualified recruits, to be Personal Advisors. Local authority careers offices and many youth centres were 'rebadged' as Connexions units and additional premises acquired. For various reasons Connexions failed to halt a rise in the numbers of those 'Not in Education, Employment or Training'. This 'failure', along with high levels of staff dissatisfaction, not least amongst youth workers forced to 'deliver' individualised interventions rather than group work, informal education and activity based programmes, and widespread managerial incompetence, resulted in the closure of Connexions in 2007. This collapse temporarily left the government without a 'youth strategy'. *Aiming High for Young People: A Ten Year Strategy for Positive Activities* surfaced a year later to fill the gap. Linked to the Extended Schools programme launched around the same time, it sought to offer all young people 'safe places to go' where they could make the most of their 'spare time'. Apart from the Extended Schools programme designed to offer school-based activities during evenings, weekends and holidays, the new strategy comprised two substantive elements. First, the Youth Service Development Fund (YSDF) with a notional £100 million to spend on projects managed by partnerships comprising statutory agencies, third-sector organisations and the private sector. Funding was to be accessed via costly bidding procedures (invariably most failed). Also all bids had to comply with specified forms of intervention and the money was time-limited to three years. Predictably, given its scatter-gun approach, YSDF failed to postpone the sector's decay. Few YSDF programmes survived the cessation of their funding, and collectively it possibly made a bad situation worse by stimulating pockets of short-term but unsustainable growth (Hodgson & Jeffs, 2013). Planned to continue until 2017, YSDF was quietly discarded in 2011. Second came the Myplace initiative with a budget of £240 million to be spent over seven years. Sixty-three capital grants were to be made, again via a costly bidding process, to establish large, well-equipped Myplace 'hubs' designed to attract youngsters from a wide catchment area. No funding was earmarked for up-keep or staffing so many quickly struggled to survive; subsequently a few have closed. As with YSDF this programme was surreptitiously discontinued-this time in 2012.

The banking crisis of 2008, and resultant austerity measures, contributed to the shelving of *Aiming High for Young People*. Central government then stepped aside, and in April 2011 transferred to local authorities a ring-fenced Revenue Support Grant of £77 per 11 to 19-year-old; barely sufficient for them to provide a barebones youth service. Then a year later, this policy was in turn discarded. Within twelve months of that decision, the 'settlement' was finally buried when the Department for Education decided it had no further interest in youth work or youth policy and dumped all responsibility for the remaining rump into the lap of the Cabinet Office – a catchall junior department devoid of ministerial clout and a substantive budget (Puffett, 2013). There it remained until July 2016 when the *Office for Civil Society*, which by now had responsibility for youth services, was transferred to the pot-pourri Department of Digital, Culture, Media and Sport.

Post-2011 expenditure levels were effectively left entirely to the discretion of individual cash-strapped local authorities. That administrative change predictably resulted in a dramatic diminution in spending upon youth services. Between 2012 and 2015, overall local government expenditure fell, primarily as a consequence of central government fiscal measures, by 27 per cent, but the pain was never evenly spread. For example, areas such as Social Care with a strong statutory base experienced reductions of 14 per cent, whereas expenditure on 'discretionary services' such as youth services and libraries fell by 45 per cent (Hastings et al., 2015). That translated into the loss of approximately 4,000 full-time youth work posts and 600 centres between 2012 and 2016 (Unison, 2016). The pace of decline has not subsequently eased. Local authority youth work budgets, according to House of Commons Library data, have declined by 54 per cent from £787 million in 2011–2012 to £365 million in 2017–2018 (Belgutay, 2017). Because local government was a strategic funder of voluntary provision that sector has similarly contracted. Even if the scale of funding cuts were to dramatically lessen during the next five years, an unlikely scenario, it is doubtful that the 'statutory' sector will survive. Irreparable damage has been inflicted to the extent it will probably suffer a similar fate to that of local authority 'liberal adult education' and become a mere distant memory. At best, all that is likely to remain will be scattered pockets of voluntary provision, plus a few far-flung 'hubs' which will function as age-specific leisure centres.

As the number of clubs and projects has waned, so likewise the super-structure telescoped. In 2017, just three per cent of youth and community work graduates secured employment in the statutory sector (Lepper, 2017) compared to

54 per cent in 1978 (Holmes, 1981). Overall, the number of students on youth and community work courses has plummeted by 52 per cent during the last six years leading to programme closures. Key organisations have similarly vanished as the base they served fell away. The National Council for Voluntary Youth Services (formed in 1936 as the National Council for Voluntary Organisations) folded in 2016; Ambition (established in 1925 as the National Association Boys' Clubs) closed in 2017; and the National Association of Youth Service Officers collapsed in 2015. Others struggle on, but for how long? The Federation for Detached Youth Workers, for example, has made its full-time staff redundant and the annual accounts show its income for 2017 as only £6,000 compared to £80,000 in 2006. The National Youth Agency and UK Youth still linger, but they, like the others, are haemorrhaging their membership base so that essentially they have become headless bodies frantically pursing corporate handouts and short-term contracts to survive. Neither appears to have a sustainable future.

Some segments, it should be noted, are doing less 'worse' than others. Notably the Scouts and Guides, although their membership remains way below what it was during their pre-war heyday, have recently enjoyed something of a minor resurgence. The former, with just over 40,000 members aged 14 to 18, appears to have turned the tide predominately by recruiting young women who now account for a quarter of their senior membership as well as a similar proportion of their leaders. The latter, whose senior section has a membership ranging from 14 to 26, recently experienced a decade of growth, admittedly from a low base, despite competition from the Scouts. In part this may be a by-product of its decision to remain single-sex and thereby offer young women a 'space of their own' to don the mantle of a 'feminist organisation' (Barnett, 2012; Palmer, 2017). Another segment that has held steady has been the 'faith sector' which probably now employs more paid workers than the statutory sector (Stanton, 2013). Reflecting this, the numbers enrolling on faith-based youth and community work degrees has 'bucked the trend' by remaining constant for the last six years (Christian Youth Work Consortium, 2016).

Moving Forward

In England, apart from the period 1939–1945 when unique circumstances prevailed, year-on-year, the average age of those involved with youth work agencies has fallen since the 1930s (Jeffs, 2018). With each passing year, youth work has therefore become less about serving 'youth' and more about 'managing' children. Indeed the new 'youth hubs' and 'youth zones' currently being opened unashamedly cater for an age range of 8 to 19. As the proportion of those under-21 in full-time education continues to expand in every industrialised nation, so the need for clubs and projects as sites for adolescent socialization diminishes. Now the pace of retrenchment has quickened as this client group acquires access to increasingly sophisticated means of electronic communication. Smartphones, tablets and computers are by the day fundamentally altering young people's lifestyles including their interactions with peers, siblings and adults (Turkle, 2011, 2015). These technological adjustments plus improvements in material well-being have produced a sharp diminution in the time spent outside the home, working part-time and physically 'hanging-out' with friends. Twenge (2017), on the basis of her longtitudinal research, argues this has resulted in the process of transition to adulthood and autonomy 'slowing down'. She found for example that 18 year olds are now acting more like 15 year olds used to, and that the latter's patterns of behaviour closely now resemble those of 13 year olds a decade ago. Alongside this trend, we appear to be living in an era when people of all ages are becoming less collectivist and more individualistic regarding their choice of leisure and social activities (Putman, 2000, 2015; Elliott & Lemert, 2006). A cultural shift that has led to communities becoming more brittle and cultivated a decline in participation in team games, group activities and social interaction, and fostered a turn towards pursuits which individuals undertake in isolation, for example, cycling, playing on a computer and visiting a gym. These and similar adjustments do not auger well for youth work's future well-being. An optimistic reading might tell us that just as youth work pushed aside boys' and girls' clubs, which in turn displaced Sunday schools, all we are now witnessing is another era of transition – during which new practice genres come to the fore i.e. *positive youth development* (Damon, 2004), *targeted youth work* (Scanlon et al., 2011), *digital youth work* (Melvin, 2015) and *missional youth work* (Kirk & Thorne, 2011).

Or maybe not; for robotics, AI, nanotechnology and computerization are all in relation to manufacturing, communications and entertainment driving forward a second 'great transformation'. Norbert Wiener as early as 1948 in his book *Cybernetics* argued that the first industrial revolution – the arrival of steam power in the eighteenth century – represented the devaluation of physical labour so that year-on-year humans increasingly found purpose as the controllers of machines in factories and on the land. Now we are witnessing a second industrial revolution whereby new technologies replace the human brain much as steam superseded muscle-power. This process poses an unprecedented challenge to all sectors of education including those segments operating beyond the confines of the formal sector. Out of the first great transformation grew what eventually became youth work and community work. As we live through that epoch's closure, so we must be prepared to acknowledge that youth work, like some other welfare formats, which emerged during the first great transformation, may have run its course. Consequently, we will need to unearth new forms of dialogical and informal education capable of addressing the social and educational challenges posed by this 'second great transformation'. We will need to confront the wholesale loss of intellectual employment (see Susskind & Susskind, 2017) as well as whole swathes of manual work, heightened social isolation, epistemic closure, generational segregation and a growing inability of many of our fellow citizens to relate to and converse directly with others. Each in turn suggest a need not for age specific forms of practice such as youth work, but for new modes of intervention that foster bonds of attachment across generational and age boundaries and promote a deep and meaningful sense of community. Faced with these new challenges, it is futile to try to reconstruct the old statutory youth service from the debris that remains. Nor is it worthwhile putting faith in the capacity of the existing 'hollowed out' youth work organizations, which ceased long ago in initiating policy. The administrative structure of English youth work that one might have described a decade or so ago has largely vanished and cannot be resuscitated. Far better to study the tributaries and backwaters of civil society where we will encounter the new forms of practice and social action that endeavour to address the fresh challenges facing us. For those looking for a helpful starting point, it is worthwhile studying the innovative forms of autonomous liberal adult education that have surfaced since the state system was dismantled. It is surely pointless to contemplate rebuilding a youth work structure formulated to address the needs of a fading era; how much more worthwhile to devote our energies at this juncture to seeking out the romance of possibility.

Scottish Perspectives on Youth Work

Foundations

Educational youth work, like school-based education, can be viewed as, 'pre-disciplinary in the sense that it is emergent and loosely and heterogeneously organised' (Deuchar, 2008: 490). In this pre-disciplinary context, it is important to present a coherent interpretation of where we have been, where we are now, and where we might be going in developing youth work practices. This section aims to make visible the evolution of youth work in the Scottish context in order to inform international perspectives on the potential for praxis which is, 'simultaneously cultural, educational, social and political, and [where] the young person is always the primary client ... [and] ... the focus of the work is always a value laden, social and moral activity' (Coburn & Gormally, 2017: 15). Understanding the context, purpose and values of practice are important in determining commonalities and distinctions that enhance possibilities for cohesion across disciplinary areas, and more importantly, for working with young people who occupy a world full of contradiction.

Devolved responsibility for education in Scotland, and a radical tradition, has set youth work on a different course. Welshman, Robert Owen, sited the world's first infant school in New Lanark. His educational and social reforms sought to alleviate ignorance through improved community-based education, leisure and social welfare to facilitate capabilities for all people to, 'exist without crime, without poverty, with health greatly improved ... and with intelligence and happiness increased a hundredfold' (Owen, 1916). Despite its utopian standpoint, the Scottish context for youth work derives from a radical political and social culture, grounded in this vision of education as key to making a good life. The evolution of youth work in Scotland has retained its focus on a radical and socialist purpose as emancipatory educational practice.

The publication of the Kilbrandon Report (HMSO, 1964), the Scottish equivalent of Albemarle (HMSO, 1960) in England and Wales, introduced professional training for youth workers and reinforced growth in local authority and voluntary sector youth work as social education, established within a holistic education system. Rather than creating a legacy of physical buildings in the Albemarle mode, Kilbrandon strengthened relationships between youth work and schooling by developing youth and community 'wings' within schools. Further, the Alexander Report (HMSO, 1975) took a lifelong learning view of education that synthesised adult education, community development and youth work to construct a new 'Community Education' service within every local authority area.

By 1984, Strathclyde Regional Council created Youth Development Teams within a collaborative framework of Area Curriculum Planning Groups, designed to integrate educational policy across pre-school, school and post-school education. Responding to the personal, educational, social and recreational needs of young people, youth work was located within 'a community development context ... concerned with the individual's role in relation to the wider society and his or her active participation in it' (SRC, 1984: 7). This framework called for a linking together of community education, education, social work, police, voluntary organisations, and leisure and recreation departments, as a catalyst for collaborative practices across professional boundaries.

Throughout the 1980s and 90s, formative grassroots development of contemporary aspects of practice was supported by the Scottish Youth Issues Unit (SYIU) under the stewardship of Marcus Liddle, who worked alongside young people and youth workers to create the prototype and impetus for internationally synthesised development of The Youth Enquiry Service, Young Scot, local Youth Councils and the Scottish Youth Parliament. The SYIU also fostered partnerships at national level that led to the development of locally-based collaborations with the NHS and Police. Further, drawing on data from across Scotland, a process-based curriculum was found to be central to youth work practice whereby the curriculum for youth work was:

– Open and flexible
– Clear in its aims and objectives
– Negotiated and responsive to the needs of young people
– Attractive to young people
– Relevant to those taking part
– Established on young people's own terms (Milburn et al., 1995: 18).

This curriculum for youth work was grounded in programmes already present in youth work (Milburn et al., 1995), but its development raised concerns about the formalisation of the informal. Grassroots participation and flexibility were key to encouraging participation and fostered alternative processes enabling engagement in contentious educational contexts including work with homeless young people or peer education projects around drugs, alcohol and sexual health. Yet, being flexible carried some risk. For example, operating at the height of concerns about the oppressive Section 28 of Thatcher's Local Government Act (1988) and working with a flexible curriculum, practitioners risked losing their jobs because the Act prevented local authorities in England, Scotland and Wales, from 'promoting' homosexuality, or from funding LGB support and campaign groups.

By the turn of the Millennium, a restructuring of local authorities and devolved Scottish Government altered the political map and changed the shape of youth work in Scotland, and for a time the language of curriculum was absent. The Community Education Service was largely re-branded as Community Learning and Development, no doubt symptomatic of neoliberal tendencies towards what Biesta (2015) has called the 'learnification' of education. This is consistent with youth and community work literature that critiques the formalisation of practices that focus on accreditation of programmes, are risk averse, focus on safe and secure measurable outcomes, and can be delivered as reduced forms of tick-box education (Batsleer, 2008; Martin, 2008). Yet, despite neoliberalism, the radical tradition has continued, but now seems more of an undercurrent than a tidal surge! Despite the unification and restructuring of local authorities and severe austerity cuts, a vibrant and now integrated youth work sector survives and continues to flourish. Youth work in Scotland remains distinct from other parts of Britain, but is aligned to core ideas on youth work as a discrete educational methodology (Harland & McCready, 2012) where the 'epistemology of youth work ... in the interest of authentic human rights for young people ... youth work can work with schools but not for schools' (Gallagher & Morgan, 2013: 46).

Where Are We Now?

Curriculum for Excellence (CfE) was initiated through the establishment of a review group that sought to implement radical change in the organisation of education for young people in Scotland, and was founded on values of wisdom, justice, compassion and integrity (Scottish Executive, 2004). CfE sets out a framework for the education of all young people, 'wherever they are being educated'. Its values are grouped around a set of core capacities that enable young people to become confident individuals, successful learners, effective contributors and responsible citizens (Education Scotland, 2014b). Synthesizing a breadth of planned learning experiences, CfE, on paper, underpins development in school, community, youth and family education.

Despite critique of the language and aspirations associated with the terms 'curriculum' and 'excellence' (Gillies, 2008), the introduction of CfE brought into view the experience and expertise of youth work educators, and was consistent with previous developments in youth work curriculum. It claims to start where young people are, and accepts that knowledge and understanding of the world are formed by influences beyond experiences in school. Whilst it does not feel like a content-driven and controlling curriculum, neither, given its focus on individual capacities, or its lack of explicit attention to collective action for social change, is it an emancipatory curriculum.

After years of campaigning, the creation of a national youth work strategy (Scottish Executive, 2007) coupled with the development of a Youth Work and Schools Partnership (drawing together partners in schools, colleges, local authority services, outdoor education, voluntary and community sectors, and national organisations such as the Scottish Youth Parliament and YouthLink Scotland) catalysed sector change. Bringing together this range of partners, has strengthened the position of youth work in Scotland (Education Scotland, 2014a).

The context in Scotland is different, in two further aspects:
- The new Regulatory framework for Community Learning and Development (CLD) (Scottish Government, 2013)
- Scotland's use of a Logic Model to measure contribution

The new Regulatory framework requires all local authorities to ensure provision of core services for young people as part of its commitment to the integration of CLD and other services. In asserting that 'Youth work contributes positively to a wide range of government policies and has a significant impact in improving the life chances of young people', the Scottish Youth Work Strategy

(Scottish Government, 2014: 8) sets out a template for youth work until 2019. Its core ambition states that:

> All young people, in every part of Scotland, should have access to high quality and effective youth work practice ... [and recognises that] ... engaging with young people must be an empowering process. It must offer young people developmental opportunities as well as the ability to lead, take responsibility, make decisions, and make a real and lasting contribution – both economically and socially.

Building on this high level of regard for youth work in Scotland, 2018 is Scotland's Year of Young People (YOYP). This is an exciting continuation of an iterative campaign to eradicate routinely negative and stereotypical discourses regarding young people. A partnership of youth work, culture and sport sectors and the Scottish Government (YOYP, 2018), promoted this special year of celebration as:

> ... an opportunity for generations to come together and celebrate our nation's young people. It is a platform for our young people (8 to 26). It will give them a stronger voice on issues which affect their lives, showcase their ideas and talents, and ultimately, aim to challenge status quo and create a more positive perception of them in society.

This high profile belief in young people, and the capacity of youth work contrasts to other parts of the UK, particularly England, where the Westminster Government has cut statutory youth work, almost to the point of extinction (Nicholls, 2018), and where outcomes-focused drivers have forced compliance with values and principles that at times appear to be at odds with youth work praxis.

Secondly, a Logic Model was introduced in Scotland, as an outcome based approach to public sector accountability (NHS Health Scotland, 2010; Wimbush et al., 2012). The rationale behind use of a Logic Model is that if short-term outcomes are achieved, this will lead to intermediate and then long-term outcomes being realised. As one example of an evaluation methodology called contribution analysis, Mayne (2012: 271) asserts that a Logic Model seeks 'to show how the intervention is expected to work or make a difference ... as part of an iterative approach to building the logic and evidence for claiming that the intervention made a contribution'. This means that where there is already evidence of success in a small scale project, then it can logically be anticipated that similar larger scale projects will be successful in future, on the understanding that adjustments can be made as projects develop over time, without having to prove cause and effect at each stage of the evaluation process. It is also logical to assume that a range of external factors and changing contexts will contribute to evolving project outcomes. While baseline information is required in order to later analyse the level and nature of change that may or may not occur over a period of time, the idea of claiming a contribution reduces pressure to provide specific causal evidence.

For example, in youth work, the collection of numeric data on participant attendance, number of interventions and tangible outputs offers no more than a superficial picture of what youth work does. It measures the easiest of things to count but does not prioritise the stories of young people and practitioners that, when applying the use of logic, clearly demonstrate how change can be achieved as part of an iterative process. Rather than measuring an extended range of quantitative evidence, it is more useful to gather and share stories about outcomes. Knowing and understanding how these were achieved, often through modification, and despite expectations, can strengthen the logic and evidence for further investment in practice.

Again, the high profile Year of Young People exemplifies this iterative process that builds the logical evidence for investment in youth work, and makes a strong case for recognising the contribution that young people make to their communities. The use of logic models and other methods of contribution analysis, are gaining credence among public sector agencies, and have been argued as reducing pressure on practitioners who are judged on performance delivery (Wimbush, Montague, & Mulherin, 2012: 312).

This shift creates possibilities for power sharing between funder and practitioner, as funding does not depend on, or guarantee, a specific output, but shows a potential contribution by linking what is done now, to the longer-term logically deduced benefits of that activity. This sits better with educational youth work where the impact of a relationship may not be realised until many years later. Taking the Logic Model seriously frames dialogue in youth work as a contributor to learning and education.

Although the Scottish context is not ideal, as it is underpinned by austerity cuts and a pervasive neoliberal condition that drives practice in a particular direction, there remains a commitment to resourcing and celebrating youth work. The new regulatory framework offers possibilities for practice and policy growth, while the application of a Logic Model means that value is not always reduced to number-crunched measurable outputs.

Where Might We Be Going?

So long as age discrimination affects young people's lives, there is a role for educational youth work as an emancipatory practice. Our Year of Young People celebrations are already challenging and changing the orthodoxies that label, stereotype and pathologise young Scots. What is clear in terms of future developments in educational youth work is that its social and democratic purpose offers a counterbalance to the neoliberal discourses that have already infiltrated schools and the wider purpose of education (Biesta, 2015; Coburn & McCafferty, 2016; Jeffs & Smith, 1982).

The Scottish position on integrated policy and practice suggests youth work as an important partner, working inside and outside of schools, using CfE as a framework for praxis. Yet, this has not brought additional or ring-fenced resources for bespoke educational youth work or for youth worker training. For example, the Education Governance Review (Scottish Government, 2017) has introduced the Pupil Equity Fund (the Scottish version of the pupil premium in England), to raise attainment in schools. This has presented opportunities for working collaboratively across school and youth work education, in school or neighbourhood based provision. However, because individual Head Teachers allocate spending, its use in developing youth work, home school partnership or family learning is sporadic at best.

In critiquing the Governance Review, Crowther (2017: 2) notes the review proposes 'the purpose of education in terms of excellence and equity says nothing about delivering social justice ... [and] ... stops short of seeking a broadly level outcome'. This is hardly surprising when, 'schools continue to operate according to mutually contradictory principles in relation to equality' (Baker, Lynch, Cantillon, & Walsh, 2009: 141) in which their equality principles are compromised in the selection and stratification of students, 'that clearly defeats certain aspects of their equality remit'. The realisation of equality in schools or youth work, is not about seeking equity or an equal opportunity of *starting at the same point*, it is concerned with equality and social justice that seeks to ensure that young people have a fair chance of *finishing at the same point* (Baker et al., 2009; Crowther, 2017).

While acknowledging an impetus for change in taking a more holistic view of education, the dominant discourse around school education and its inherent power hierarchies remain. This makes it difficult to predict whether this view of education will be extended, or if school education will continue to assimilate all forms of education with young people through the arbitrary application of a 'school-age' construct, whereby educational youth work is subsumed within the mainstream.

Community Education and CLD have made collaborative work a high priority, but this does not mean a fully integrated practice. So far, this has worked in school-based practices which offer programmes or projects that compliment schooling education. However, there is room for improved understanding of the contribution that distinct youth work practices make in crossing educational boundaries between formal and informal methodologies. For example, in seeing young people as assets in their communities, informal educational youth work is different from formalised work with young people that is located in services for employability, health, policing, and social work wherein young people who are routinely engaged via referral, or are required to attend, through formalised processes that identify or label young people as deficient or in need of 'intervention'.

Seeing the young person as the primary client, according to Sercombe (2010: 26), 'places youth work in radical distinction to most other forms of engagement with young people ... [where the role is] ... to balance the interests of different stakeholders'. However, despite the distinctiveness of specific practices, professional or disciplinary boundaries are often blurred, for example, in the use of common language and informal educational methods to engage with young people in community, health, school and social contexts. This blurring of boundaries can create a useful starting point for understanding and collaboration. Engaging in purposeful dialogue across disciplinary boundaries could achieve new synergies in multi-disciplinary practices, across Great Britain and internationally.

Wenger (1998) suggests that learning about meaning and understanding are shaped by time and place, by physical environment, by social relationships, and by the individual and collective ideas of everyone engaged in the learning process. Understanding that the world is not fixed, and that people are guided by different ideas or beliefs, or live in different cultural and social circumstances, creates boundaries and borders between people and practices. If these boundaries and borders are socially constructed, then they may be socially deconstructed. Deconstructing boundaries and borders involves working within and outwith current discourses to create new ideas and alternative forms of knowledge (Giroux, 2005, 2009).

In youth work, a complex set of cultural and social relations assist young people to learn by mixing across cultural and social boundaries in order to create new identities and understandings of the world, (Coburn, 2013). Boundary crossing can raise young people's awareness of commonality, by showing how they are connected through shared characteristics, for example, in gender, ability and style grouping. In this sense, youth work facilitates the consolidation and development of new ideas and identities among young people. Youth work's capacity for the development and consolidation of ideas are key to understanding its distinctive methodology for engaging with young people on their own terms as part of a power sharing negotiated relationship (Coburn, 2013; Coburn & Gormally, 2017). The assertion of youth work as a distinctive methodology (Harland & McCready, 2012) could be linked to Wenger's (1998: 95) ideas on the evolution of social practices, which are achieved through a mutual alignment of, 'repertoire, styles and discourses'. Understanding how youth work operates at the boundaries of practice assists in showing how it works across borders in order to build new ideas and perspectives. Wenger calls this affirmation and consolidation of practice a 'duality of boundary relations' (Wenger, 1998: 104). This is useful in conceptualising youth work, but could also encourage thinking beyond current practice boundaries, in order to consider possibilities for change. Thus, borders and boundaries hold the potential to become sites of *professional* transformation (Coburn, 2010, p. 33). Thinking about youth work as a border pedagogy (Coburn & Gormally, 2017; Coburn & Wallace, 2011) helps young people and practitioners to explore the nature of practice and identity as *becoming*.

This is particularly useful, as today's young people and youth workers live in 'interesting' times, and, despite a changed world since the heyday of youth club work, possibilities remain for flexible and responsive youth work. Technology is used to connect, create, learn and meet partners (in every sense); this places social media and Internet activity at the core of young people's lives. Reported shifts in young people's political involvement and their increased contribution to communities through volunteering (Payne, 2017), give optimism for new means of engagement. Yet, these shifts sit alongside persistently high rates of suicide and an increasing number of violent deaths among young people. They also sit within a context where the decision to leave the EU was not strongly supported by young people. They now have to live with the consequences of something for which they did not vote (Coburn & Gormally, 2017). This is compounded in the Scottish context by the additional Independence Referendum, where the outcome was also inconsistent with the younger vote (Coburn & Gormally, 2017).

In some sense, this range of 'interests' creates a perfect storm for youth work. It is beginning to be revisited politically – arguments for rebuilding a 'statutory youth service' seem to be taking hold as there appears to be an increasing political will towards investing in youth work (Nicholls, 2018). Yet, whether a statutory youth service offer is a means of responding to contemporary interests is contested, and raises questions about the kind of service and practices that are imagined or rebuilt. What kind of youth work is fit for purpose in this post-industrial and emerging-technological age? Are current professionally qualifying programmes fit for purpose in this new era? Does the current liminal state of youth work (Coburn & Gormally, 2017), afford space for personal and professional transformation, where ideas can be discussed, and shifts in different directions can be imagined in creating futures that are not yet known?

Neoliberal developments in public policy and the management of services have sought to regulate practice through, for example, use of function-by-function competences, and the creation of occupational standards for youth work (LLUK, 2008). While these include basic competencies such as, being able to 'communicate effectively and develop rapport with young people' or 'identify and secure resources for youth work', they also include more complex elements, such as 'lead change' or 'support young people in taking action and tackling problems'. These more complex elements present opportunities to counteract the social control agendas that have become more explicit and dominant in recent practice (Jeffs & Banks, 2010) and to challenge dangerously tokenistic forms of participation that are sold as 'citizenship activity' (Fyfe, 2010).

As state intervention in the lives of young people has increased (Mizen, 2004) and youth work has become, 'increasingly prescriptive, intrusive and insistent' (Davies & Merton, 2009: 46), the future development of educational youth work as an emancipatory practice remains precarious. Yet, developing such practices is vital to strengthening the logic for extending emerging national and international youth work.

Developing National and International Perspectives

Proposing youth work as educational methodology (Harland & McCready, 2012), offers possibilities for re-asserting a vision for youth work as border pedagogy that opens doors and crosses thresholds into a new ways of thinking about the future. A commitment to such praxis is needed, if, as a society, we are serious about respecting young people's right to equality and social justice.

The neoliberal project impacts on all aspects of life in Scotland, the rest of the UK, in Europe, and in the wider world. Challenging this will take more than a global coalition for educational youth work. However, youth work can logically claim a contribution to social change in areas of equality and social justice. At both micro-levels and in global contexts, structures for facilitating this already exist. These include local community practices, youth councils, youth work projects, and campaigns such as Youth Work Changes Lives and In Defence of Youth Work. It also includes global organisations such as the Commonwealth Alliance of Youth Workers' Associations, SALTO Youth, and worldwide youth parliament networks.

Thus, what is needed is not a new structure or means of connecting people. Instead, it would make sense to consider commonalities in order to develop scope for a UK-wide response to contemporary contexts, enhancing co-ordination of effort and resources through more deliberate cooperative endeavour.

1. *Youth Work Technologies and Social Media*
Youth work uses technologies to reach out to, and stay in touch, with young people. We could do more to share, consider and create technologies and social media to develop new process-based practices, tapping into campaigns for social justice. 'Learning in association with others' no longer requires young people's 'in-room' presence. Of course this does not replace youth work practices in the physical environment, but it could extend and inform the development of new virtual learning environments that currently reside within software companies that do not share socially democratic value bases or emancipatory educational purpose.

2. *Youth Work as Political Education*
In some Scottish contexts, youth workers have been instructed to steer clear of politically divisive topics, such as Brexit and the referenda on Scottish Independence. This has always been the case. Practitioners have either operated in more political environments, or have worked within such structures, but outwith their remits, to engage dialogically with young people regarding political processes, in order to develop their capacity to critique social policy and analyse power that sustains the status quo. Given this period of 'all-level political renaissance', it is time to re-acknowledge that all education, including youth work, is always political and value-laden.

3. *Youth Work for Equality, Social Justice and Well-Being*
Reflecting Robert Owen's vision for community-based education, leisure and social welfare as the key to making a good life, a focus on work associated with a radical practice remains important in creating conditions for equality and social justice. The provision of a few hours respite from lives that are impacted by poverty, poor health and isolation are not sufficient to bring about the kind of social change required for this social democratic vision. Rather than focus on *how* we do youth work, our energies should also be re-dedicated to its core purpose of achieving and sustaining equality and social justice. The lessons of this Year of Young People in Scotland should be shared more widely to show its impact in rejecting stereotyping and pathologising views of young people, disseminating this work internationally and contributing to wider global movements for equality, social justice and well-being.

Conclusion
Drawing on a radical and socialist cultural tradition, the youth work curriculum in Scotland has evolved over time to sit quite comfortably within Curriculum for Excellence where educational youth work is identified as a

discrete CLD practice. This examination of Scottish perspectives shows differences and commonalities, in historical and contemporary contexts. At a time of political, social and economic change, recognising such differences goes some way towards understanding, for example, why practitioners in Scotland, are inclined to accept school-based youth work than practitioners in other parts of Britain.

The introduction of a regulatory framework for CLD in Scotland, and continued use of Logic Models in the development of policy and practice, has forged collaboration across professional boundaries. Yet, questions remain in regard to the position of educational youth work, as part of CLD within a Curriculum for Excellence and an educational governance review, that acknowledges the youth work contribution, but does not bring the level of resourcing required to shift dominant discourses that see education as schooling in preparation for employment. Border pedagogy can assist youth workers to see different perspectives and to cross professional and geographical boundaries as a means of reconceptualising practice. Sharing methodologies and stories of success, as evident in Scotland's Year of Young People, offers hope in the reification of youth work practice and building the logic for youth work education. United by existing commonalities in youth work technologies and social media, the political nature of praxis, and the struggle for equality and social justice, can afford youth work a chance to retain its distinctiveness and to reach beyond current boundaries. This offers hope for ongoing development of an international community of practice for youth work.

A Perspective from Northern Ireland

> And admit that the waters
> Around you have grown ...
> Then you better start swimmin'
> Or you'll sink like a stone
> For the times they are a-changin'.
> (Bob Dylan: *The times they are a-changin'*)

Introduction

The conversation went something like this: "There is a wave coming ... for some this wave will gently lap their ankles and they will scarcely feel it, for others this wave will rage over their head and they will be engulfed by it and they will not know what hit them; we need to prepare now for the change that this coming". This metaphor is attributed to a senior officer in the statutory youth service in

Northern Ireland in the early 2010s discussing the change they expected in the youth service in the near future. Youth work has been described as diverse or disparate (McCready & Loudon, 2015) or weakly classified and loosely structured (Scott-McKinley, 2016). However Northern Ireland's distinct context and history have shaped its statutory youth service today.

Youth Work Foundations
Pre-Partition Youth Work in Ireland

Youth work in Ireland in the latter 19th century echoes the development in other parts of the UK. Industrialisation and young people's increased leisure time led to the emergence of a relationally-driven service[1] (Davis, 1999; McCready & Louden, 2015). Practice was informed by concern for the spiritual, moral (character formation) and physical development of young people, motivated variously by evangelical Christianity and the political concerns of the British state and empire (McCready & Loudon, 2015). In addition, Irish Nationalism's campaign for self-government led to the Home Rule crisis at this time.[2] The Easter rising of 1916 was quickly followed by the partitioning of Ireland.[3] The civil unrest of the troubles in the 1960s and 1970s is rooted firmly in this period. Throughout this unsettled period, youth work was largely the domain of the philanthropic and religious.

Post Partition in Northern Ireland

McCready and Loudon (2015) point out that, there was little legislative or apparent interest in youth work by the Northern Ireland State post World War 1 and prior to the onset of World War 2. During this time, the Ministry of Education enacted grant making powers to 'reputable' voluntary organisations involved in promoting positive recreation for young people.[4] The voluntary sector continued to consolidate its infrastructure with SCOYO (The Standing Conference on Voluntary Youth Organisations) being established in 1939. SCOYO was broadly interested in 'collaboration, promotion of the service, research and the drive to serve young people' (McCready & Loudon, 2015: 50).

However, post WW2, following the Youth Welfare Act (NI) 1947, emerging state interest led to 'a vibrant period' (McCready & Loudon, 2015: 33). A newly established Youth Committee produced annual reports on the youth work sector; training was established, and the sector was consulted and surveyed, and recommendations were made on areas such as juvenile delinquency and recognition of youth leadership as a profession.

In the late 1950s and early 1960s, there was significant cultural change in the UK. In England and Wales, the Albermarle Report saw substantial investment and expansion in government sponsored youth work. A year later in 1961 the white paper on The Development of the Youth Service in Northern Ireland was produced. This led to the Youth Welfare and Physical Training and Recreation Act (NI) 1962, which established the Youth and Sports councils and made grants available for up to 75% running costs and 90% of salaries of full-time youth workers.

The 'Troubles' and Emergence of the Statutory Youth Service

Northern Ireland's youth work commenced its significant deviation from the rest of the UK in the early 1970s as a direct consequence of the sectarian powder-keg that exploded in 1969. The period 1969 to 1976 accounts for over half the deaths of the whole Troubles through shootings, bombings, riots and as a result of the social fragmentation that occurred. Young people often bore the brunt of this turbulence, and there was concern that they would be drawn into rioting, paramilitary activity and conflict (Smyth & Hamilton, 2003; Smyth, 2007: 49). The regional government in Stormont was prorogued, and power was transferred to Westminster in 1972. Government was now by direct rule in London.

Youth workers during this time were increasingly engaged in delivering diversionary programmes aimed at keeping young people, particularly young men, off the streets and away from violence. This was effectively a peace-keeping role. However, under direct rule, there were significant changes in local government structures, as responsibility for housing, education, health and social services were transferred to sub-regional professional public bodies. Within Education, these bodies became the five Education and Library Boards. It was at this time, under the Education and Library Board (NI) Order 1972, that the statutory basis of youth work was established. This was followed by the Recreation and Youth Service (NI) Order 1973, which formed a youth committee to advise the Department of Education. This, in effect, produced the structures and functions of the modern youth service. At the same time, the first dedicated professional qualification emerged in 1972, with a two-year full-time Diploma in Youth and Community work commencing in 1973. The state's annual budget for youth work rose from £125,500 in 1972 to £3.5million during 1975/1976 and to £8 million in 1980. 'This funding resulted in 143 purpose built youth centres, a host of full-time youth work posts and an increase in professional training' (DENI, 1986: 5). The Youth Service positioned itself as reactive and needs-responsive, an approach which government appeared to endorse. Although this created a safer environment for young people, there was recognition of an over-emphasis on sport and recreation aimed at catering for the assumed needs of young men (Harland & Morgan, 2003), and keeping young people off the streets.

Stability, Curriculum, Care and Maintenance

The 1980s were characterised by reduced riots and street violence, signalling a change in the intensity of the ethnic conflict (Smyth & Hamilton, 2003: 19). Government interest in youth work remained high, as did investment. But with interest and investment comes expectation. In the late 1980s, government expectations of the Youth Service were made more explicit. These expectations are expressed clearly in the 1987 document a 'Policy for the Youth Service in Northern Ireland' (DENI, 1987) commonly referred to as 'The Blue Book'. This document introduced a central core curriculum for youth work in Northern Ireland. In addition, it signalled the creation of the Youth Council for Northern Ireland with its statutory function to directly advise the Minister of Education concerning youth work. The policy included two concepts that were central to monetarist Conservative policy makers at the time, the introduction of a central core curriculum, and a contract culture. These concepts were linked to a wider policy push for value for money, demonstrable effectiveness and efficiency. Youth Service managers were asked to be 'explicit about the value of youth work' at a time when budgets were constrained and costs were rising (Carter et al., 1995; McCormick, 1998; Scott-McKinley, 2016). The policy also recognised the reconciliation and cross community work that youth workers had been engaged in, before, and since, the outbreak of the Troubles.

As this policy bedded in, seismic shifts in the political environment were underway; this culminated in the political settlement of the Belfast Agreement in 1998. The Agreement paved the way for a return to devolution and the removal of direct rule. Northern Ireland politicians were once again in control, only this time, within a power sharing assembly. 'Power sharing' required mandatory coalition government including the main political parties from across nationalism and unionism. One of the first tasks of the administration was a root and branch 'Review of Public Administration' signalling another shake-up of local government and the sub-regional structures supporting youth work. This was a slow and meandering process that was typical of the political climate of the time; civil servants have dubbed this as a period of 'continuation on a care and maintenance basis' (Knox, 2008).

Where Are We Now? Current Context and Challenges

Changing Priorities ... Shifting Sands

In the relative political stability that emerged, a key development in the youth sector in Northern Ireland, has been the introduction of Priorities for Youth: Improving Young People's lives (DE, 2013). Priorities for Youth (PfY) focuses on economic imperatives and realigns youth work with Department of Education formal education priorities concerning underachievement, raising standards and addressing the performance gap in qualifications evident for many young people in Northern Ireland. PfY appears to have the hallmarks of a more integrated departmental youth policy, with clearer links to other education policy and priorities. The focus is on securing the 'strategic alignment of youth work with Department of Education Priorities'. As in the late 1980s, we hear the identification of 'disorder' and the justification for the political corrective of discipline, and a further technical, rational intervention. The Department of Education Minister, John O'Dowd, sets out the major policy challenge it seeks to address; "youth work could no longer be allowed to remain a separate policy, detached from the overall education priorities". Bunyan (2012) argues that all governments seek to shape the discourse of social change. As youth workers, there is the potential for social policy discourse to outflank our work, as power affects the reality of practice. PfY is a significant re-orientation of emphasis towards formal education and away from informal education and associational and emancipatory practice.

Beattie et al. (2017) recognise that 'the inference was that youth work needed to 'compliment' the formal education agenda; rather than having any distinct merit in and of itself'. Despite all the positive statements, it was clear that youth work was now to fulfil a subordinate role supporting formal education.

In addition, a very explicit message was communicated to the statutory Youth Service. PfY clearly states the primacy of the voluntary youth sector in Youth Service delivery: 'The voluntary sector will be encouraged and supported to provide those youth services assessed as needed and the statutory youth sector will continue to deliver youth services where there is no viable alternative' (DE, 2013: 16). Large teams of statutory workers are now uncertain about their future roles.

The second impact of PfY has been substantial structural change; this is the outworking of the Review of Public Administration, which is still ongoing. The generation-old structures of the five Education and Library Boards and the Youth Council for Northern Ireland (YCNI) were radically overhauled. The five ELBs were amalgamated into a single Education Authority. Discussion continues to ensue about 'convergence' and alignment of everything from internal financial procedure, human resources policies, through to child protection policies and procedures. This has caused significant upheaval within the new organisation, with various regional emphases sometimes in competition. The Education Authority (EA) was established under the Education Act (NI) 2014 and became operational on 01 April 2015. It is a non-departmental body sponsored by the Department of Education. EA is responsible for ensuring that efficient and effective primary and secondary education services are available to meet the needs of children and young people, and to support the provision of efficient and effective youth services. The budget and staff of the Youth Council for Northern Ireland were transferred to the Education Authority, signalling the closure of the YCNI.[5] The Youth Service now has a new internal structure, an expected reduction in middle management youth officers, a reduced management hierarchy and an explicit mandate from government.

One way that this mandate was actioned was the establishment of a new Regional Advisory Group (RAG). The role of the RAG is to consider and provide advice to the Education Authority Youth Service on the delivery of youth services which reflect regional needs and priorities for both universal provision (raising standards for all) and targeted provision (closing the performance gap) and meet the needs of specific groups of young people. RAG includes stakeholders with interest and expertise in Youth Service policy including representation from young people, voluntary organisations and other government departments assisted by statutory partners.

A key focus for RAG is the development of a Regional Youth Development Plan (RYDP). This is a three year, strategic plan for the Youth Service across Northern Ireland, 'responding to assessed need and focused on outcomes to address the priorities and actions identified in Priorities for Youth' (EA, 2017: 2). The RYDP makes clear how PfY is interpreted: 'Priorities for Youth directs that Youth Work must be planned in response to the assessed need, prioritised age ranges and other identified groups' (EA, 2017: 7). The new age ranges for EA funded youth work are aligned more closely to formal education key stages, 4–8, 9–13, 14–18, 19–21 and 22–25 with the key age bands for intervention being 9–13 and 14–18 (DE, 2013: 17). Therefore, needs assessment becomes a key feature in providing a transparent and accountable justification for the allocation of resources. Under the new structures, needs assessment takes place at three levels – within very localised provision, at area level undertaken by a Senior Youth Officer (planned to be co-terminus with the 11 local councils) and at Northern Ireland level. The first Regional Assessment of Need covers the period 2017–2020. 'The purpose of this needs assessment therefore has been to identify the key issues affecting young people in Northern Ireland, especially those most marginalised and disadvantaged and to give an indication of where resources may be best focussed to meet their needs' (EA, 2016: 3). The process uses survey methods (both online and offline) and consulted with 11,937 young people, 795 youth workers and 862 parents. It provides detailed lists of issues of concern raised by young people, and can be broken down by age, gender and local council area. Such centralised identification can be clearly powerful and useful to policy makers, and can inform managers' and workers' decision making. However, stakeholders have consistently raised concerns that an over-reliance on government statistics and quantitative surveys can mean identification of need can be missed, especially in respect of rural young people, youth crime and minority groups, for example LGBT+ young people. However, there appears to be evidence within the first annual Addendum to the Regional Assessment of Need (EA, 2018: 4) that the needs of young people who identify as LGBT+ have been acknowledged.[6] The Foreword acknowledges that the first assessment may have 'lacked detail as to the extent of concern that stakeholders attributed to these issues'. What is evident is that the quality of the methodologies used to identify need will become increasingly important. In addition, there is serious risk for practitioners, with youth workers' pedagogical preference to 'start where young people are at' being set aside. There is potential for workers to feel trapped in addressing pre-identified needs with pre-identified target groups in meeting pre-identified outcomes: a kind of youth work dystopia. Youth workers have to be flexible, creative and disruptive, finding ways to trouble and question while they muddle through. They play the system, and 'ride two horses', shoehorning practice into targeted language, but this can present ethical dilemmas. The challenges are clear, how can needs identification be clear and concise, but inclusive of qualitative evidence? How can pre-identification of need for a three-year plan be flexible for practitioners responding to the needs of young people at the point of contact? And how can youth work managers be flexible and supportive of their staff in responding to the tensions that are created? Finally, the terminology of 'need', even though important, nourishes deficit constructions of how we understand young people.

These new emphases and structures pave the way for the third major development – the prominence given to new managerial methods. Central to this is a new funding distribution mechanism, presently in draft and stalled because of the current political impasse in Northern Ireland. In the words of the minister, "I now want to ensure that by providing a clear policy remit, planning and performance will improve and provide increased evidence of the value of youth work and a stronger case". In addition to the regional approach, youth workers have faced an 'increased focus on proving outcomes and impact through 'scientific', quantifiable models and measurement tools is gaining traction to the exclusion of most other means' (Beattie et al., 2017). A key feature of this will be the targeting of resources and reporting systems that have 'clear performance indicators and measurable evidence of progress'. The challenge for the youth sector will be to maintain an understanding of a pedagogy that is process-focused, when the policy shift appears to be (like the late 1980s) towards more instrumental approaches. This re-orientation to measurable outcomes and accreditation, thrusts youth work into a more calculable and product orientated form of practice with the inherent danger of values drift, prescription and additional transaction costs. Coupled with the push to central management information systems, centralised quality assurance and performance moderation, performativity becomes a predominant experience of semi-professional and professional youth workers. As practitioners internalise and individualise the language of performance, adhering to its regime of truth results in the profession stepping further away from the collective and emancipatory basis of practice. Undeniably, the riposte by management is that such change is crucial to ensure continued funding for youth work.

Devolution and Youth Service Budgets

It is notable that in the area of funding, devolution presents challenges and opportunities for youth work. The devolution experiment, which started in the UK in 1998, has enabled greater divergence in youth work policy, funding and practice. The overall budget available to spend in Northern Ireland is still set in Westminster by the UK government. This is allocated using the Barnett formula.[7] Northern Ireland politicians have had limited influence on this budget (until recent influence by the Democratic Unionist Party in the Hung Parliament, 2018). However, local politicians can shape how the money is spent. The budget is 'unhypothecated'. In other words, not specified in any way, meaning that, Northern Ireland politicians have discretion and can prioritise differently from the UK Government's decisions concerning England.

Northern Ireland politicians have chosen to prioritise health and education, with the allocated education budget reaching approximately £2bn per annum. Youth Service budgets are structured within the Department of Education, and because of its statutory basis, these budgets are ring-fenced. The Youth Service is allocated approximately 1.8% of this budget, and has remained remarkably stable during a time of austerity.

TABLE 2.1   Total Youth Service Budgets

2013–2014	2014–2015	2015–2016	2016–2017	2017–2018
£34,081,000	£34,940,000	£32,864,000	£32,881,000	£33,431,000

(SOURCE DEPARTMENT OF EDUCATION)

The policy and structural changes discussed, have had little impact on overall youth service spending. This brings us back to the metaphor of the tidal wave lapping at the feet of some and engulfing others. If youth work is in an area of deprivation (normally the top 15% of SOA[8] in the Northern Ireland Multiple Deprivation Indicators), remains within the PfY targeted age groups and specified targeted strategic areas, and can comply with new managerial outcome demands, then funding is likely to remain stable. Outside these parameters, funding may change dramatically. With the scale and pace of change, and the rapid movement of personnel, there is always the risk that institutional memory will be lost. The challenge for the sector is to ensure that policy makers and senior managers in the Education Authority remain informed about youth work's statutory basis and ring fenced funding. The dangers of competitive tendering and commissioning of services looms with the inherent problems of short-termism and the salami slicing of budgets.

The Beginning of Making Everything Clear ...

> How I manage, it's not clear, dear dear, you say it's not clear, something is wanting to make it clear, I'll seek, what is wanting, to make everything clear, I'm always seeking something, it's tiring in the end, and it's only the beginning. (Beckett, 2010)

It would be too easy to underestimate the information demands currently being placed on the youth service. There is an epistemic shift occurring for statutory youth service managers, which is impacting youth work. This represents a change in the nature and quality of collected data, and how this is used as evidence to inform their decisions about practice. Managers and youth work practitioners are expected to respond with increasing speed, to an expanding variety of information requests from politicians and local and regional government officials, about resources and their deployment, outputs, and, most importantly, outcomes. Youth workers are increasingly using outcomes-based accountability, which is part of a wider approach by the NI government (NIA, 2016); this mirrors developments in Scotland.

The shift for managers has been a significant rise in demand to produce tertiary artefacts,[9] as managers request finer detail from youth workers for outcomes based reporting (in the form of quality assurance processes moderation, inspection and other reporting regimes). The challenge for managers is how to aggregate the increasing amounts of information in digestible forms for politicians, funders and policy makers. Managers face the challenge of how they can outline, explain, justify and account for the needs of young people, plan responses to those needs, and ensure the service produces outcomes for young people, (or perhaps more accurately, outcomes in young people for government). This shift from inputs and outputs to outcomes is a significant challenge for the youth work sector. It raises the potential for payment by results style contracts between the statutory and voluntary sector.[10]

This creates a great tension for youth service managers. Third level arte-facts (accessible documents that provide area or regional information in a summary form concerning needs identification, plans or outcome reporting) require knowledge and evidence from youth workers that is 'mobile, immuta-ble and combinable' (Latour, 1988). Priorities for Youth explicitly recognises this need, and requires the Education Authority Youth Service to create a management information system (DE, 2013: 17–21). However, it is important to caution that the forms of information and knowledge that meet this need are often orientated to statistical quantification. The boundary here for youth workers, and their managers, is the need to insist on numbers *and* narrative, stories of transformation *and* statistics. There may also be some opportunities as the Youth Service is challenged to work to Open Data principles.[11] This may provide much needed public transparency concerning statutory Youth Service operation. The danger of course is an over-simplification of how youth work practice is represented. An example is the current internal use of Youth Service scorecards, where target outcomes are monitored using single page spread-sheet dashboards with traffic light colours for managers. This is an exogenous culture orientated towards managerialism.

However, it is important to remember that youth work is context driven, and interested in the specifics of young people's experiences, needs and aspira-tions. As such, youth work is concerned with the particular (Ord, 2016). A shift in discourse to the reasoning of industrial production, market competition and management are problematic for youth work. Decision making becomes more hierarchical and is framed within bureaucratic-administrative systems. The role of management is increasingly highlighted and promoted as a means of organisational control, and engenders and 'justifies' the need for greater effi-ciency, effectiveness and value for money (Ord, 2011). Managerialism becomes not only likely, but unavoidable. Youth workers and youth work organisations must justify themselves and their work in terms of its adherence to externally defined management principles and central policy imperatives. Consequently, youth workers and young people become objectified subjects to be controlled, organised, classified and verified.

Conclusion

You must go on. I can't go on. I'll go on. (Beckett, 2010)

According to Priorities for Youth (DE, 2013: 2); youth work is particularly rel-evant for young people 'at risk of disengaging from society, those who become disaffected at school, those at risk of committing an offence, those who could become non-stakeholders in their own community, and those adversely affected by the legacy of the conflict'. This policy discourse means that youth work is in danger of becoming part of a system that re-defines young people legally, medically and pastorally as 'deficit subjects'. Some are within formal education, where youth workers in schools will intervene; others are exiled outside of formal education, where youth workers will work in alternative education programmes. We have become a form of 'triage' for formal education. In terms of practice, the focus will be on underachievement, youth workers will be expected to engage with and practice increasingly within the formal school environment, for example The Learning Together Programme. For those young people impacted by the legacy of the conflict, there will be a new strand of work associated with Fresh Start funding[12] were statutory youth workers alongside teachers and voluntary sector youth workers work in the most deprived communities to address paramilitarism. It is expected that this work will include aspects of Global Service Learning to re-engage young people in their communities. For the wider youth population, the funding associated with Together Building a United Community[13] (T: BUC) presents a new opportunity for the statutory Youth Service to lead and set the agenda for community relations work within the youth work sector. These programmes are very much 'signature' projects, some with a high degree of specialization. For the statutory Youth Service, they have the potential to raise its profile and kudos within the Education Authority. However, as targeted programmes, they risk undermining and damaging the associational nature of existing open access provision.

For some youth workers, the re-orientation, re-structuring and epistemic shifts discussed in this section are a form of 'existential threat' to practice. They see the potential for youth work to lose its relevance, meaning, connection, dialogue and generative process. Conversation is replaced by session plans; ongoing dialogue is replaced by 6, 8 or 12-week pre-planned programmes. Often workers remain true to the purpose, values, ethics and methods of youth work, while doing so in an alien policy, organisational and accountability culture.

Northern Ireland youth work has become increasingly classified and more tightly structured as it has developed. Priorities for Youth constricts this classification further in the service of formal education. Moreover, streamlined structures narrow control to a single Education Authority. Funding commitments from Government remain stable, so it can be argued that clearer classification and simplified structures have been effective in maintaining a statutory Youth Service. The question we may need to ask is: 'what will the nature of youth work be that keeps swimming?'

Welsh Perspectives: The Future of Youth Work in Wales – Back to the Future or Forward to the Past?

Introduction

Where youth work is going in Wales in 2018 is partly the product of its history and partly the result of the commitment and enthusiasm of countless young people, youth workers and managers in both voluntary and maintained sectors; but the battle for the heart and soul of youth work is likely to be won or lost in the context of policy decisions at local and national levels. The current policy context for Youth Work in Wales is dominated by recent elections and the European referendum, the ongoing effects of austerity, a series of Welsh Government (WG) reviews of aspects of youth work, and the emergence of the Education Workforce Council.

Wales continues to follow a similar path to England in seeing significant cuts to youth services and restrictions to grants to voluntary organisations. Some local authorities have dispensed entirely with their youth services, others are in the process of investigating trusts and social enterprises, and others still are struggling on as Youth Services; but all are significantly affected by the shift from open-access provision towards targeted, case-load style work, focused around the drive to reduce the number of young people not in education, employment or training (NEET). Voluntary organisations, perhaps being more used to accommodating the demands of funders, are undertaking targeted, outcome-driven work with young people, whilst retaining open-access work as far as they are able. Both, according to the 2017 review of the National Strategy for Youth Work in Wales, have been more heavily influenced by the 2013 Youth Engagement and Progression Framework (the NEETs agenda), than by the WG's strategies for Youth Work in Wales.

The Political Context for Youth Work in Wales

The construction of a new policy context in Wales arose from the election of New Labour to UK government in 1997, and the establishment of the National Assembly for Wales (NAW) in 1999. The new Assembly was created by the Welsh Government Act 1998 and assumed responsibility for a wide range of policies and public services previously controlled by the UK Government through the Secretary of State for Wales.

In the most recent Welsh Assembly Government elections held in May 2016, the Labour Party remained the largest party as it has been since the first elections in 1999. However, as it did not have a majority, it needed to look for cross-party support, which included making the single Liberal Democrat Assembly Member Cabinet Minister for Education. With regard to local government, the WG, continues to consult on a reforming agenda, with a number of models being proposed, including significant reductions to the current 22 local authorities, a regional approach, and developing greater co-operation between the existing local authorities. A report commissioned by the WG from consultants rezolvPS in 2015, 'A National Approach to Youth Work in Wales' (WG, 2015) explored various models for the delivery of youth services in the context of local government reform: including a national Youth Service, regional arrangements, and the status quo with enhancements such as hypothecation of funding, statutory guidance, inspection of youth services, and the creation of an independent strategic body for Youth Work in Wales, along the lines of YouthLink Scotland. Serious consideration of such proposals could radically shift the policy context for Youth Work in Wales in the future.

Throw into this political mix the decision by British voters to end their membership of the European Union, with its concomitant effects on European funding streams such as Communities First that have become increasingly vital for many Welsh youth organisations, initiatives and projects, and the result is a volatile combination of factors, the outcome of which is hard to predict. Clearly, there will be implications for all areas of policy development related to young people in Wales, and major effects on how services for young people are funded, organised and delivered in future.

Policy Drivers and Debates

The new political era brought about by Welsh devolution allowed amendments to Section 123 of the Learning and Skills Act 2000, enabling the National Assembly in Wales to direct Welsh local authorities, through the seminal Extending Entitlement strategy (2000) and Extending Entitlement Direction and Guidance (2002), to 'provide, secure or participate' in the provision of 'youth support services'.

These pieces of legislation, which still obtain, set out the Welsh Government's intention for universal entitlement for all young people aged 11 to 25 to take advantage of employment opportunities, and participate in education and the life of their communities. Extending Entitlement directed the 22 local authorities in Wales to set up Young People's Partnerships (YPPs) as the primary vehicle for maximizing multi-agency activity to deliver a series of ten stated entitlements for 11–25 year olds.

This approach was driven at local authority level by a Young People's Partnership Plan underpinned by the United Nations Convention on the Rights of the Child (UNCRC, 1989), which, since 1999, had become the basis of all work for children and young people in Wales, and contributed to the appointment of a Children's Commissioner in 2001.

Young People's Partnerships and Plans were quickly superseded by the production of the Children Act (2004) whose guidance required local authorities to co-ordinate collaborative working arrangements (from 2008) in an overarching Children and Young People's Plan for all 0–25 year olds, incorporating the collaboration and planning requirements for 11–25 year olds set out in Extending Entitlement.

The ensuing National Youth Service Strategy was much anticipated. In its Foreword, Jane Davidson, Minister of Education, Lifelong Learning and Skills at the time, described the Youth Service as 'an important part of the vision for Extending Entitlement – that all organisations providing services for young people should work together to provide a network of support and experiences to all young people' (WAG, 2007:1). It was rooted in the values and standards of the National Occupational Standards for Youth Work (LSIS, 2012), and crucially contained action plans and lines of accountability for Welsh Government, local authorities, the WLGA (Welsh Local Government Association), voluntary organisations and the FE and HE sectors. The strategy recognised the 'experience and achievements' of the Wales Youth Agency prior to its subsumption by the Welsh Government. However, the loss of its independent voice has been much debated, and is regretted by many.

In 2012, the Welsh Government challenged local authority areas across Wales to improve the way they worked together by developing a Single Integrated Plan (SIP) to streamline arrangements for partnership working and reduce the possibility of local authority plans working in isolation. The SIPs were to replace the proliferation of other partnership plans, including the Children and Young People's Plan.

Continuing the policy direction towards multi-agency youth support services for young people in Wales, WG brought out the Youth Engagement and Progression Framework (YEPF) and Implementation Plan (WG, 2013), which provided non-statutory guidance towards reducing the numbers of young people not in education, employment or training (NEET). Whilst the YEPF recognised youth workers' status 'for their engagement, brokerage and lead worker skills' (WLGA, 2015; p2), a collateral effect was to focus youth services on the systems and targets of the YEPF, rather than on the Youth Strategy, thus increasing the focus on targeted youth work, and away from open-access provision.

In the same year, a partnership of maintained and voluntary sector youth work stakeholders produced 'Youth Work in Wales: Principles and Purposes' (Youth Work in Wales Review Group, 2013), a re-affirmation of the unique methodology, values and professional practice of youth work. This continued the to and fro between government and the youth work sector with regard to policy direction. The Principles and Purposes document built on the

Curriculum Statement for Wales, added a fifth pillar, 'inclusive', to the well-established four pillars of youth work – educative, expressive, participative and empowering. The subsequently revised National Youth Work Strategy for Wales (WG, 2014), set out a four-year vision for youth work in Wales, and continued the clear policy linkage with the Youth Engagement and Progression Framework, requiring the contribution of youth work organisations to be better connected with broader support services, as a means of ensuring a more consistent and integrated offer to young people.

However, it also firmly links targeted work with open-access services, describing them as 'highly valued by many young people for the continuity of support they offer within communities' (WG, 2014: 2). Open-access provision is seen as 'vitally important ... to effectively connect young people with more targeted or specialised support' (ibid.: 2).

The Strategy identifies youth work as being beneficial in providing safe places for young people to relax and have fun, gain personal and social skills essential for future employment and responsible community membership, and, where potentially vulnerable young people can access support. It also recognises youth work as being well placed, and having the necessary skill sets, to provide the 'lead worker' role for a number of young people as part of the Youth Engagement and Progression Framework.

Forward to the Future
Into the changeable winds blowing around Youth Work, an educational policy super-tanker sailed into view. The review of schools' curriculum in Wales by Professor Graham Donaldson (WG, 2015), styled 'Successful Futures', was described by then Minister of Education Huw Lewis as a "compelling, exciting and ambitious vision for a new curriculum for Wales". It calls for greater focus on 'social competencies', and criticises a current over-emphasis on assessment, qualification and performance management (WLGA, 2016). Vanessa Rogers (2016), in her Evaluation of Youth Work in (Welsh) Schools, found significant benefits to young people of the presence of youth workers in schools. Tom Wylie in his position statement 'Developing Youth Work in Wales' suggested 'youth work should aspire to having a complementary role with schools'(WG, 2016: p3), and included 'co-ordinated provision for youth workers in all secondary schools and colleges' in the Welsh Youth Work Charter (WG, 2016: 4). Do these luminaries indicate the future direction of Welsh Government youth policy, and an opportunity for youth work to make a greater contribution to formal education in schools? A recent report (NAW, 2016) certainly felt that both voluntary and statutory sectors should play a central role in curriculum reform. Others would see such a move towards youth work in schools as a

further erosion of the foundational principles of youth work, and a shift away from informal learning in community settings available to all young people on a voluntary basis, an approach which characterises the majority of the Welsh Youth Work Charter.

Another recent policy pointer for the future direction of Youth Work in Wales, the Well-being of Future Generations (Wales) Act 2015, proposes to make public bodies think more about the long term, work better with people, communities and each other, and take a more joined-up approach to preventing problems. The title of the Act would certainly suggest a commitment by the Welsh Government to young people as the future generations of Wales.

And Coming into View ...

A number of other factors have come together more recently, which prompt both cautious optimism and evidence-based skepticism. WG initiated a comprehensive series of reviews, including Extending Entitlement, the impact of the National Youth Work Strategy for Wales 2014–2018, the Youth Work Strategy Support Grant, the funding of national voluntary organisations, the effectiveness of the Council for Wales of Voluntary Youth Services (CWYS), and the functions of ETS Wales.

These reviews have taken place in the wake of a trenchant report from the Children and Young People's Committee (CYPC) of the National Assembly for Wales (NAW) (the scrutiny function for WG). The 'What type of youth service does Wales want? Report of the inquiry into Youth Work' (NAW, 2016), calls for a national model for youth work 'encompassing statutory and voluntary provision' (NAW, 2016: 9). The Committee is 'concerned that targeted provision has been prioritised at the expense of open-access provision' (NAW, 2016: 5–6) and argues for a balance. It concludes that there is a pressing need for major intervention from WG to maintain universal entitlement for Welsh young people amongst continued funding cuts.

The review of the 2014–2018 Strategy for Youth Work in Wales (WG, 2017), rooted in consultation with youth workers, young people and strategic bodies from both maintained and voluntary sectors, reached the same conclusion regarding open-access provision.

The CYPC report also called for a new national body for Youth Work in Wales 'to provide the impetus for a new way of working based on co-ordination of the voluntary and statutory sectors' (NAW, 2016: 26). The irony of the Wales Youth Agency having been disbanded as an independent body in 2005 on the advice of Welsh Government officials for, amongst other things, being too focused on the youth work sector, continues to rankle with some in the sector in Wales. The Youth Strategy review (WG, 2017) found a similar lack of strategic leadership for youth work, and a disparity between the funding of services in the voluntary and maintained sectors: it recommended, *inter alia*, that where voluntary organisations are better placed to provide services, funding should go to them.

As part of their commendable series of reviews, Welsh Government commissioned Margaret Jervis, doyenne of voluntary sector organisation Valleys Kids, to look again at Extending Entitlement, the provisions of which regarding youth support services in Wales, although never rescinded, had largely been superseded by subsequent measures. She produced a hard-hitting reminder of the value of youth work in supporting young people and delivering youth support services (Our Future – a Review of Extending Entitlement (2017). She acknowledges the complex environment young people currently encounter, quoting Public Health Wales' (WG, 2017: 11) startling revelation that 47% of children in Wales have been exposed to adverse childhood experiences, and the consequent need for targeted child protection services; but she asserts that 'only open-access community-based and universal youth work provision can offer an effective response to problems that occur on this scale' (WG, 2017: 11). Her challenge to government, and the sector, is how to ensure the availability of open-access provision for all young people, whilst providing targeted services for those young people who need extra support.

All the reviews agree on the need for a long-term strategy for youth work in Wales that is founded on the needs and voices of young people, the contributions of both voluntary and maintained sectors, the means of ensuring quality of provision, and the protection of, and accountability for the funds intended for youth work.

The compulsory registration of all full-time professional youth workers and youth support workers working for local authorities, in schools and other formal education contexts, adds to this atmosphere, bolstering the youth work profession, and causing employers to seek JNC recognised professionally qualified youth workers and youth support workers. The net effects have seen recruitment at Welsh Higher Education Institutions offering professional qualification courses in youth work remaining firm, clear recognition of JNC recognised youth work qualifications as the requirement for those wishing to work in the sector, and youth work sitting alongside teaching within the Education Workforce Council, which has replaced the General Teaching Council for Wales.

Déjà vu or a View of the Future?

We wait anxiously to see, but with greater optimism and anticipation than of late. Why? A new Minister responsible for Youth Work in Wales has been appointed. At a WG conference for Youth Work in Wales on 21 March 2018,

Eluned Morgan asked the assembled company to commit with her to Youth Work in Wales, and announced a new strategic direction. We should learn from the past: she undertook to publish a review of youth work finances, of the Youth Work Strategy for Wales, of the review of Extending Entitlement, and hoped their messages would challenge us. She promised to place young people at the centre, for there to be clear measurable actions, clarity in the role youth work could play in wider WG policies, an elevated position for the youth work profession as a strategic service, and parity of esteem for the voluntary and statutory sectors. There was a distinct impression that she and her officials had been listening to what the sector had been saying – suspension of disbelief hung in the air ...

For she also announced an action to take this forward – the establishment, not of a Youth Support Services Board, but of a Youth Work Board, with a remit for future youth work strategy and the formal steps that would be required. Every young person deserves a champion, she asserted; and Youth Work in Wales is a great vehicle to achieve this.

Before we get too carried away though, we have been here before in Wales. There is reference to sufficiency assessments being required in each local authority (NAW, 2016), which may demonstrate the gaps in youth work provision, but we are yet to see if more resources will be made available to achieve the vision. Youth work methods and values may influence wider Welsh Government policies; or youth work methodology may be further subsumed in targeted approaches dealing with young people's pathologies, rather than their holistic life needs. Much hangs on the work of the new Youth Work Board, and the clout it holds with politicians, the youth work sector, and, critically, with young people.

Climb aboard folks – one more time ....

Acknowledgement

Steve Drowley would like to extend his gratitude to John Rose for his helpful contributions in enabling the writing of the section on youth work in Wales.

Notes

1   The YMCA founded in London in 1844, followed 6 years later in Belfast in 1850, Carrickfergus in 1873 and Dublin in 1893. Similarly, the YWCA founded in London on 1855 followed 17 years later in Dublin in 1872. This pattern is repeated with the Girls

Clubs (England, 1861; Bray, 1877), the Boys Brigade (Glasgow, 1861; Belfast, 1888), the Scouting Association (England, 1904; Belfast, 1907) and the Guides in Ulster in 1910.

2   'Home Rule', resulted in Home Rule bills in Westminster in 1886, 1893 which were defeated and 1912 which was enacted, but suspended do to the outbreak of World War 1.

3   War of Independence 1919 to 1921 and the Government of Ireland Act (1921) partitioned Ireland creating Northern Ireland (6 Northern Counties) and finally the Anglo-Irish Treaty (26 Southern Counties) which ended British rule in most of Ireland.

4   Physical Training and Recreation Action (NI) 1938.

5   The closure of the Youth Council for Northern Ireland will require primary legislation. Tensions within education policy made this difficult, therefore only its statutory advisory function to the Minister of Education was retained with a small budget of £40,000 per annum.

6   This has been supported by formal advice from the Youth Council for Northern Ireland.

7   The majority of the devolved administrations' spending is funded by grants from the UK Government – the block grant being the largest. Since the late 1970s the non-statutory Barnett formula has determined annual changes in the block grant. More information here http://researchbriefings.parliament.uk/ResearchBriefing/Summary/CBP-7386 and http://www.bbc.co.uk/news/uk-northern-ireland-38077948

8   Super Output Areas (SOAs) were a new geography that were developed NISRA to improve the reporting of small area statistics more information available https://www.nisra.gov.uk/support/geography/northern-ireland-super-output-areas

9   Primary artefacts may be the recording, sessions and programme plans produced by workers, secondary may be considered the service level agreement produced by workers for a centre or local project.

10 This is already a feature with European funding.

11 A cultural shift to ensure that government data is transparent and publically available. https://www.opendatani.gov.uk/about

12 £0.5 billion funding for shared and integrated education projects combating paramilitarism, £150,000 per annum for Youth Service.

13 Approximately £1.5 million per year to youth service, https://www.executiveoffice-ni.gov.uk/articles/together-building-united-community

References

Baker, J., Lynch, K., Cantillion, S., & Walsh, J. (2009). *Equality: From theory to action* (2nd ed.). Basingstoke: Palgrave Macmillan.

Barnett, E. (2012, November 15). Girl guides new chief "we are the ultimate feminist organisation". *Daily Telegraph.*

Batsleer, J. (2008). *Informal learning in youth work*. London: Sage Publications.

Beattie, G., Erwin, D., Luke, J., McFeeters, M., McArdle, E., & Neill, G. (2017). *Squeezed out: The value of stories in youth work's growing measurement landscape*. Retrieved April 3, 2017, from https://sites.google.com/view/youth-work-dialogue-ni/critical-voice-articles

Beckett, S. (2010). *The unnamable*. London: Faber and Faber.

Belgutay, J. (2017, November 6). Youth work sector devastated by cuts. *Times Educational Supplement*.

Biesta, G. (2015). What is education for? On good education, teacher judgement, and educational professionalism. *European Journal of Education, 50*(1), 75–87.

Bunyan, P. (2012). *Partnership, the big society and community organising: Between romanticizing, problematizing and politicking community*. Oxford: Oxford University Press.

Burke, E. (1791). *Reflections on the revolution in France*. London: J. Dodsley.

Carter, N., Klein, R., & Day, P. (1995). *How organisations measure success: The use of performance indicators in government*. London: Routledge.

Christian Youth Work Consortium. (2016). *Report of the consultation: Christian youth work and ministry across the UK*. London: CYWC.

Coburn, A. (2010). Youth work as border pedagogy. In J. Batsleer & B. Davies (Eds.), *What is youth work?* Exeter: Learning Matters.

Coburn, A. (2013). *Learning about equality: A study of a generic youth work setting* (Unpublished doctoral thesis). University of Strathclyde, Glasgow.

Coburn, A., & Gormally, S. (2017). *Communities for social change: Practicing equality and social justice in youth and community work*. New York, NY: Peter Lang.

Coburn, A., & Gormally, S. (2017a). Cohesion, commonality and creativity: Youth work across borders. In S. Dzigurski (Ed.), *Europe in transition: Diversity, identity and youth work*. London: British Council, SALTO Cultural Diversity Resource Centre/ European Commission. Retrieved March 8, 2018, from https://www.salto-youth.net/downloads/4-17-3716/EuropeInTransition.pdf

Coburn, A., & McCafferty, P. (2016). The real Olympics games: Sponsorship, schools and the Olympics – The case of Coca Cola. *Taboo: The Journal of Culture and Education, 15*(1), 23–40. Retrieved May 14, 2018, from http://www.freireproject.org/download/journals/taboo/06coburnmccafferty.pdf

Coburn, A., & Wallace, D. (2011). *Youth work in communities and schools*. Edinburgh: Dunedin Press.

Crowther, J. (2017). Education governance in Scotland: A response. *Journal of Contemporary Community Education Practice Theory (CONCEPT), 8*(2). Retrieved May 3, 2018, from http://concept.lib.ed.ac.uk/article/view/2465/3590

Damon, W. (2004). What is positive youth development? *Annals of the American Academy of Political and Social Science, 591*(1), 13–24.

Davies, B. (1999). *From voluntaryism to welfare state: A history of the youth service in England* (Vol. 1). Leicester: Youth Work Press.

Davies, B., & Merten, B. (2009). *Squaring the circle? Findings of a 'modest inquiry'into the state of youth work practice in a changing policy environment.* Leicester: De Montfort University.

DE (Department of Education). (2003). *Youth work: A model for effective practice.* London: Department of Education for Northern Ireland.

DE (Department of Education). (2013). *Priorities for youth.* London: Department of Education for Northern Ireland.

DENI. (1986). *Northern Ireland youth service: A review.* London: Department of Education for Northern Ireland.

DENI. (1987). *Policy for the youth service in Northern Ireland.* London: Department of Education for Northern Ireland.

Department for Education. (2017). *Participation rates in higher education.* London: Department for Education.

Deuchar, R. (2008). Facilitator, director or critical friend? Contradiction and congruence in doctoral supervision styles. *Teaching in Higher Education, 13*(4), 489–500.

Donaldson, G. (2015). *Successful futures: Independent review of curriculum and assessment arrangements in Wales.* Cardiff: Welsh Government. Retrieved from https://gov.wales/docs/dcells/publications/150225-successful-futures-en.pdf

Education Authority. (2016). *Youth service regional assessment of need 2017–2020.* Retrieved from http://www.eani.org.uk/_resources/assets/attachment/full/0/52935.pdf

Education Authority. (2017). *Youth service regional development plan 2017–2020.* Retrieved from http://www.eani.org.uk/_resources/assets/attachment/full/0/59618.pdf

Education Authority. (2018). *Regional assessment of need draft addendum.* Retrieved from http://www.eani.org.uk/_resources/assets/attachment/full/0/52935.pdf

Education Scotland. (2014a). *Our ambitions for improving the life chances of young people in Scotland: National youth work strategy 2014–2019.* Retrieved May 29, 2018, from https://education.gov.scot/Documents/youth-work-strategy-181214.pdf

Education Scotland. (2014b). *What is curriculum for excellence?* Retrieved February 5, 2018, from https://education.gov.scot/scottish-education-system/policy-for-scottish-education/policy-drivers/cfe-(building-from-the-statement-appendix-incl-btc1-5)/What%20is%20Curriculum%20for%20Excellence

Elliott, A., & Lemert, C. C. (2006). *The new individualism: The emotional costs of globalization.* London: Routledge.

Fyfe, I. (2010). Young people and community engagement. In L. Tett (Ed.), *Community learning and development* (3rd ed., pp. 69–86). Edinburgh: Dunedin.

Gallagher, S., & Morgan, A. (2013). *The process is the product (Part one): Is there a need for measurement in youth work?* Edinburgh: University of Strathclyde.

Gillies, D. (2008). Quality and equality: The mask of discursive conflation in education policy texts. *Journal of Education Policy, 23*(6), 685–699.

Giroux, H. (2005). *Border crossings*. Oxon: Routledge.

Giroux, H. (2009). Critical theory and educational practice. In A. Darder, M. Baltodano, & R. Torres (Eds.), *The critical pedagogy reader* (pp. 27–51). London: Routledge.

Harland, K., & McCready, S. (2012). *Taking boys seriously—A longitudinal study of adolescent male school-life experiences in Northern Ireland*. Jordanstown: University of Ulster, Department of Justice, Northern Ireland.

Harland, K., & Morgan, T. (2006). Youth work in Northern Ireland: An exploration of emerging themes and challenges. *Youth Studies Ireland, 1*(1), 4–18.

Harland, K., Morgan, T., & Muldoon, O. (2005). *The nature of youth work in Northern Ireland: Purpose, contribution and challenges*. Belfast: Ulster University/Queens University.

Hastings, A., Bailey, N., Bramley, G., Gannon, M., & Watkins, D. (2015). *The cost of cuts: The impact on local government and poorer communities*. York: Joseph Rowntree Foundation.

HMSO. (1960). *The youth service in England and Wales* (*The Albemarle report*). Retrieved November 15, 2008, from http://www.infed.org/archives/albemarle_report

HMSO. (1964). *Children and young persons in Scotland* (*The Kilbrandon report*). Edinburgh: HMSO.

HMSO. (1975). The Alexander report: The challenge of change. In C. McConnel (Ed.), *The making of an empowering profession*. Retrieved June 24, 2018, from http://cldstandardscouncil.org.uk/wp-content/uploads/The_Making_of_An_Empowering_Profession_-_3rd_Edition_-_pdf.pdf

HMSO. (1988). *The local government act 1988* (*Chapter 9), section 28. Prohibition on promoting homosexuality by teaching or by publishing material*. Retrieved June 24, 2018, from http://www.legislation.gov.uk/ukpga/1988/9/contents

Hodgson, T., & Jeffs, T. (2013). *Evaluation of MOBEX network school inclusion project*. London: Paul Hamlyn Foundation.

Holmes, J. (1981). *Professionalisation: A misleading myth?* Leicester: National Youth Bureau.

Horgan, G. (2010). The making of an outsider: Growing up in poverty in Northern Ireland. *Youth and Society, 43*(2), 453–467.

Jeffs, T. (2018). Pearl Jephcott: Girls' club worker. *Women's History Review*. doi: 10.1080/09612025.2018.1472891

Jeffs, T., & Banks, S. (2010). Youth workers as controllers: Issues of method and purpose. In S. Banks (Ed.), *Ethical issues in youth work* (pp. 106–123). London: Routledge.

Jephcott, P. (1948). *Rising twenty: Notes on ordinary girls*. London: Faber and Faber.

Jephcott, P. (1954). *Some young people*. London: Allen and Unwin.

Kirk, B., & Thorne, J. (2011). *Missional youth ministry*. Grand Rapids: Zondervan.

Knox, C. (2008). Policy making in Northern Ireland: Ignoring the evidence. *Policy and Politics, 36*(3), 343–359.

Latour, B. (1988). *Science in action: How to follow scientists and engineers through society.* Cambridge, MA: Harvard University Press.

Learning and Skills Act. (2000). *Section 123.* Retrieved from http://www.legislation.gov.uk/ukpga/2000/21/contents

Learning and Skills Improvement Service. (2012). *Youth work national occupational standards.* London: LSIS. Retrieved from http://www.youthworkwales.org.uk/wp-content/uploads/2017/11/youth_work_national_occupational_standards_1_.pdf

Lepper, J. (2017, August 14). Youth work student numbers fall to record low. *Children and Young People Now.*

Lifelong Learning UK (LLUK). (2008). *Skills for learning professionals: Youth work.* Retrieved May 19, 2017, from http://www.lluk.org/3132

Martin, I. (2008). *Reclaiming social purpose in community education: The Edinburgh papers.* Edinburgh: Edinburgh University. Retrieved April 20, 2018, from https://criticallychatting.files.wordpress.com/2008/11/theedinburghpapers-pdf.pdf

Mayne, J. (2012). Contribution analysis: Coming of age? *Evaluation, 18,* 270–295.

McCormick, J. (1998). *An enquiry into the process involved in the formulation of a new youth work curriculum and considerations for it implementation* (MSc. thesis). University of Ulster, Faculty of Education, Jordanstown.

McCready, S. (2001). *Empowering people: Community development and conflict 1969–1999.* Belfast: HMSO, The Stationery Office.

McCready, S., & Loudon, R. (2015). *Investing in lives: The history of the youth service in Northern Ireland 1844–1973.* Belfast: Belfast Youth Council for Northern Ireland/Corporate Document Services.

Melvin, J. (2015). Youth work in digital age. In G. Bright (Ed.), *Youth work: Histories, policy and contexts.* Basingstoke: Palgrave Macmillan.

Milburn, R., Clark, J., Forde, L., Fulton, K., Locke, A., & MacQuarrie, E. (1995). *Curriculum development in youth work.* Edinburgh: SOED.

Mizen, P. (2004). *The changing state of youth.* Basingstoke: Palgrave Macmillan.

National Assembly for Wales/Children, Young People and Education Committee. (2016). *What type of youth service does Wales want? A report of the inquiry into youth work.* Cardiff Bay: NAW. Retrieved from https://www.assembly.wales/laid%20documents/cr-ld10870/cr-ld10870-e.pdf

NHS Health Scotland. (2010). *Prevention 2010, logic modeling.* Edinburgh: NHS Scotland. Retrieved June 12, 2018, from http://www.healthscotland.com/documents/1645.aspx

NIA (Northern Ireland Assembly). (2016). *Outcomes-based government paper 41/16 Northern Ireland assembly research and information service briefing paper.* Retrieved from http://www.niassembly.gov.uk/globalassets/documents/raise/publications/2016-2021/2016/executive_office/4116.pdf

Nicholls, D. (2018). Wining a statutory youth service. *Journal of Youth and Policy.* Retrieved May 10, 2018, from http://www.youthandpolicy.org/articles/winning-a-statutory-youth-service/

Ord, J. (2011). *Critical issues in youth work management.* London: Routledge.

Ord, J. (2016). The importance of Aristotle's phronisis in resisting instrumentality in youth work in England. In L. Siurala, F. Coussée, & L. Suurpää (Eds.), *The history of youth work in Europe* (Vol. 5). Strasbourg: Council of Europe.

Owen, R. (1816). *Address to the inhabitants of New Lanark.* Retrieved from http://www.robert-owen.com/

Palmer, K. (2017, May 18). Modern guides: From cooking to campaigning for sex education. *BBC.* Retrieved from http://www.bbc.co.uk/news/uk-39952566

Payne, C. (2017). *Changes in the value and division of unpaid volunteering in the UK: 2000 to 2015.* Retrieved March 15, 2018, from https://www.ons.gov.uk/economy/nationalaccounts/satelliteaccounts/articles/changesinthevalueanddivisionofunpaidcare-workintheuk/2015

Puffett, N. (2013, July 3). Cabinet office takes control of youth policy. *Children and Young People Now.*

Putman, R. (2000). *Bowling alone: The collapse and revival of American community.* New York, NY: Simon and Schuster.

Putman, R. (2015). *Our kids: The American dream in crisis.* New York, NY: Simon and Schuster.

Reed, B. (1950). *Eighty thousand adolescents: A study of young people growing up in Birmingham.* London: Allen and Unwin.

rezolvPS. (2015). *A national approach to youth work delivery in Wales: Report prepared for and on behalf of the Welsh government.* Abergavenny: rezolvPS Ltd.

Rogers, V. (2015). *An independent evaluation of youth work in schools in Wales.* Retrieved from https://beta.gov.wales/sites/default/files/publications/2018-02/an-independent-evaluation-of-youth-work-in-schools-in-wales-vanessa-rogers-may-2016.pdf

Scanlon, M., Powell, F., Geoghegan, M., & Swirak, K. (2011). Targeted youth work in contemporary Ireland. *Youth Studies Ireland, 6*(1), 3–16.

Scottish Executive. (2004). *A curriculum for excellence: The curriculum review group.* Retrieved March 15, 2018, from http://www.gov.scot/Resource/Doc/26800/0023690.pdf

Scottish Executive. (2007). *Moving forward: A strategy for improving young people's chances through youth work.* Edinburgh: St. Andrew's House.

Scottish Government. (2013). *The requirements for community learning and development (Scotland) regulations 2013.* Retrieved February 10, 2018, from http://www.legislation.gov.uk/ssi/2013/175/pdfs/ssi_20130175_en.pdf

Scottish Government. (2014). *Developing the young workforce: Scotland's youth employment strategy.* Retrieved February 10, 2018, from https://beta.gov.scot/publications/developing-young-workforce-scotlands-youth-employment-strategy/

Scottish Government. (2017). *Education governance: Next steps empowering out teachers, parnets and communities to deliver excellence and equity for our children.* Edinburgh: Scottish Government. Retrieved March 17, 2018, from http://www.gov.scot/Resource/0052/00521038.pdf

Scottish Government. (2018). *Year of Young People: What is YOYP?* Retrieved March 17, 2018, from http://yoyp2018.scot/what-is-yoyp/

Scott-McKinley, A. (2016). Youth work curriculum in Northern Ireland: A history. In F. Coussée, L. Suurpää, & H. Willisons (Eds.), *The history of youth work in Europe* (Vol. 5). Strasbourg: Council of Europe.

Sercombe, H. (2010). *Youth work ethics.* London: Sage Publications.

Smith, M.K. (1982). *Creators not consumers: Rediscovering social education.* Retrieved January 6, 2018, from http://infed.org/archives/creators/index.htm

Smyth, M., & Hamilton, J. (2003). The human costs of the trouble. In O. Hargie & D. Dickson (Eds.), *Researching the troubles: Social science perspectives on the Northern Ireland conflict* (pp. 15–36). Edinburgh: Mainstream.

Smyth, P. (2007). The development of community relations youth work in Northern Ireland: 1968 to 2005. In D. Magnuson & M. Baizerman (Eds.), *Work with youth in divided and contested societies.* Rotterdam/Taipei: Sense Publishers.

Stanton, N. (2013). Faith-based youth work – lessons from the Christian sector. In S. Curran, R. Harrison, & D. MacKinnon (Eds.), *Working with young people.* London: Sage Publications.

Strathclyde Regional Council. (1984). *Working with young people.* Glasgow: Strathclyde Regional Council.

Susskind, E., & Susskind, D. (2017). *The future of the professions: How technology will transform the work of human experts.* Oxford: Oxford University Press.

Turkle, S. (2011). *Alone together.* New York, NY: Basic Books.

Turkle, S. (2015). *Reclaiming conversation: The power of talk in a digital age.* New York, NY: Penguin Press.

Twenge, J. (2017). *Igen: Why today's super-connected kids are growing up less rebellious, more tolerant, less happy – and completely unprepared for adulthood.* New York, NY: Atria.

UNICEF. (1989). *The United Nations convention on the rights of the child.* London: UNICEF. Retrieved from https://downloads.unicef.org.uk/wp-content/uploads/2010/05/UNCRC_united_nations_convention_on_the_rights_of_the_child.pdf?_ga=2.196698604.1101297996.1530806088-249526639.1530806088

Unison. (2016). *A future at risk: Cuts in youth services.* London: Unison.

Walkey, F. J., Wills, W. H., & Motley, H. (1931). *Methods in youth work.* London: Kingsgate Press.

Welsh Assembly Government. (2002). *Extending entitlement: Support for 11–25 year olds in Wales direction and guidance.* Cardiff: Welsh Government. Retrieved from https://gov.wales/docs/dcells/publications/160108-extending-entitlement-en.pdf

Welsh Assembly Government. (2007). *Young people, youth work, youth service: National youth work strategy for Wales.* Caerphilly: Welsh Government. Retrieved from http://www.childreninwales.org.uk/news/news-archive/national-youth-service-strategy-launched-16307-w/

Welsh Government. (2013). *Youth engagement and progression framework*. Cardiff: Welsh Government. Retrieved from https://gov.wales/docs/dcells/publications/131007-ye-framework-implementation-plan-en.pdf

Welsh Government. (2014). *The national youth work strategy for Wales*. Llandudno Junction: Welsh Government. Retrieved from https://gov.wales/topics/educationandskills/skillsandtraining/youth-work/national-youth-work-strategy-for-wales/?lang=en

Welsh Government. (2015). *Well-being of future generations act*. Cardiff: Welsh Government. Retrieved from https://gov.wales/docs/dsjlg/publications/150623-guide-to-the-fg-act-en.pdf

Welsh Government. (2016). *Developing youth work in Wales*. Cardiff: Welsh Government. Retrieved from https://gov.wales/topics/educationandskills/skillsandtraining/youth-work/?lang=en

Welsh Government. (2016). *Wales charter for youth work*. Cardiff: Welsh Government. Retrieved from https://gov.wales/about/cabinet/cabinetstatements/previous-administration/2016/youthcharter/?lang=en

Welsh Government. (2017). *Review of the national youth work strategy for Wales 2014–2018*. Cardiff: Welsh Government. Retrieved from https://gov.wales/topics/educationandskills/skillsandtraining/youth-work/youth-work-reports/review-of-the-national-youth-work-strategy-for-wales-2014-2018/?lang=en

Welsh Government. (2018). *Our future: A review of extending entitlement*. Cardiff: Welsh Government. Retrieved from https://gov.wales/topics/educationandskills/skillsandtraining/youth-work/youth-work-reports/our-future-a-review-of-extending-entitlement/?lang=en

Welsh Local Government Association (WLGA)/Principal Youth Officers' Group (PYOG). (2015). *The role and value of youth work in current and emerging agendas in Wales*. Cardiff: WLGA. Retrieved from http://www.wlga.wales/SharedFiles/Download.aspx?pageid=62&mid=665&fileid=574

Wenger, E. (1998). *Communities of practice: Learning, meaning and identity*. Cambridge: Cambridge University Press.

Wiener, N. (1948). *Cybernetics: Or control and communication in the animal and the machine*. Cambridge, MA: MIT Press.

Wimbush, E., Montague, S., & Mulherin, T. (2012). Applications of contribution analysis to outcome planning and impact evaluation. *Evaluation, 18*, 310–329.

WLGA/PYOG. (2016). *Curriculum for life: What contribution can youth work make to a new curriculum for Wales?* Cardiff: WLGA. Retrieved from http://www.wlga.wales/SharedFiles/Download.aspx?pageid=62&mid=665&fileid=738

Youth Work in Wales Review Group. (2013). *Youth work in Wales: Principles and purposes*. Retrieved from http://www.wlga.wales/SharedFiles/Download.aspx?pageid=62&mid=665&fileid=568

Youth Work and Cartographic Action: Re-naming Paradoxes – Mapping Utopian Futures

Graham Bright and Carole Pugh

Introduction[1]

Using Foucauldian and Freirean frameworks, this chapter seeks to re-name inherent paradoxes in the history and development of youth and community work, and map ways in which these continue to influence contemporary practices. In highlighting these intrinsic dilemmas which result in amoral praxes, the chapter begins to promote an imaginary that not only recognises youth work's current precarious predicament, but which draws upon and synthesises Trickster typologies and perspectives from Utopian studies to consider and affirm new ways ahead for the Profession which re-state its commitment to critical interruption.

At the heart of youth work lies a commitment to empower young people to think and act critically, democratically and morally in agentially shaping *their* worlds (Young, 2006). Yet:

> Most commentators seem to agree that an agenda of control has become more explicit and more dominant within youth work in recent years ... there is an on-going debate about whether youth workers should embrace this control agenda as providing a socially recognised and valued rationale for the work, or whether it runs contrary to the values of youth work and corrupts its essential nature. (Jeffs & Banks, 2010: 106)

This critique, together with continuing debates over the future of the Profession, and the hollowing out of its purpose, raise questions over whether state-funded youth work has any future at all (Jeffs, 2015). This chapter furthers this discussion by developing cartographic imaginaries that map the roads travelled, plot new routes, and assess potential destinations. Drawing on Utopian thought, we seek to dream and name new ways of working that reclaim Professional purpose.

© KONINKLIJKE BRILL NV, LEIDEN, 2019 | DOI:10.1163/9789004396555_003

The Journey So Far ...

From the emergence of youth work as a philanthropic social movement that took hold in the wake of the industrial revolution, paradoxes of emancipation and control, although epochally denied, have never been far from the Profession's collective pre-conscious (Bright, 2015a). Youth work's pioneers, moved by the 'plight' of poor and working-class young people growing up in the challenging environments of Victorian and Edwardian Britain, were stirred to action by what many saw as the potential of young people to bring about change in their own lives and communities, *and* by the perceived threat posed by the 'moral underclass' to the established order of control. Youth work's founders undoubtedly laid a seed-bed for collaborative engagement that has enabled the transformation of generations of young people's lives. Yet, undeniably, the Profession was born in, and continues to occupy complex and contradictory spaces (Batsleer, 2010) in which young people are both empowered *and* controlled (Coburn, 2011).

The New Labour government of 1997–2010 and its commitment to neoliberal economics and third way policy (Sercombe, 2015) tattooed its influence on youth work. Critical deconstruction of the most notable of New Labour's policies– Every Child Matters (ECM) privileges 'Economic Wellbeing' above the achievement of all other outcomes. Presented under the guise of concern for the wider ecology of children and young people's lives, ECM can be seen as a mechanism of state pastoral power (Smith, 2014), designed to promote self-governing and self-reliant citizens (Chandler & Reid, 2016). ECM was fundamentally tethered to discourses of *social* exclusion, a discursive mechanism that expressed a *universal* responsibility for people experiencing 'multi-faceted syndromes of disadvantage' (Coles, 2006: 93). Joined-up problems required joined-up solutions (Social Exclusion Unit, 1998), and as successive policy initiatives flooded out of Whitehall, youth work was 'invited' to play its part in the unfolding drama of mitigating the socio-economic disease of the age. New Labour's vision for youth work as set out in *Transforming Youth Work* (DfES, 2002) represented a level of state investment arguably not seen since the heady days of Albemarle (HMSO, 1960). Yet with funding came expectation and regulation. Youth work could have its 'place at the table', but like so many other players was required to uncritically do the state's bidding in order to justify its position.

Whilst ostensibly youth work under New Labour represented a gateway for young people's positive participation in the new social order, in actuality, the Profession became a cog in the machinery of neoliberal control. Symptoms of multifarious social ills were treated with prescriptive policy pills which supposedly represented a person-centred approach to (young) people's lives. Yet in reality much intervention was framed by positivistically uniform processes (Hine, 2009) that did little to address many of the underlying structural issues which caused them. Young people discoursed at greatest risk were subject to increasingly rigorous forms of surveillance, intervention and control. Resultantly, much youth work became targeted to this end (Cooper, 2012; Lehal, 2010). When young people didn't 'improve', they became increasingly subject to tacit and overt processes of responsibilisation. Services too were responsibilised, with those failing to meet imposed outcomes deemed inadequate. The remedy to this 'inadequacy' was the enforcement of closer partnerships, which demanded increased information sharing, monitoring, surveillance and targeting. This coerced individual youth workers to comply, or self-identify as 'failing'.

The shift in approach introduced by the Coalition (2010) and Conservative (2015) governments heralded the development of a non-approach to youth work. The combination of the financial crisis and a dogmatic commitment to a neoliberally induced decimation of the state in the name of fiscal sensibilities, radically altered the landscape of many public and welfare services. This has resulted in a real threat to the continued existence of state sponsored youth work beyond 2020 (Davies, 2017)

New youth work providers were expected to emerge from a much wider field, with increased priority given to community leaders and volunteers, over local government. Businesses were also identified as potential providers highlighting the continuing shift towards a closer allegiance with the private sector, who saw the potential of provision as an effective, and efficient model to 'reach and engage' young people for corporate, rather than educational purposes. Statutory investment in the National Citizen Service, has further diverted state support from local authority work, towards the contractual delivery of narrower forms of provision (de St Croix, 2011, 2015).

The continuing shift toward commissioning extended the reach of state-focused obsessions regarding surveillance, targeting and outcomes to the Voluntary and Community Sector (vcs), (DfE, 2012; Norris & Pugh, 2015), thus undermining its strengths and independence (Buchroth & Husband, 2015). Having effectively 'tamed' statutory provision, the state now appeared determined to also co-opt the vcs.

Naming Landscapes

The position that youth work currently finds itself in is therefore beyond a few wrong turns. The surrounding landscape is fundamentally changed.

In examining this in more detail, we seek to understand the forces that have reformed the terrain and identify where we may find some safer ground on which to re-group.

Youth workers have always worked in partnership (Bunyan & Ord, 2012; Wood et al., 2015). Traditionally, these partnerships have been grounded in flexible and *generative* processes that are responsive to grass-roots needs and developments. However, partnerships under recent successive governments have become monolithically *generated* and imposed structures, methodologically designed to ensure synergised professional and organisational conformity. Partnership and integrated working thus remain central to curative, controlling and panoptical endeavours.

Trends towards the formalisation of partnerships can be seen in a growing number of examples since the 1980s (Rhodes, Tyler, & Brennan, 2003). Whilst these rhetorically linked empowerment with partnership, they have increasingly become aligned with competitive processes (Atkinson, 1999).

Under New Labour, the organisation of partnerships across economic sectors and organisational boundaries was structured by neoliberal ideals which were sold on the basis of third way pragmatism – it mattered little who did the work, as long as it was managed with the greatest 'efficiency'. Partnership and joint working, it was contended, would enable synergised approaches to practice that eliminated duplication, 'ensuring' the better utilisation of resources; whilst competition would lead to improved standards, choice and value for money. Processes of tendering and commissioning required that organisations demonstrated a commitment to agendas, outcomes and managerialism, whilst continuing to feed off, and contribute to, negative discourses about young people, in order to justify their work. The result of these combined processes saw youth work being driven by inputs, targets, outcomes, spreadsheets and inspection frameworks which represented the panoptic gaze of new public managerialism (Burton, 2013; DfES, 2002). Ever-increasing forms of 'efficiency' and capricious rationalisation has inevitably led to evermore being required of ever fewer people. Those left, find themselves required to engage in a puppetry of performativity that repeatedly bashes 'at risk' young people with state's subjugating truncheon.

Ever 'closer' and increasingly contrived forms of *multi-agency* and interprofessional working, have resulted in the subsumption of distinct services into generic 'early intervention teams' or locality based 'hubs'. Practitioners from different disciplines have been homogenised into genericised structures, and coalesced around a bland skills/competency-ruled middle ground, focused on similarity and compromise. The existence of distinct professional values is denied, thus silencing contestation and critical debate.

Multi-disciplinary structures have become oppressive deprofessionalising mechanisms which systematically strip practitioners of their phronetic agency and individuality (Ord, 2014). Whilst government calls for a unity of purpose, aggressive marketisation of the sector allows the state to govern organisations (and through them young people) by stealth. This undercurrent is perhaps best expressed as a process of 'divide and conquer'. Exacerbated by cuts and fear of reprisals, many youth workers no longer dare speak out (Hughes et al., 2014). The reach of neoliberal rationality in silencing voices (Couldry, 2010) has extended to youth work. It has muted, or at least quietened, a profession founded on enabling others to name the world (Freire, 1972) and 'come to voice' (Batsleer, 2008: 5).

Neoliberal Terraforming

This unfolding discussion points us towards the application of Foucauldian analyses of governmentality, a concept which critiques ways in which states, directly through policy diktat, and more importantly indirectly through a 'bundle of discursive practices' (Hearn, 2012: 90) direct the lives, practices and subjectivities of their citizenry. Discourses surrounding young people and what they 'ought' to be, how they 'should' behave and what they 'must' do, have, and continue, to punctuate policy and practice. For Dean (2010: 17ff) governmentality can be summed up as 'the conduct of conduct', the processes through which individuals control, govern and responsibilize self in relation to the normative discoursed requirements of an external body, usually the state (Chandler & Reid, 2016; Olssen, 2008). The modern state is thus 'individualising and totalising'; it is concerned with the welfare of 'each and all' (Smith, 2014: 13). While ECM is no longer promulgated as formal policy, it perhaps represents the most obvious example of governmentality in action – its mantra continues to run through professional discourse like letters through rock.

Neoliberal governmentality has re-formed the landscape surrounding practice. Like a well-constructed traffic management system with new, smooth, clearly-defined, and fast moving highways, the route taken feels 'natural', well-integrated and effectively managed. It channels and directs practice, and warns of areas to be avoided. It shepherds, shapes and ultimately controls the route taken. Its real effectiveness however, is its subtlety – slow incremental changes have substantively avoided the outcry of professional concern, and resulted in an environment that invisibly controls professional behaviour. Youth work has found itself re-positioned miles from its original location.

Analyses of governmentality thus highlights the ways in which youth work has been programmed to uncritically pursue the 'welfare' of 'each and all' (op. cit.). Utilisation of these frameworks therefore suggests that the Profession has, in various ways played a significant, but not always self-critical role in imbuing, pedalling and perpetuating often narrow constructions of socialised self-governance in young people's lives. The Profession was once sanctioned and privileged for this expertism by the state, society *and* young people. The dynamics of its position have however changed: neoliberal rationalities have rendered youth work an enclave within the complexities of wider partnership and integrated practice. Organisations are compelled to compete aggressively (Buchroth & Husband, 2015) for ever-smaller funding pots designed to meet incrementally narrower agendas which increasingly prescribe how young people should self-govern. Neoliberal youth work has been co-opted in the service of the state, at the expense of serving young people (Sercombe, 2015).

Much youth work has acquiesced. It operates within the confines of pre-scribed *configurations*, in order to survive, and, perhaps, if lucky, attempt to speak critically from within. Yet all of this comes at a cost. Youth work, under the auspices of 'citizenship', 'safeguarding', 'NEETness', 'inclusion' and various other discursive practices has become part of a mechanism of surveying the lives of *all* young people, whilst focusing on those who the state deems are at (or, perhaps more accurately pose) greatest risk (Belton, 2009; de St Croix, 2010).

Mechanisms of targeted multi-disciplinarity have become the panoptical instrument by which the state surveys practice, in the surveillance of young people's lives, and have thus become instruments of moral containment, rather than creative spaces for shared learning and critical praxis. Hall (2013) argues this point eloquently, contending that targeted youth support work is increasingly required to approach integrated practice as case management. This, it is argued, moves youth work away from its grounding in informal education, towards the realms of 'second class social work'.

Analysis of the relationship between much of youth work's governed position within current multi-disciplinary, interagency and integrated frameworks is therefore essential. Present organisational mechanisms appear fundamentally grounded in performative governmentality: they attempt to ensure youth work governs itself in line with state agendas, in order that young people do the same.

Regaining the Steering Wheel

Mapping this terrain highlights paradoxes and uncomfortable contradictions in youth work's recent history and contemporary practices. It is a profession that espouses a critical and emancipatory praxis with people; yet analysis demonstrates that recent practice has navigated a route that steers closer to perpetuating and supporting dominant structural hegemonies, and avoids the more difficult terrain involved in challenging these (Tilsen, 2018). Youth work must, in line with its roots in critical pedagogy, continue to name the world; yet it must also name itself. Failure to do so risks rendering youth work complicit in the systems it should interrogate.

Coburn (2011: 62) argues that: 'The starting point for critical pedagogy is the learner and not the teacher or the state'. Critical pedagogy however calls us not only to 'name' but to act (Cho, 2013). English youth work faces continuing disassemblage (Youdell & McGimpsey, 2014). Undoubtedly, there are important practical and organisational decisions to be made regarding how to proceed. Yet of more fundamental importance are the moral and ethical mazes the Profession must orienteer in its regeneration and 'reassemblage' (ibid.).

In many instances, youth work has presented itself to young people as one thing, whilst in reality being something else. For a profession founded on principles of relational trust (Seal & Frost, 2014), such Janus-like behaviours are amoral. Others, however, might argue this as a protean, chameleon-like necessity – a requirement to subversively support young people's informal and critical education. To this end, Tucker (2006: 81ff) points out youth work is involved in a 'game', the rules of which are ambiguous and ever-changing. In Foucauldian terms, 'games of truth' must be deconstructed in order to illuminate them for what they are. This is a game which throws youth workers and young people into a matrix of discourse-fuelled power relations that entwines a range of institutions (Nicholls, 2012). It is a game played by the state's rules, in the eternal pursuit of moral self-discipline. It simultaneously seeks to involve and include young people whilst holding them at a distance until they socialise themselves into compliance. It is a game through which youth workers and young people are manipulated for performative purposes –a game that must be named to be challenged. In revealing its tacit and illusionary rules (Tucker, 2006), youth workers stand a better chance of 'tipping [the] balances of power and control in young people's favour' (Davies, 2010: 3). The Profession, has an ethical duty to work alongside young people to recognise and expose the game's changing nature.

Trickery? Redrawing the Map

Analysis of the game however ought not to result in fatalistic capitulation. Deconstructive processes illuminate 'realities' and open up possibilities for agential action. Whilst 'ignorance' conveniences the presumption of power, knowledge holds the potential to challenge systems and catalyse change – turning 'powerlessness' toward empowerment (Apple, 2013; Schirato et al., 2012).

These ideas of games and power, point towards re-considering the potential of youth work as a typology of trickery (Richards, 2014). The trickster in mythology represents a being who utilises covert knowledge in order to usurp powerful systems and undermine convention. Such a notion is of course not new to youth work – which is grounded in principles of interruption (Belton, 2010), and embodies a commitment to sabotaging critical naivety (Bright, 2015b). Tricksters are driven to bend the rules for their own or others' benefit. They operate according to the terrain – often by stealth, but sometimes through brave, outlandish (and occasionally apparently foolish) public displays. These are playful characters who understand, but question the validity of rules '... the trickster figure serves as a chaos-inducing element intent on challenging the existing order of things' (Bassil-Morozow, 2015: 11). They are critical, adaptive, shape-shifting operatives who expose and disable assumed and constructed fallacies. Tricksters are engaged in the clever disruption of power and oppression – a notion youth work claims it aspires to.

Trickster narratives often begin with the protagonist feeling trapped, or restricted. They want to feel free, and, like the youth work ideal, engage in audacious border or boundary crossings (Coburn, 2010) that seek to re-draw the maps of possibility. Bassil-Morozow (2015: 16) notes that: 'The trickster's boundary-breaking and map-redrawing activities can be malicious, playful or heroic – and sometimes all three at once'. Youth work, needs to engage playfully and passionately in extending and re-drawing the once expansive boundaries of its practice, in order that it might generate new critical imaginaries of just possibility. Learning from tricksters may well be vital for survival.

Plotting Utopia?

Before navigating the possibilities of a new youth work cartography, some dreaming is required and some questions are demanded. At its best, what could, and should, contemporary youth work look like? How does this imaginary fit with, or challenge social realities and possibilities? All societies require engineering. Olssen (2010) argues that two forms of engineering exist: the piecemeal and the utopian. Whereas, the piecemeal pays attention only to the most obvious and urgent of ills, the utopian expresses a holistic blueprint of the future and explores ways of getting there. Ontologically, utopian thought is grounded in an ideal of 'imagination otherwise' – it holds that new imaginaries of possibility are better than what currently exists. Drawing on Riceour (1986), Levitas (2011: 89) contends therefore that 'the function of utopia is challenge, the best aspect being the exploration of the possible ...'. Utopic purpose is 'to expose the credibility gap wherein all systems of authority exceed ... both our confidence in them and our belief in their legitimacy' (Riceour in Levitas, op. cit.). In this way utopia represents 'the refusal to accept that what is given is enough' (Levitas, 2013: 17).

A key role in utopian analysis is to raise consciousness of 'estrangement' – to create spaces and generate language that critically calls out the actualities of experience as it is lived and constructed, in order to set it in stark contrast with prophetically longed for futures. Thus, utopic thought concerns the possibilising of change and the subjective and relativist potentials of social transformation through the dreamt reclamation of futures (ibid.). By drawing on Bloch's (1986) idea of, *docta spes* (educated hope) Levitas (2013: 5) further highlights critical educative capacity of the utopic in the enactment of change – an idea that has clear synergy with the Freirean frameworks which drive critical youth work praxis.

Whilst many might yearn for the utopia of a radically different society, utopian thought teaches us to map the territory towards a new imaginary of aspirational possibility. There are of course totalitarian dangers in utopic dreaming, but incapacitating inertia in not. As Levitas (2011: 4) notes: 'The elision between perfection and impossibility can serve to invalidate all attempts at change, reinforcing the claim that there is no alternative, [thereby] sustaining the status quo'.

New Destinations

Cartographic conversations and action in mapping youth work futures are challenging, but crucial. Politically however, the array of utopian possibility is vast. Whereas right wing conceptualisations tend to be grounded in the individualising, libertarian socio-economic ideals of market rationality which result in widening social and economic inequity and alienation, the range on the left varies from the social democratic to varying flavours of radical Marxist thought. Whilst many Marxists tend to view utopia pejoratively as an abstract, mythical notion, that hinders true, radical social transformation, the socialist utopic has a long and distinguished history. Levitas (2011: 42ff) contends utopian socialists like Henri Saint-Simon (1760–1825) and Robert Owen[2] (1771–1858) painted pictures of different possibilities in which society is more equitably and coherently advanced through localised communities which foster 'cooperation, association and harmony'. These are ideals which underpin youth and community work practice. It is this *socialist* ideal of grass-roots localism which we believe speaks direction to youth work's current predicament. As such, 'Organic restructuring [that] necessitates the development of a network of cooperative settlements which go beyond simple consumer or producer cooperatives' (ibid.: 53) needs to be considered in advancing alternative youth work futures.

Youth and community work needs to regain its status as a beacon of civil society, one which draws on utopian ideals of 'spontaneous social self-organization independent of the market and state' (Levitas, 2013: 164). This is the cooperative landscape in which youth work originates. Whist the now defunct 'Big Society' seemingly rediscovered this space, in reality it represented the vacuous neoliberal co-option of these spaces by the market and state. Practice must be re-imagined in order that we can collectively become architects of separate, creative, community-shaped spaces. Such localised 'uncoupled' cooperative spaces, hold the potential at least, to enable the anarchic interruption of systems (de St Croix, 2014), and, 'replace market and state with an alternative economy and society' (Levitas, 2013: 165).

Navigating New Routes

Let us, for a moment, therefore, play a game with mapping new imaginaries of practice. Presently, the Profession engages in the trickery of Janus-like behaviour which presents its work to the state in one way, and to young people in another. The Janus typology however speaks to youth work in other ways. Janus as the Roman God of transition represents liminality – one face looks to the past, the other to the future. Janus' liminality speaks of the permanence of change: it is always with us. Whilst this signifies a truism, youth work (like so many other professions) currently faces a particularly striking transitory moment in its history in which three 'game options' are available.

Firstly, youth work can continue to be played unwittingly within the existing system, accepting its continuing co-option in return for status and employment. However, the extent to which this form of practice can claim to be located within the Profession's values and pedagogies is highly questionable. Continuing down this track, might generate a range of people who 'work with young people', yet without youth and community work's distinctive ethos. This will inevitability lead to the Profession's physical and moral destruction.

Secondly, youth and community work could elect to play the game within the existing habitus, but with the explicit intention of manipulating and usurping it on young people's behalf. This is a version of the game which many youth workers have played from the origins of the Profession, navigating a course between liberation and control, balancing the needs of agencies, the wider community and young people. Starting where young people are – but seeking to move them forwards, through conversation, creative action and engagement in a direction that is negotiated – but agreed generally to be forwards (Rosseter, 1987; Jeffs & Smith, 2005). However, this form of practice requires some space in which to create these educative processes – the question is whether 'disassemblage' (Youdell & McGimpsey, 2014) has created an external environment that renders these kinds of survival tactics ineffectual. Workers may, occasionally, be able to punch a hole through the hedge to create a new route, or redefine locations that 'should' be headed towards – but fundamentally these choices are becoming more restricted, and the paths narrower. At an individual level playing the game this way provides a rationale and claim to professional integrity, but a failure to engage with this and organise collectively appears to have steered youth work to the 'end of the road'. If we are to play the game, but aim for more than individual survival, the Profession must re-imagine itself once again as a transformative movement.

For those who remain in state-controlled (or commissioned) youth work, its disassemblage may yet provide the impetus to begin conversations that re-shape the basis of the work, enabling the Profession to form its own definitions – rather than clinging to those it has been ascribed.

Redundancies and redeployment have led to workers taking up posts in different arenas. There has been on-going interest in the skills offered by youth workers in housing and re-settlement, 'information and support' roles, and with young people who are educationally disengaged (Coburn & Gormally, 2015; Smith, 2013). Whilst still under the control of state funded agendas, workers may be able to find more elbow room in these kinds of provision. For example, while housing projects may have stated goals around re-settlement and employment, there is time and space for conversations that are more open-ended in nature. Workers are able to take advantage of this space to co-create educative opportunities. Perhaps these forms of practice, while not radically re-shaping the map, provide enough space for workers to continue to effectively play the game, and usurp the status quo, with and for young people. The re-deployment of youth workers, in different sectors, with differing approaches and traditions, should therefore be seized as an opportunity to reconsider the values and approaches that are central to practice, and how these might be named.

New Modes of Transport and Travelling Companions?

Finally, youth work as an act of defiance and ultimate trickery might choose to *consciously uncouple* from the present game, in order to develop a new one which privileges rules of engagement negotiated by young people themselves. In this vision, the Profession engages in *actively chosen* processes of 'disassemblage' and 'reassemblage' (Youdell & McGimpsey, 2014) which enable the reclamation of its shared moral authority with young people, and a recovery of its truer ethos. Whilst this idea for some may have particular moral and vocational traction, it is a high risk strategy. There are a number of issues in plotting this direction of travel. These relate to three broad, yet interrelated themes: provision, resourcing and profession. *Initial speculative* discussion regarding these is offered here.

Firstly, reassemblage of youth work in this fashion would have an undoubted impact on direct work with young people, with a likely disparity in levels of provision. Some localities with better established independent and voluntary sector provision could see practice flourish where new partnerships and creative pedagogical practices inform the work. Areas with better established access to social, democratic, civil and economic resources could see provision survive and grow, with disadvantaged areas risking the loss of youth work entirely.

However, demand by communities for provision may well be higher and more vocally demonstrated in some more marginalised areas. Collaborative and co-productive endeavour between independent funding bodies, charities, civil society (for example, theatres, arts groups, sports, libraries) and local communities in these spaces might well provide fertile ground for renewal, and enable *new forms* of co-operative diversity.

At a local level, there is some evidence of workers re-assembling. In some cases offers of voluntary redundancy have led to the creation of social enterprises, community interest companies, mutuals or charities where workers attempt to establish their own forms of organisation and practice (de St Croix, 2014). The pathways between processes of control and informal education still need to be negotiated; yet workers are re-claiming virtue and agency in its navigation. Whilst this might offer localised hope, socially just reassemblage requires the establishment provision that actively questions and crosses the borders of parochial utopias.

Another potential version of reassemblage concerns broadening the definition of 'youth work'. A scan of local youth providers reveals sports, arts, theatre and music-based provision beginning to feature more prominently, providing more activities, in wider locations, and in more universal terms. While the starting points for this provision are often focused around interest and skill development, as work expands, and becomes more accessible, these new providers are finding the need to respond to the ideas, concerns, and issues that young people themselves bring. Examining this practice identifies where there are similarities in values and approaches. Perhaps, once uncoupled, youth work needs to seek new partners and form new alliances, whilst simultaneously re-generating its value bases and creating a new language rooted in civil society (Jeffs, 2015).

Universities, which were at the forefront of what would become youth and community work (McGimpsey, 2001), should also be seen as potential partners. Reimagining the Settlement Movement in which universities, as an expression of their commitment to social justice, engage with their local communities through practice should not be beyond the realms of possibility. Such an approach would allow opportunities for students to develop experience, and enable universities to widen participation and promote good research in the field. Reimaging university involvement would also meet practitioner need for collegiate spaces where people can breathe, consider, rejuvenate and generate critical and collaborative imaginaries of practice (Hughes et al., 2014).

The second issue that must be contended with is resourcing – a problem that has beset youth work from its beginnings. State investment in youth work must continue to be fought for; however, the terms of any new settlement need to be carefully, debated and considered (Davies, 2017). Perhaps reassemblage of the work, which incorporates ethical value-based social enterprises, can be fashioned in ways that connect self-financing, with forms of income generation that are cognisant of the need to challenge dominant neoliberal discourses. Issues of financial resourcing may be difficult to resolve, but it is essential that reassemblages re-engage critically with ethical issues associated with funding sources, requirements and discourses.

In reassembling practice, it is important to look at resourcing beyond financial terms. Recreating partnerships based on co-operation and co-production will be essential. These new alliances hold the potential to re-form wider networks and re-engage young people with adults in their communities.

The increasing 'professionalisation' of the work, with degree level entry and re-formed roles has led to the loss of the traditional part-time worker. These are the individuals who did another job alongside youth work, but contributed regularly, over the long term, bringing differing experiences to the work, and communicating its value back to a wider audience. Historically, the involvement of a wide range of adults in youth work generated benefits beyond what happened in its buildings: by engaging and investing their time, these adults became advocates for informal education, and young people (Jeffs, 2015).

In recent years however, volunteering itself has been subject to neoliberal rationality, with many now seeing it as a means to personal advantage in a competitive jobs market (Rochester, 2013). Locally, numbers of volunteers appear to have increased, supporting statutory services in delivering 'more for less'. Reconstructing practice therefore involves wider debates, not only about the utilisation of volunteers, but also regarding the reframing of voluntary action as an expression of collectivity, community and democracy – values which underpin youth work practice.

Finally, we must consider what youth work as a reclaimed profession might look like in the uncoupled game. The neoliberal project has rendered youth work, like society, diffuse and 'atomised' (Bauman, 2009) to the point vaporisation. In pursuing the uncoupled game, there is no longer a need to fear the *loss* of a distinct collective professional identity, which has already ceased to exist outside the boundaries of the Profession's own consciousness. Energy instead needs to be focussed on reimagining the phoenix of professional autonomy, collectivity and the potential of renewed public recognition in the new ecologies of practice. This demands that youth work engages in conversations regarding professional re-orientation and re-organisation.

Traditional notions of 'profession' are, to some degree, externally shaped. The ascription, by the state, of 'professional status' as an ideal and legitimising mode, fluctuates in line with the vagaries of social and economic mores. This can be seen especially in professions like youth work, which can be arbitrarily deemed non-essential. Youth work's recognition as a profession was hard won, and, while external recognition is undoubtedly important, solely externalised categorisations of 'profession' can be prescriptive and limiting. They fail to take account of the potential of internal identities and shared phronetic agency in shaping occupational futures. In this vein, Banks and Gallagher (2009) argue that professions need to continually, agentially and reflexively construct themselves in response to external *and* internal forces. In this view, the notion of the Profession is not solely reliant on external prescription and validation, (as has been seen in recent processes of de/professionalization); rather, it requires that youth work reimagines forms of internal validation, which critically draw on the Profession's ethos and rich history in facing contemporary challenges.

In this way, professions can rebuff the singular, essentialist fettering of external logic and move to reclaim themselves as 'moral communities or practices that have notions of the good or human flourishing built into them in the form of their core purpose or service ideal' (ibid.: 48). Movement in this direction enables youth workers to reclaim their practice as an ideal that is committed to working and thinking critically *with* young people. 'This, in essence, is why workers are professional. It is not a question of status. [Good] youth workers, whatever their employment or volunteering situation, want to do a job well' (Nicholls, 2012: 103). Youth work is a passionate and resistant profession (de St Croix, 2013, 2016) that must be committed to imagining different futures with young people. It must re-envision and reorganise itself in line with that commitment.

Youth work has a long and distinguished history of promoting collective self-organisation. It should not, therefore, be beyond the realms of possibility to consider ways in which the Profession might re-imagine and re-order *itself.* Generative and interconnected networks abound in youth work. Synergistically, these hold the cooperative potential to contribute towards promoting the internal consciousness and validity of the Profession in the new uncoupled world. Collaborative organisation is however key. Regular local, regional and national fora which *intentionally* catalyse critical, creative and cohesive communities of practice (Wenger, 2013) in the service of young people and their communities must be prioritised. Such spaces could offer renewed hope, and the potential of *generative* partnerships which reclaim professional ethos, autonomy and internal regulation.

Conclusion

This chapter has sought to map and acknowledge terrains of practice, imagine new places to play and rules to play by. Although game-playing can be fun, it can also be socially problematic, psychologically damaging (Berne, 1964) and politically dangerous. Sometimes players who attempt to subvert games end up dead or morally ruined (Bassil-Morozow, 2015). The next moves that the Profession makes need to be thought about carefully. The stakes are high. We are after all playing with young people's lives and democratic futures. Undoubtedly however, the Profession is currently involved in a game in which many practitioners and young people are being *played.* Morally, youth work needs to *actively* play the game with and for young people, whether overtly or covertly, in order to re-shape the agenda towards them. The unpalatable alternative is to continue to be passively played by the state for *its* increasingly narrow and performative agenda. The Profession must be true to its heritage and ethos, yet responsive in meeting the needs of today's young people. It must decide the versions of the game that it is willing to play, and rules it is willing to play by. Collective, resistant and grass-roots renewal is needed in plotting new possibilities. It is time to dialogue, map, and act. Let the games begin!

Notes

1 The notion of cartographic action draws on ideas from geography, reflecting the idea that the drawing, naming and categorising of the terrain is, in itself, an act that shapes the landscape. This chapter uses this metaphor to consider the extent to which youth work has allowed the landscape it operates within to be redrawn around it, resulting in a sense of disorientating displacement. Cartographic action calls us to map routes and imagine destinations that lie beyond the known. Such activity makes possible the reclamation of practice.

2 Owen's attempt to generate this ideal can still be seen in his new model village at New Lanark.

References

Apple, M. (2013). *Can education change society?* Abingdon: Routledge.

Atkinson, R. (1999). Discourses of partnership and empowerment in contemporary British urban regeneration. *Urban Studies, 36*(1), 59–72.

Banks, S., & Gallagher, A. (2009). *Ethics in professional life.* Basingstoke: Palgrave Macmillan.

Bassil-Morozow, H. (2015). *The trickster and the system.* London: Sage Publications.

Batsleer, J. (2008). *Informal learning in youth work.* London: Sage Publications.

Batsleer, J. (2010). Youth work prospects: Back to the future? In J. Batsleer & B. Davies (Eds.), *What is youth work?* Exeter: Learning Matters.

Bauman, Z. (2009). Identity in the globalizing world. In A. Elliott & P. du Gay (Eds.), *Identity in question.* London: Sage Publications.

Belton, B. (2009). *Developing critical youth work theory.* Rotterdam, The Netherlands: Sense Publishers.

Belton, B. (2010). *Radical youth work.* Lyme Regis: Russell House Publishing.

Berne, E. (1964). *Games people play: The psychology of human relationships.* London: Penguin.

Bloch, E. (1986). *The principle of hope* (Vol. 3). London: Basil Blackwell.

Bright, G. (2015a). The early history of youth work practice. In G. Bright (Ed.), *Youth work: Histories, policy and contexts.* London: Palgrave Macmillan.

Bright, G. (2015b). In search of soul: Where now for youth and community work? In G. Bright (Ed.), *Youth work: Histories, policy and contexts.* London: Palgrave Macmillan.

Buchroth, I., & Husband, M. (2015). Youth work in the voluntary sector. In G. Bright (Ed.), *Youth work: Histories, policy and contexts.* London: Palgrave Macmillan.

Bunyan, P., & Ord, J. (2012). The neoliberal policy context of youth work management. In J. Ord (Ed.), *Critical issues in youth work management.* Abingdon: Routledge.

Burton, M. (2013). *The politics of public sector reform*. Basingstoke: Palgrave Macmillan.

Chandler, D., & Reid, J. (2016). *The neoliberal subject: Resilience, adaptation and vulnerability*. London: Rowman and Littlefield International.

Cho, S. (2013). *Critical pedagogy and social change*. Abingdon: Routledge.

Coburn, A. (2010). Youth work as border pedagogy. In J. Batsleer & B. Davies (Eds.), *What is youth work?* Exeter: Learning Matters.

Coburn, A. (2011). Liberation or containment: Paradoxes in youth work as a catalyst for powerful learning. *Youth and Policy, 106*, 60–77.

Coburn, A., & Gormally, S. (2015). Youth work in schools. In G. Bright (Ed.), *Youth work: Histories, policy and contexts*. London: Palgrave Macmillan.

Coles, B. (2006). Welfare services for young people: Better connections? In J. Roche, S. Tucker, R. Thompson, & R. Flynn (Eds.), *Youth in society* (2nd ed.). London: Sage Publications.

Cooper, C. (2012). Imagining 'radical' youth work possibilities – Challenging the 'symbolic violence' within the mainstream tradition in contemporary state-led youth work practice in England. *Journal of Youth Studies, 15*(1), 53–71.

Couldry, N. (2010). *Why voice matters*. London: Sage Publications.

Davies, B. (2010). What do we mean by youth work? In J. Batsleer & B. Davies (Eds.), *What is youth work?* Exeter: Learning Matters.

Davies, B. (2017). Beyond the local authority youth service: Could the state fund open access youth work – and if so, how? A speculative paper for critical discussion. *Youth and Policy, 116*, 24–44.

Dean, M. (2010). *Governmentality* (2nd ed.). London: Sage Publications.

Department for Education. (2012). *Statutory guidance for local authorities on services and activities to improve young people's well-being*. Retrieved May 7, 2015, from http://www.learning-southwest.org.uk/wp-content/uploads/2014/11/statutory-guidance-on-la-youth-provision-duty.pdf

Department for Education and Skills. (2002). *Transforming youth work: Resourcing excellent youth services*. London: DfES.

de St Croix, T. (2010). Youth work and the surveillance state. In J. Batsleer & B. Davies (Eds.), *What is youth work?* Exeter: Learning Matters.

de St Croix, T. (2011). Struggles and silences: Policy, youth work and the national citizens service. *Youth and Policy, 106*, 43–59.

de St Croix, T. (2013). I just love youth work! Emotional labour, passion and resistance. *Youth and Policy, 110*, 33–51.

de St Croix, T. (2014, June 28). *What does it mean to be radical in youth work today? The example of the voice of youth co-op*. Paper presented at British Educational Research Association Youth Studies and Informal Education Special Interest Group, Newman University, Birmingham, UK.

de St Croix, T. (2015). Volunteers and entrepreneurs? Youth work and the big society. In G. Bright (Ed.), *Youth work: Histories, policy and contexts*. London: Palgrave Macmillan.

Freire, P. (1972). *Pedagogy of the oppressed*. London: Penguin.

Hall, K. (2013). The future of targeted youth support as second social work. *Youth and Policy, 111*, 77–81.

Hearn, J. (2012). *Theorizing power*. Basingstoke: Palgrave Macmillan.

Hine, J. (2009). Young people's lives: Taking a different view. In J. Wood & J. Hine (Eds.), *Work with young people*. London: Sage Publications.

HMSO. (1960). *The youth service in England and Wales (The Albermarle report)*. London: HMSO.

Hughes, G., Cooper, C., Gormally, S., & Rippendale, J. (2014). The state of youth work in austerity England – reclaiming the ability to 'care'. *Youth and Policy, 113*, 1–14.

Jeffs, T. (2015). Innovation and youth work. *Youth and Policy, 114*, 75–95.

Jeffs. T., & Banks, S. (2010). Youth workers as controllers: Issues of method and purpose. In S. Banks (Ed.), *Ethical issues in youth work*. Abingdon: Routledge.

Jeffs, T., & Smith, M. (2005). *Informal education: Conversation, democracy and learning*. Nottingham: Educational Heretics Press.

Lehal, R. (2010). Targeting for youth workers. In J. Batsleer & B. Davies (Eds.), *What is youth work?* Exeter: Learning Matters.

Levitas, R. (2011). *The concept of Utopia*. Oxford: Peter Lang.

Levitas, R. (2013). *Utopia as method*. Basingstoke: Palgrave Macmillan.

McGimpsey, I. (2001). Durham house settlement: Its history and place in the settlement movement. In R. Gilchrist, T. Jeffs, & J. Spence (Eds.), *Essays in the history of community and youth work*. Leicester: Youth Work Press.

Nicholls, D. (2012). *For youth workers and youth work*. Bristol: Policy Press.

Norris, P., & Pugh, C. (2015). Local authority youth work. In G. Bright (Ed.), *Youth work: Histories, policy and contexts*. London: Palgrave Macmillan.

Olssen, M. (2008). Understanding the mechanisms of neoliberal control: Lifelong learning, flexibility and knowledge capitalism. In A. Fejes & K. Nicoll (Eds.), *Foucault and lifelong learning: Governing the subject*. London: Routledge.

Olssen, M. (2010). *Liberalism, neoliberalism and social democracy*. Abingdon: Routledge.

Ord, J. (2014). Aristotle's phronesis and youth work: Beyond instrumentality. *Youth and Policy, 112*, 56–73.

Rhodes, J., Tyler, P., & Brennan, A. (2003). New developments in area-based initiatives in England: The experience of the single regeneration budget. *Urban Studies, 40*(8), 1399–1426.

Riceour, P. (1986). *Lectures on ideology and Utopia*. New York, NY: Columbia University Press.

Richards, W. (2014, June 28). *A silent revolution: The trickster as an autonomous adaptive agent*. Paper presented at British Educational Research Association Youth Studies and Informal Education Special Interest Group, Newman University, Birmingham, UK.

Rochester, C. (2013). *Rediscovering voluntary action: The beat of a different drum*. London: Palgrave Macmillan.

Rosseter, B. (1987). Youth workers as educators. In T. Jeffs & M. Smith (Eds.), *Youth work*. London: Macmillan.

Schirato, T., Danaher, G., & Webb, J. (2012). *Understanding Foucault* (2nd ed.). London: Sage Publications.

Seal, M., & Frost, S. (2014). *Philosophy in youth and community work*. Lyme Regis: Russell House Publishing.

Sercombe, H. (2015). In the service of the state: Youth work under new labour. In G. Bright (Ed.), *Youth work: Histories, policy and contexts*. London: Palgrave Macmillan.

Smith, M. K. (2013). What is youth work? Exploring the history, theory and practice of youth work. *The Encyclopedia of Informal Education*. Retrieved March 15, 2015, from http://www.infed.org/mobi/what-is-youth-work-exploring-the-history-theory-and-practice-of-work-with-young-people/

Smith, M. K. (2014). *The government of childhood*. Basingstoke: Palgrave Macmillan.

Social Exclusion Unit. (1998). *Bringing Britain together: A national strategy for neighbourhood renewal*. London: The Stationery Office.

Spence, J., & Devanney, C. (2006). *Youth work: Voices from practice*. Leicester: National Youth Agency.

Tilsen, J. (2018). *Narrative approaches to youth work*. London: Routledge.

Tucker, S. (2006). Youth working: Professional identities given, received or contested? In J. Roche, S. Tucker, R. Flynn, & R. Thomson (Eds.), *Youth in society*. London: Sage Publications.

Wenger, E. (2013). A social theory of learning. In S. Curran, R. Harrison, & D. Mackinnon (Eds.), *Working with young people*. London: Sage Publications.

Wood, J., Westwood, S., & Thompson, G. (2015). *Youth work preparation for practice*. Abingdon: Routledge.

Youdell, D., & McGimpsey, I. (2014). Assembling, disassembling and reassembling 'youth services' in austerity Britain. *Critical Studies in Education, 56*(1), 116–130.

Young, K. (2006). *The art of youth work*. Lyme Regis: Russell House Publishing.

CHAPTER 4

Youth Workin' All over Europe: Moving, Associating, Organising and Providing

Howard Williamson and Filip Coussée

Introduction

Youth work in Europe is a heterogeneous practice, as numerous documents testify and as the Declaration of the 1st European Youth Work Convention held in 2010 confirmed.[1] Throughout Europe, youth work is characterised by diversity. This diversity is a strength but also a weakness. The strength lies in the fact that young people with very different backgrounds, characteristics and attitudes are attracted to some form of youth work and find a meaningful context there – a space and possibilities that they do not find in their schools or families or elsewhere in their lives. As Cohen (1986) once said, leisure is the weak link in the chain of socialisation, less controlled or regulated (when compared to family, school or work) and so allows space for greater youth self-determination and autonomy. This may create both opportunities and problems for young people and the societies and communities in which they live. Youth work operates primarily in that leisure space, working in many different ways with young people in their leisure time. The diversity of youth work (from the work of self-governed youth organisations, through open clubs and special projects, to street-based practice) makes it easier to reach out to all young people, including those in more marginalised and excluded circumstances. The apparent lack of specificity and clarity as to what youth work is and does, however, makes it more difficult to command a certain social status (unlike teaching, social work or counselling).

This diversity in method, shape and target group derives from youth work's history, a history that, despite its variety, also has surprisingly striking similarities across many countries. There are, of course, different cultural accents derived from diverse social, political and economic contexts, but usually we see two prevailing generic factors in youth work *avant la lettre*: young students' self-organisation on one hand, and the social and pedagogical organisation of working (class) youth on the other hand (Van de Walle et al., 2011). The students' emancipatory movement drew attention to a youth question: 'What is the role and contribution of young people in our society?' Pedagogical initiatives

© KONINKLIJKE BRILL NV, LEIDEN, 2019 | DOI:10.1163/9789004396555_004

directed towards working class youth generated a social question: 'How can the integration of the lower social classes into the existing social order be assured, and their perceived (and sometimes more real) threat to the social cohesion of society be avoided?' This provided a different focus for the evolution of youth work. These questions carried different weight in the divided Europe before 1989, but remained significant on either side of that divide. It was this tension between emancipation and pedagogisation that lay at the core of youth work. Given its self-declared heterogeneity, it may continue to be difficult to define youth work, but understanding the tensions at the heart of practice can help youth workers to comprehend, explain and strengthen the significance of their practice on individual and on societal levels.

Defining or Understanding Youth Work

In the past decade, a great deal of ink has flowed on the question of defining youth work. Peter Lauritzen (2008: 369–370) produced what many consider to be as plausible and persuasive a definition of youth work as is likely to be achieved:

> The main objective of youth work is to provide opportunities for young people to shape their own futures. Youth work is a summary expression for activities with and for young people of a social, cultural, educational or political nature. Increasingly, youth work activities also include sports and services for young people. Youth work belongs to the domain of 'out-of-school' education, most commonly referred to as either non-formal or informal learning. The general aims of youth work are the integration and inclusion of young people in society. It may also aim towards the personal and social emancipation of young people from dependency and exploitation. Youth Work belongs both to the social welfare and to the educational systems. In some countries it is regulated by law and administered by state civil servants, in particular at local level. However, there exists an important relation between these professional and voluntary workers which is at times antagonistic, and at others, cooperative. The definition of youth work is diverse. While it is recognised, promoted and financed by public authorities in many European countries, it has only a marginal status in others where it remains of an entirely voluntary nature. What is considered in one country to be the work of traditional 'youth workers' – be it professionals or volunteers – may be carried out by consultants in another, or by neighbourhoods and families in yet another country or,

indeed, not at all in many places. Today, the difficulty within state systems to adequately ensure global access to education and the labour market, means that youth work increasingly deals with unemployment, educational failure, marginalisation and social exclusion. Increasingly, youth work overlaps with the area of social services previously undertaken by the Welfare State. It, therefore, includes work on aspects such as education, employment, assistance and guidance, housing, mobility, criminal justice and health, as well as the more traditional areas of participation, youth politics, cultural activities, scouting, leisure and sports. Youth work often seeks to reach out to particular groups of young people such as disadvantaged youth in socially deprived neighbourhoods, or immigrant youth including refugees and asylum seekers. Youth work may at times be organised around a particular religious tradition.

This broad depiction captures the huge diversity in methods, issues, contexts and target groups that might be within the orbit of youth work policy and practice. It also touches on the many tensions and debates that have dogged youth work throughout its history. Youth work belongs to both educational and social welfare systems, although it is neither school nor social work. Youth work can be voluntary and/or professionalised. Youth work aims for social inclusion, but also fosters individual choice and emancipation. Youth work is a universal practice, but may reach out to specific groups, based on deprivation, religion, gender, circumstance or policy priority. As one quasi-youth work policy initiative once put it, the goal is to provide a 'universal service differentiated according to need'.

In some respects it is good to have such an encompassing *description* – rather than a *definition* – of practice, but the many tensions that come across in Lauritzen's description cry out for a better understanding of youth work. Of course youth workers on the ground have an idea of the significance of their particular work, but as a policy domain, youth work remains difficult to grasp. Politicians and the wider public may proclaim the value of such 'recreational' services and activities (youth clubs, youth projects, youth outreach work, youth organisations) but, when it comes to difficult decisions within public administration relating to budgets, youth work is invariably considered low down in the hierarchy of priorities, and provision is often left primarily to charitable agencies (the 'voluntary' or NGO sector). All European nations provide a minimum of ten years free schooling, some much more, but far fewer see the importance of funding youth work. In those countries that do, the precarious position of youth work is highlighted in times of austerity, where much of the provision has been cut in order to protect 'core programmes' (Jeffs, 2011). These are the political challenges faced by youth work. Understanding youth work at an individual educational level *and* on a societal-political level not only enables youth workers to improve their practice, it also helps to improve the social position and recognition of youth work in the very different contexts in which it has evolved across Europe. To that end, it is important to identify the shared, specific and essential characteristics of youth work that encompass its diverse practices. It is essential to identify those common defining features in order to preserve distinctive, but vulnerable and often hard to understand, *youth work* interventions, because these, cannot be provided in the same way by other players in the social and educational field.

A first step in the identification of youth work's significance is, therefore, a socio-political analysis. This analysis has to precede the organisation of any pedagogical provision, for we cannot discuss the quality of social and pedagogical work if it is divorced abstractly from the socio-political context in which young people grow up. A second set of building blocks is provided by the historical reconstruction of youth work practice and policy, because history brings to the surface those elements that have been instrumental in not only cementing and sustaining successful youth work, but also influencing the shifting policy conceptions of what 'successful' means.

It is up to youth workers, researchers and policy makers to discuss the worth of these building blocks today. This is of paramount importance, as in many European countries, youth work is under significant pressure to formalise its curriculum and outputs, and to inscribe itself within employability, 'anti-radicalisation', and risk-reduction/management agendas, in addition to cultivating critical engagement, both with young people, and those who otherwise shape their lives. If youth work practice is *dominated* by these agendas its potential to reach out to all young people and to contribute to a wealthy and healthy democratic system will be limited. The challenge for contemporary youth work is to connect with these agendas without reneging its essential 'life-world' orientation.

The Social and Political Context of Youth Work Practice

In the aftermath of World War Two, most European nations (certainly those to the 'west') developed welfare regimes that aimed – in various ways – to reconcile capitalist market economies with values of equity and equality (Esping-Andersen, 1990). Although globalisation and systems of supranational governance have diminished the power of nation-states, many of these welfare regimes have remained fairly resilient. Given the rise of neoliberalism and the impact of austerity, this may come as some surprise, but analyses still reveal a significant continuity in states' choices in balancing interdependencies between social expenditure and economic performance (Saint-Arnaud & Bernard, 2003). However, as the traditional pillars of the Keynesian, 'passive' welfare state – full employment, stable jobs, and male-breadwinner families – were steadily eroded from the 1980s onwards, the majority of European nations have transitioned towards active welfare statism. Social inclusion, defined in the first place by labour market participation, became a central concept which engendered a growing emphasis on individual responsibility and ever-tightening links between rights and duties. Yet, after a decade characterised by welfare cuts and increasing social exclusion and poverty (Piachaud & Sutherland, 2001), the 1990s saw the birth of the 'social investment state': a welfare state that does not compensate for failure, but invests in future success. These shifts in the relation between government and citizens are well documented and articulated in discourses of the 'enabling state' (Gilbert, 1989) and the employment-first welfare state (Finn, 2003). Social workers involved in pedagogical practices saw their roles and tasks redefined in this new context. As taking opportunities and individual responsibility increasingly became the duty of the moral citizen, social workers came to focus on individual activation and re-moralisation, with policy shifting practice towards individual outcomes. For quite some time, youth work seemed to escape these pressures (partly because of its already peripheral and uncertain status in the 'professional' world); however, youth work practice was increasingly narrowed, especially in countries in which it had become an almost statutory practice. The war on drugs, the fear of radicalisation, the decline in decent jobs, the influx of increasing numbers of migrants, amongst other things, made the contexts for youth work far more complex than previous decades. Youth workers, where their role was to some extent recognised and their presence visible, were now expected to contribute to the 'fight' against significant social problems.

These trends mean that youth workers are increasingly confronted not only with old actors close to their field (such as social workers, careers advisers or school teachers) but also with new actors (such as specialist NGOs, and, indeed private sector businesses), many of which seek to bring new evidenced-based approaches into the field of 'working with young people'. On the pretext of joined-up and evidence-based thinking, youth workers are increasingly asked to cooperate with these actors, further fuelling tensions that have always prevailed in youth work. This often brings practitioners into uncomfortable situations in balancing rights with obligations, the interests of young people with those of parents, and the objectives of labour market partners with children's health agencies. The emphasis on joined-up thinking seems though to feed a rather controlling attitude towards 'vulnerable' people; it is more concerned with papering over the cracks, than with re-constructing the foundations (Warin, 2007). All these confused and interwoven developments hold promise for youth work's 'autonomy through dependency' position (see Siurala et al., 2016), but also make youth work extremely vulnerable. Some youth workers suffer from 'Calimero syndrome': 'It's not fair. They are big and I am small'. Others simply seem to acquiesce without concern or complaint to the continual re-boundarying of their work. This raises questions regarding whether these processes are a matter of strategy, opportunistic trimming or powerlessness (Jordan, 2004). We argue that youth workers (and young people) are far from powerless. Youth work practices are not only an answer to social problems, but they are closely connected to the definition of these problems. As a result, their interventions help to create a 'horizon of legitimate expectations' (Mahon, 2002: 360). Many youth workers fail to defend the value and parameters of their work; rather they tend to assimilate and embrace current policy imperatives in order to survive. Youth workers need the consciousness, insight and knowledge regarding the political character of their practices in order to be more explicit and credible about their pivotal and essential role in democracies. Addressing false expectations of what is possible through youth work will not be achieved through turning our backs on (usually local) governments and withdrawing to a position in which youth work practices continue on the goodwill of patronage or sponsorship and are carried by volunteers 'doing good by stealth' (Lister, 2001).

The reframing of welfare states from passive to active, re-emphasises the moral and pedagogical role of youth work, social work and community development. As such, their job is more valued than in times where policymakers apparently only asked them to get the 'dirtbags' off the street (Jeffs & Smith, 1996). Nevertheless, in such circumstances, many workers across these fields struggle to cope with the inherent paradoxes and dilemmas they consequently face in their work. Their feelings of uncertainty are reinforced by the dominance of 'Third Way' philosophies (Giddens, 1998) that tend to depoliticise social and pedagogical practices. Poverty and social fragmentation are no longer seen as symptoms of social inequality, but as consequences of non-participation in the labour market, with its focus on the individual skills acquisition requisite for integration into the existing social order (Levitas, 1998). If youth work subscribes uncritically to this agenda, it will find itself colluding in strengthening inequality between 'the established' and 'the outsiders' (Elias & Scotson, 1994), just as the schooling system already does. Contemporary youth work is no longer concerned with social inclusion, but rather with the management of social exclusion (Scherr, 1999). Such a teleological loss also indicates the erosion of essential social pillars: human rights and democracy. The current hegemony risks restricting broader social-pedagogical strategies, limiting practice to the organisation of care and support. In this way, access to social rights is reduced to access to social provision. This, in turn, produces an individualised and de-contextualised understanding of youth work, leading to a reductionist approach that focuses on little more than reaching out to young people in order to secure individual results: getting them back on track, particularly back into education, employment or training. The social and political context disappears, and an institutionally driven agenda imposes itself on what needs to be a life-world driven practice. Such reductionism decimates practices that focus on informal learning and positive development, the part where the focus is on learning to live a life, rather than merely earn a living (Macalister Brew, 1968). The focus needs to shift therefore from the accessibility of youth work provision, towards questions regarding how 'useful' youth work can be, for the wellbeing of individuals, groups, communities, and, ultimately society, on their own terms. The question therefore is not how we can motivate young people to participate *in* youth work, but how young people can participate, engage and develop *through* youth work. This remains an abstract question, because it can only be answered in concrete situations, with real young people. Nevertheless, there are still some general characteristics of youth work that bind our practices together and help us understand its individual and societal value. Moreover, some historical insights enable us to better understand the unique, if often ambivalent, position of youth work in the field of social and pedagogical practices.

Historicising Youth Work Practice and Policy

Although not all languages and communities have a noun to 'name' the practice of working with young people in their life-world, these practices can be identified in all countries, and are characterised by two features. Firstly, they work in the social sphere of society (the sphere that bridges the private aspirations and life-worlds of people and public expectations and spaces). Secondly, they work with young people in their leisure time, and are committed to their practices being guided by, sometimes led by, young people themselves.

Across Europe, 'youth work' has developed along two main branches. The first branch is connected to the social questions that have evolved since the middle of the 19th Century. The already existing social and pedagogical strategies to educate the lower working classes in order to prevent alcoholism, poverty and immorality were strengthened by drastic social transformations driven by the industrial revolution. The pedagogical and cohesive power of 'natural' living environments (the family, the village, the church and community association) came under pressure through processes of industrialisation and proletarianisation. Driven by a crisis in the agricultural economy, people migrated in huge numbers to towns and cities. The relatively predictable traditional agricultural society gave way to a class society in which a new sense of community needed to be 'organized'. Caritas and control, the two main mechanisms of imposing social cohesion, no longer seemed capable of coping with the new challenges. Therefore, in order to answer this 'social question' the focus shifted to the creation of a broad social sphere (Donzelot, 1984), the main aim of which was to integrate people through education and care. As a result, all social problems emerging from industrial capitalism (proletarianisation, urbanisation, idleness, ignorance, illness, squalor, criminality, poverty and destitution) were transformed through social and pedagogical work into pedagogical questions. Examples of this kind of youth work *avant la lettre* are the patronages in Italy, France and Belgium (based on Don Bosco's model of the oratorio in Turin), and the Boys' and Girls' Brigades in the United Kingdom. Don Bosco was deemed a genius, because he saw social problems as fundamentally symptomatic of a lack of education. Through education, young people learn to behave as good citizens should. The pedagogical work in the social sphere is thus instrumental to the realisation of a societal project and focuses on the assimilative participation of all citizens in that project. This suggests that social and pedagogical work is essentially and inevitably political, as it contributes to a society that is permanently 'under construction'. In this process of construction, the borders between private and public are constantly discussed, although it is clear that some groups in society have greater possibilities than others to transform their private troubles in public issues (Wright Mills, 1959).

It is clear that most of the social and pedagogical interventions that might be called 'youth work' at that time were aware that their interventions were rarely neutral. These interventions were deliberately focused on the adaption of 'maladapted youth'. There were of course also critical voices arguing that social and pedagogical provision could intervene in a corrective and compensatory manner, whilst at the same time challenging and questioning the existing social order, rather than just confirming it through individual integrative work. International youth work organisations such as the YMCA/YWCA and the Catholic Working Youth for example, were critical of young people's working conditions.

The second branch in the evolution of youth work developed not so much in the context of the education of the working class, but in the milieu of student youth. Student movements had already developed in the middle ages, but in the 19th century they claimed an increasing role in debating the position of young people in society. One well-known example is the Wandervögel Jugend in Germany, a rather loose movement that inspired the formation of activist student movements in many other European countries. This, has often been called the first real youth movement, because it sprang from youthful ideals rather than adult concerns, as in the case of Sunday Schools, Boys' and Girls' Brigades, and Patronages. There were, of course, often also adults working behind the scenes, trying to channel youthful engagement in an acceptable way, rendering their actions more cultural than social. These youth movements were gradually transformed into a method of youth work, through which educators started to appreciate the pedagogical possibilities of youthful engagement. Underpinned by theories of adolescence advanced by Stanley Hall (1904) and others, most of these organisations and associations were reframed as a youth question. Youth was constructed as a distinct stage in life and a distinct group in society. Adolescence was seen as a necessary period of 'Sturm und Drang' (storm and stress). The question was how to foster and guide young people's enthusiasm and engagement into something that was productive to cultural renewal, whilst ensuring the political stabilisation of the existing social order. This youth question became the focus of a distinct youth (work) policy, one concerned essentially with the participation of young people in society. The social question did not disappear, but emphasis on it faded.

Becoming a Method. Closing the Debate?

The social sphere is essential for a vibrant democracy. A society 'under permanent construction' is, however, also exhausting and causes social unrest. There are, therefore, always forces at work that want to, at least temporarily, close social and political debates. These forces focus on anchoring existing power (im-)balances and containing 'social movements'. As a result, the welfare state is always a delicate balance between renewal and stabilisation. Continuities in society are always confronted by pressures for social change. The establishment and expansion of cooperatives at the beginning of the 20th century improved the fate of workers and farmers. A series of social laws and children's laws were approved: the prohibition of child labour, Sunday rest, retirement pensions, decent working hours, a ban on night work for women. In many countries, the general (male) right to vote was obtained. This was not only a period of gradual democratisation through social legislation, but a time when a range of socio-cultural initiatives were being developed: libraries,

Sunday Schools, sports associations, youth organisations, theatres, and more. The initial diversity of social-pedagogical initiatives thereby found a stable environment in which to grow and specialise. They distinguished themselves from each other and started to lead their own, sometimes quite introspective and self-referential lives, turning attention away from a social context that seemed quite stable, but in doing so disconnecting from their own histories and shared roots. Many of them became detached from their initial, quite distinct political mission and have subsequently become methods of social work, cultural work, or sports activity. Some youth work initiatives lost themselves completely. Many of them became attracted to – or displaced by – a new form of youth movement spreading throughout Europe at the beginning of the 20th Century: Scouting. In elaborating his method of youth work, Baden-Powell did not at first think of a separate movement. He wanted to help youth leaders, such as those from the Boys' Brigade, make their 'outdoor life and character building' more attractive. The Scouting method, however, quickly grew into a movement, one that spread rapidly and unprecedentedly all over the world. Its smooth dissemination was successful particularly because of its political neutrality. It does not question the political, religious and cultural order. On the contrary, it became embedded and renamed, within the youth structures of politically diverse organisations. Catholic patronages and the socialist Red Falcons applied the Scouting method, as well as state organisations such as the fascist Opera Nazionale Ballilla (Italy) and the Nazi Hitler Jugend (Germany); the communist Komsomol in the Soviet Union and Hungary also adopted the new method. The methodical, seemingly apolitical, nature of Scouting was appealing to the somewhat orphaned existing initiatives in the youth field that saw many of their related social and pedagogical activities (in sports, education and culture) go their own separate ways, quite often deleting their original missions from their identity.

The new concept of youth work, at the turn of the 20th century was no longer founded in a 'social question', but came to be based on a 'youth ideology': all young people, whether workers or students, have to pass through the *ideal* youth phase. A certain period of 'Sturm und Drang' was seen as part of a natural development. As a result, ideal types of youth care and youth movement came together in the 'public school model' on which Baden-Powell based a private youth world isolated from adults. Adults hold the reins, but transfer the responsibility for concrete activity to young people. Baden-Powell emphasised pedagogical principles such as 'self-government' and 'learning by doing', but his method was intended and excellently suited to transmitting the values and norms of the existing social order. As Van Uytfanghe et al. (1988: 26) have argued, 'If the public schools were prepared to lead, the Scouts must produce young people ready to follow'. Even the student movements felt attracted to this new method of youth work based on outdoor life, adventure, teamwork, learning skills, self-organisation and working for others.

In this way, 'youth questions' replaced 'social questions' in youth work's unfolding development; its focus shifting from redistribution of opportunities between rich and poor to redistributing possibilities between old and young. Emphasising age criterion inevitably diminished attention to the socio-economic fault lines in young people's lives.

From this moment on, youth work became a method, and youth work debates focused on methodical techniques: group work, creativity, models of participation, and learning crafts, skills, and leadership. Its underpinning ideology, rooted in the social question, seemed to disappear. This has continued to make youth work practices extremely vulnerable to instrumentalising agendas (that seek to subordinate youth work, or enlist its methods for the realisation of other goals). Many youth work organisations have therefore gone from being heads of movements, to becoming the arms of the state (Maunders, 1996).

Keeping up the Tensions

From the 1970s onwards, youth workers – and 'social' workers in general – observed that social inequality, exclusion and poverty were not marginal concerns, and, as a result, reflected increasingly on the content and focus of their practices. Influential social educators such as Giesecke (1970) and Freire (1970) criticized youth work (and social work in general) for becoming a middle-class instrument of social control, rather than engaging critically with existing systems, and so failing to fulfil its promises of equality. Many young people now have greater possibilities in their leisure time than they once did; this makes them less dependent on a youth work offer to fulfil their aspirations. At the same time, in many countries, youth work has developed a 'service' mentality, one in which it is seen as 'a service for youth where it is needed: home, class, playground, office ...' (Davies, 1970: 6).

Youth workers need to revisit some of the early purposes of practice and reconnect with those initial missions. They need to consider roads not taken and learn to confront prevailing inclusion discourses with the lived reality of young people's experiences. This may involve highlighting and challenging the inequality and injustice experienced by many young people that actively exclude them. Why should youth workers address employability, if it is only to guide young people towards hamburger jobs, precarious work in offices, or short-term temporary jobs without any chance of enabling young people to build a dignified life? Of course, it is legitimate for youth work to cooperate with labour market institutions that aim to integrate young people, but youth work has a different mission based in informal and social learning. Youth workers need to uncover and unravel how a system based on competition inherently excludes certain groups of young people and to support young people (and policymakers) to find creative and innovative solutions and alternatives to programmes and approaches that have proven not to work sufficiently for all young people.

Re-Socialising Youth Work Practice and Policy

In current policy, there is a tendency to neglect the inevitability of these tensions and dilemmas. A plea is heard, instead, for a more structured, individualised, professionalised and outcome-focused youth work, especially with regard to 'vulnerable' young people. In this approach, youth work is increasingly constructed only as part of the infrastructure providing a transit zone between the private lifeworld and the public system, which focuses on individual development and smooth integration into existing society. Youth work then, does not start where young people are, but where society wants them to be.

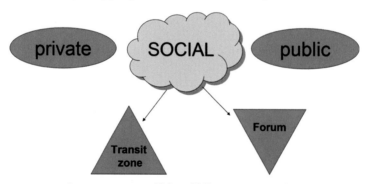

FIGURE 4.1   Between system and lifeworld (from Coussée et al., 2010)

Youth work is however as much a social forum as it is a transit zone (Verschelden et al., 2009). Youth workers may help to adapt young people to social change, to new challenges, and to the 'risk society' (Beck, 1992), but at the same time, they analyse and question with young people in order to enable understanding of the impact of these challenges and changes on young people's lifeworlds. What are the consequences of a changed and changing society? Are they in the interest of all young people? Whether we speak about youth associations and organisations, detached youth work, youth centres and services, or playgrounds, youth work in all its forms and shapes has both a transit and a forum function. And while there is no doubt that recreation is a main carousel of youth work activity, sometimes youth workers focus on this part of their job at the expense of the social and the pedagogical aspects of their work. This imbalance reduces youth work, to the cruel, but perhaps apt, depiction of adolescent child-minding.

Youth work's power is its ability to create free spaces for young people that are characterised by safety, a sense of belonging, bonding and bridging, the art of conversation, challenge, friendship and relationships. In striking contrast to the contemporary school system, youth workers create places where young people can explore themselves and their environment. Youth work contexts should be places where young people find the motivation to learn. This may not be concerned in the first place with measurable skills, but it does play an important role in young people's holistic development. This additional value is exactly the reason why, over a century ago, educational thinkers, youth leaders and policy makers established a youth work framework which gathered together all distinctive and differentiated practices that focused on the positive development of young people outside school time. This is an important message to today's youth policy makers at all levels: youth work policy has never been only about achieving predefined outcomes, nor was it about fixing predetermined issues. Alongside schooling and welfare systems, youth work practices are instrumental to the ongoing process of democratisation. Youth work facilitates genuine discussions with young people on their terms, about *their rights, duties, and place in society; the organisation of society's institutions; their relationships with other people and groups, and relationships within families and schools.*

Conclusion

Characterised in the 1st History of Youth Work in Europe publication as both 'forum' and 'transit zone', youth work remains a concept that is full of internal tensions, not least its struggle to balance emancipation and control. Yet it remains an important driving force in the smooth integration of young people into society, and in promoting their emancipation. The internal tensions within all forms of youth work lead to constant struggles between integrative and emancipatory poles, but also between the quest for the recognition of youth work as a contributor to broad package of social provision for young people, and a desire for it to develop a more fluid (and independent) position as a critical movement. Some youth work initiatives profile themselves as rather loose associations where dialogue and deliberation are central; others are rather more strictly organised in ways where discipline and training lie at their heart.

In attempting to find consensus, the 2nd European Youth Work Convention, in 2015 sought to identify some 'common ground' across the diversity of youth work practices, proposing that youth work provides *spaces* for young people's identity and autonomy and *bridges* for young people's transitions towards full participation in economic and civic life. This common ground helps youth workers to cherish necessary diversity whilst celebrating youth work as a distinct, fundamental educational practice (supporting the positive development of young people), and, as a practice that is supportive of social cohesion and the process of democracy itself.

Despite or possibly (and probably) because of its diversity, youth work practice today demonstrates a remarkable resilience to changing times and contexts. Its core principles and practices have remained relatively stable over time and space, despite its variety of shapes and methods. In this chapter, we described the heart of youth work as a tension between inter-related, but conflicting concepts, derived from a dual perspective on young people: as valued (to be promoted, a 'resource to be managed') or as vulnerable or even villainous (to be protected or punished, a 'problem to be solved'). Youth work throughout Europe, has at different times, and in different ways, directly endeavoured, or been expected to take on different, potentially competing, and, even conflicting roles: diversion, dialogue, development, association, aspiration and assimilation.

Almost fifty years ago, a conference in the then state socialist eastern Europe, focused on young people as 'factors in' social change; thirty years later, a united democratic Europe held a conference on young people as 'actors for' social change. Youth work has represented both the holy grail for *both* emancipation *and* control, and been viewed as a poisoned chalice for precisely the same activity. Its social context is everything. As youth work moves with the times, promoting youth association, facilitating youth organisation, or providing activities and advice, its identity, recognition and status will be mirrored in the social and political expectations of its place within wider 'youth policy' contexts. Youth work must continue to determine how it will respond to the tensions between 'the social question' and 'the youth question', and, the other inherent dilemmas it routinely faces. This in turn will determine how society values its ongoing contribution, *and* whether or not, youth work remains true to itself.

Over the past decade, the 'crisis' and austerity measures have produced, in many (though by no means all) parts of Europe, dramatic public sector cuts in budgets for youth work provision. This has been draconian in those countries where youth work had, to that point, acquired a professional status and become almost a statutory service. England is the most striking example of youth work's fall from grace. Youth work has manifestly been very vulnerable when confronted with a discourse drenched in an atmosphere of austerity, where problem-focused, outcome-driven policies ask for a return on investment in terms of fewer problems caused or experienced by young people. Two European Youth Work Conventions, seven seminars, and subsequent books on the History of Youth Work in Europe, have, during this time, created a solid body of knowledge and insights that can provide a social and pedagogical alternative to this neoliberal economic discourse. In this alternative scenario, it is emphasized that youth work is a distinct intervention in the lifeworld of young people. In addition to schools and families, this third milieu of socialisation and transition, can make a positive difference in the development of children, young people and their communities, even though that difference can rarely be 'monetarised' or expressed in economic terms. It is of utmost importance that this European discourse seeps down into local youth work. Local youth workers must understand their own practice in social and pedagogical terms, build alliances with other provision and organisations in the social and pedagogical field, and keep in touch with their local policy makers. It is essential that youth workers support young people in illustrating the difference youth work can make through extending distinctive opportunities and experiences, thereby supporting young people in gaining a broader and deeper comprehension of themselves, their environments and society as a whole. Youth work does not have to be fully professionalised to do this, but it does merit professional recognition as a significant social and pedagogical provision.

Note

1   See https://www.salto-youth.net/downloads/4-17-2803/2010_Declaration_European_youth_work_convention_en.pdf

References

Beck, U. (1992). *Risk society, towards a new modernity*. London: Sage Publications.
Cohen, P. (1986). *Rethinking the youth question*. London: Institute of Education.

Coussée, F., Verschelden, G., Van de Walle, T., Medlinska, M., & Williamson, H. (Eds.). (2010). *The history of youth work in Europe and its relevance for youth policy today* (Vol. 2). Strasbourg: Council of Europe Publishing.

Davies, B. (1970). Changing conceptions of youth work. *Jeugdwerk Nu, 2*(21), 5–7.

Donzelot, J. (1984). *L'invention du social: essai sur le déclin des passions politiques*. Paris: Fayard.

Freire, P. (1970). *Pedagogy of the oppressed*. New York, NY: Herder and Herder.

Giddens, A. (1998). *The third way: The renewal of social democracy*. Cambridge: Polity Press.

Giesecke, H. (1970). *Die Jugendarbeit*. München: Juventa Verlag.

Jeffs, T. (2011). Running out of options: Re-Modelling youth work. *Youth & Policy, 106*, 1–8.

Jeffs, T., & Smith, M. (1996). 'Getting the dirtbags off the streets' – Curfews and other solutions to juvenile crime. *Youth and Policy, 52*, 1–14.

Jordan, B. (2004). Emancipatory social work? Opportunity or oxymoron. *British Journal of Social Work, 34*(1), 5–19.

Lauritzen, P. (2008). Defining youth work. In A. Rothemund & Y. Ohana (Eds.), *Eggs in a pan. Speeches, writings and reflections by Peter Lauritzen*. Strasbourg: Council of Europe Publishing.

Levitas, R. (1998). *The inclusive society? Social exclusion and new labour*. London: Palgrave Macmillan.

Lister, R. (2001). Doing good by stealth: The politics of poverty and inequality under new labour. *New Economy, 8*(2), 65–70.

Macalister Brew, J. (1968). *Youth and youth groups*. London: Faber and Faber.

Mahon, R. (2002). What kind of "social Europe"? The example of child care. *Social Politics, 9*(4), 342–379.

Maunders, D. (1996). Head of a movement or arms of the state? *International Journal of Adolescence and Youth, 6*(2), 175–194.

McKeen, W. (2006). Diminishing the concept of social policy: The shifting conceptual ground of social policy debate in Canada. *Critical Social Policy, 26*(4), 865–887.

Saint-Arnaud, S., & Bernard, P. (2003). Welfare regimes in advanced countries: Convergence or resilience? *Current Sociology, 51*(5), 499–527.

Scherr, A. (1999). Transformations in social work: From help towards social inclusion to the management of exclusion. *European Journal of Social Work, 2*(1), 15–25.

Siurala, L., Coussée, F., Suurpää, L., & Williamson, H. (Eds.). (2006). *The history of youth work in Europe, Volume 5: Autonomy through dependency: Histories of co-operation, conflict and innovation in youth work*. Strasbourg: Council of Europe.

Stanley Hall, G. (1904). *Adolescence: Its psychology and its relations to physiology, anthropology, sociology, sex, crime, religion, and education* (Vols. I & II). New York, NY: D. Appleton & Co.

Van de Walle, T., Coussée, F., & De Bie, M. (2011). Social exclusion and youth work. From the surface to the depths of an educational practice. *Journal for Youth Studies, 14*(2), 219–231.

Van Uytfanghe, M., Crivit, R., & Samijn, D. (1988). *Funkties van het jeugdwerk, historisch bekeken.* Gent: FOJOD.

Warin, J. (2007). Joined-up services for young children and their families: Papering over the cracks of re-constructing the foundations. *Children & Society, 21,* 87–97.

Wright Mills, C. (1959). *The sociological imagination.* New York, NY: Oxford University Press.

CHAPTER 5

The Future of US Youth Work

Dana Fusco and Michael Baizerman

Going There from Here?

It might be odd to ask about the *future* of youth work in the US given that youth work has no commonly understood or robust *presence*. The cultural narrative for youth work, at best, lies in the distant periphery of public discourse. This is in part due to the fact that historically US youth work has been situated in different communities of practice yielding no common lexicon from which to garner support. There is also no sole jurisdiction for youth work; it belongs both to no one and to everyone. Each of the six federal offices within the US government responds to youth-related issues from within their mission, purview, and priority. For example, the Department of Health and Human Services provides funding for programs for drug use and abuse, teen pregnancy, and prevention of HIV and AIDS, depending on heightened or diminished concern; the Department of Labor funds youth employment and career programs; and the Department of Education funds formal and informal education programs. Youth work is not language that one would find in any policy or request for proposal from any of these chief federal departments. What one will find is funding for youth programs that target 'vulnerable' youth populations: homeless youth, 'disconnected' youth, youth in foster care or involved with the juvenile justice system, youth with disabilities, indigenous youth populations, pregnant teens, and the like. In fact, there is a rather robust system of nonprofit organizations within the US that offers a variety of youth-related programming in response to these requests. These can range quite drastically in scope, content, and pedagogy. While internationally many of these would not be considered 'youth work', in the US we accept a broad range of youth-related services and programs within the category of youth work (Fusco, 2012; Pozzoboni & Kirshner, 2016) – though, this is contested space, as there are no agreed upon youth work tenets or principles across the various settings and contexts. Then, our discussion of the future of US youth work is contextualized in two realities: there is both no such thing as a unified profession or labor of 'youth work' in the US and, there exists a vast diaspora of youth work practice in communities throughout the nation.

So, how does one think about a future of youth work for this oddly scattered practice? We turn briefly to the history of midwifery as an interesting corollary.

© KONINKLIJKE BRILL NV, LEIDEN, 2019 | DOI:10.1163/9789004396555_005

In midwifery, a complex set of factors drove its demise and then (marginal) rebirth as a semi-profession. At a time when men could not attend child birthing, midwives were seen as competent (enough) in dealing with women's health issues. Births occurred at home under the care and competency of the midwife. There was an accepted cultural arrangement between midwives and pregnant women contextualized in acceptable vocational roles for women at the time. The first shift in this arrangement occurred in the late 1700s with the onset of medicine and formal medical training. When licensing for midwives emerged, women could not take advantage of advanced education as many were illiterate and could not afford the cost of tuition. Men started attending midwife training and legitimized midwifery as a branch of the medical profession, rather than a vocational trade. A second shift occurred when public hospitals were built and medical training proliferated. Birthing at home no longer had public support, particularly among the middle and upper classes who shifted their trust of birthing to the male physician and the hospital. By the 1920s, only half of all births were attended at home by midwives. Perceptions of childbirth had gradually changed from a natural process to a traumatic one requiring a drug-induced state. But in the 1960s, there was a rebirth of midwifery when feminist movements spurred new thinking: women wanted to reclaim power over their bodies. Today, though there are fewer midwives, they receive a unified curriculum and have a professional association – 15,000 midwives today oversee 10% of US births. The perceptions of women in history, available societal and vocational roles for women, competing professions and the place for men within them, as well as changing views of childbirth itself, all are interwoven to tell a story of the ebbs and flows of a profession (Rooks, 1999).

While it is not possible to know the future of youth work in the United States with any certainty, there are some weighty considerations to be learned from this history: including the perceptions of youth and youth roles in society; the vocation of youth work and who can(not) become a youth worker; the authority and mission of professional bodies of youth work; alternative, even competing, youth-related practices to youth work; and public awareness and buy in for youth work, to name a few. Such factors would play no singular role in future events but might coalesce to yield the demise or (re)birth of youth work, or neither. We can also assume that motion is a dynamic force. Small actions can ripple through time, even turn into historical social movements, and it is impossible to know in advance what the 'magic moment' or 'tipping point' (Gladwell, 2006) will be. With no singular cause, actions get triggered and either take root or fizzle out, die and get replaced with something else.

Of course, one cannot discuss the future of youth work without also asking: what sort of practice(s) with young people is likely to continue into the future? As discussed, youth work in the US maps onto a large geographically, culturally and politically diverse landscape of practices with young people. There is not one youth work or one type of youth worker within and across contexts. There are differences by spheres of practice and within spheres of practice, such as delinquency, health, education, recreation, and religion, for example. Youth work directly with a young person, or a group of young people; and indirect youth work on behalf of youth are named differently depending on the sphere of practice. Thus in juvenile justice, youth workers are probation officers; in medicine and health, adolescent nurses; in mental health, counselors; in ministry, youth ministers, for example. Therefore, we must distinguish between 'the future' and futures, as multiple and alternative. Henceforth, we use 'futures' to always mean 'possible and multiple futures'. We do this because our actions can help craft proximate to distal futures for youth work as such, as well as for individual young persons.

This chapter will examine some key considerations in order to reflect and project on US youth work futures. Also, a caveat is presented: hypothesizing and mapping various scenarios, however likely or unlikely, puts us in a 'wait and see' mode. Though the mapping itself might hold value (e.g., make us more critically aware of the complex interplay of factors that affect youth work and its future/potential) we might also envision the future we want and then set about to create it. We believe in analysis and choice, in prioritization and in decisions – in human action. Thus, we believe that the futures in our youth work world will be in part (or more) a result of our goals, acts, and actions: we have agency, and power and, hopefully, a call to use these for, on behalf of, and with young people. This chapter will then also humbly put forth a proposal for considering youth work outside of vocational, organizational, and professional roles; that is, as one of 'stance' – one taken up with and behalf of young people.

The Futures of Youth Work: Key Considerations

Youth, the Youth Problem and Garnering Public Attention

There are 56 million young people, ages 12–24 years old, in the US; that is almost one-fifth of the total US population, according to the 2015 census. More than half of the world's population is under the age of 30 (USAID, 2012). This 'youth bulge' has received international consideration demanding also the attention of the US. In 2012, former Secretary Clinton stated 'responding to the needs and aspirations of young people is a crucial challenge for the future' (USAID, 2012: 1).

While the size of the youth population matters, size plus 'problems' matter more for garnering support for youth-related policies and services, and, for
youth work. Depending on geographical location, 19–25% of young people live
below the federal poverty line (in extreme poverty) and 41% of adolescents
are categorized as low income (Actforyouth, 2013). Teens in rural and urban
areas (about half of all teens residing in the US) experience greater poverty
and diminished opportunities than teens living in suburban (more privileged)
areas. Teens of color also experience a higher incidence of poverty than their
white counterparts. Sixty-one percent of Black teens, 60% of Hispanic teens,
and 58% of Native American teens live in low-income families (Actforyouth,
2013). Recent estimates report over 1.5 million 'unaccompanied' youth (homeless or runaway); most between the ages of 15 and 17 (National Coalition for the
Homeless, 2008).

This alone should get the public's attention. But, alas it often does not. There
are a myriad of interrelated factors that draw public awareness and attention
to youth issues. While it is impossible to predict the exact causal direction, it
seems that often awareness begins with a compelling story. The 'story' might be
in the form of one case (a 10-year old who commits suicide because of online
cyber-bullying) or many. Effective stories illuminate an important social issue
and can attract a champion. Champions can be those victimized and/or their
families, celebrities, advocacy or practice organizations that deal with the
issue, politicians, researchers, or professional organizations. Social media has
helped stories to 'go viral' and gain a critical mass of support. The online public petition polls also provide a way to track the number of people who will
support and get behind an issue. It is numbers that will turn an issue into a
national crisis and get the attention of policy makers and funders.

Video games are an example. In 1999, two teens killed 13 people in the Col-
umbine High School mass shooting: the worst high school shooting in US history at that time. The investigation revealed that the two shooters were avid
players of a very violent video game. Two years later, an 'empirical' analysis
was conducted linking violent video game usage with antisocial behaviors
(Anderson & Bushman, 2001). In 2005, the American Psychological Association (APA) released a statement advocating for the reduction of violence in
video games marketed to young people as well as an increase in media literacy
and transparent depiction of harmful effects to be posted on products of the
entertainment industry, and this resolution was updated in 2015 (APA, 2015).

While not unworthy actions, such responses to moral panic are *issue-driven
responses*. Issue-driven responses offer token solutions and show that 'something is being done' without really addressing the broader societal and macro
conditions that are also driving the concerning behavior. We worry about the

effects of violent video games, but never ask why teens are drawn to such games in the first place (e.g., maybe it is because there are fewer and fewer free recreational spaces and interesting programmatic activities for teens; maybe society has created multiple institutions that reinforce the passive nature of 'adolescence' – that is, teens have little opportunity to enact agency in ways that can contribute to their communities; maybe, society reinforces notions of aggression particularly in males, etc.). Any of these might lead to broader societal responses in which youth work would certainly have a significant role to play. Else the issue passes.

More recently, the number of 'disconnected' youth (those not associated with either an institution of school or work) has received considerable attention. Here we have a social issue that is getting attention at a policy level due to: both the size of the population (2.4 million youth ages 16–24 met the definition of being disconnected in 2014) (Fernandes-Alcantara, 2015) and a perceived problem (significant loss of active and productive adult citizens contributing to societal functioning as well as exorbitant costs associated with adults who will need a range of social services to live).

A response for youth work will be to uncover the youth veil in order to see young people, the realities of their lives as lived, and their 'disconnected-ness' in the context of not just being 'youth', but being youth in this adult world. To us a good but oblique definition of youth is: 'What does it mean to do and to be a _____ year old _____ around here, now'? To compound this a little, consider that 'youth' is a socially, culturally, economically constituted social role, and that the word 'youth' is also used as a metaphor, symbol, and in other ways as shorthand for a variety of conditions, people, states of mind, and more. All of this abstraction must be located in the policy-funding-services structures and process, in social science, and in relation to the realities of being and doing youth-hood, as well as the facts of the status of the youth population. This distinction matters because to the extent that youth workers and the field take on the responsibility to shine lights on the lives and conditions and futures of youth, then any diminishment of youth work as social institution and profession will very likely result in a dimmer illumination of how young people do their youth-hood and live forward into their personal and collective futures: less attention to youth and less centrality to youth work field, again. To lose youth work is to lose light and voice and public, communal, and adult attention and presence for youth during their youth-hood and into their futures as adults.

These are the sociopolitical, sociological, and psychological drivers that impact the potential of youth work as a social response to the 'youth problem'. Within the field itself, vocational, organizational and professional drivers of change also emerge.

Youth Work Organizations, Vocations, and the Quest for Profession

Organizations have to be ready to respond to socially defined issues, like what to do with these 'disconnected' youth while remaining vigilant about not absorbing the pathological deficit perspectives associated within such definitions of youth. In fact, youth work in the US is an organization based practice and cannot be fully understood without considering this. To know its theories, practices independent of this organizational and hence political context is not to know 'it'.

Yet, for many, the future of youth work does not rest on thriving youth organizations with vocational opportunities, but on the professionalization of youth work. The claim is that professionalizing youth work would help it gain a legitimate space in society alongside professions such as law or teaching. This might be so, but collectively we are still sorting the unintended consequences (Johnston Goodstar & Velure Roholt, 2013); the benefits and detriments of gatekeeping (Vachon, 2013); and the potential loss of diversity in the workforce (Moore, 2013). Then there are the obvious questions such as: what does it mean to professionalize? Whose and what kind of knowledge counts (Walker & Walker, 2012)? Professionalization is contrite with battles over power and prestige, including self-interest in laying claim to a body of knowledge, the marginalization of unskilled workers in the process, even the need to pathologize the client in order to 'show up' with the cure (Abbott & Meerabeau, 1998).

While there have been attempts to professionalize youth work, there is no one professional association or national hub for youth workers. The largest association for professional youth work is within the genre of youth work known as 'child and youth care' (CYC). It would not be correct to equate CYC with youth work, though it is fairly accurate to recognize CYC as one of the most organized and vocal arms. This is due to its long and robust history, rigorous theoretical and empirical practice frameworks, strong presence in higher education, niche within the residential youth settings, and professional association with an online journal and plenty of national and international conferences from which membership grows. The language of 'child care' is also publicly embraced and adding 'youth' to the mix was a successful strategy for gaining broader public appeal. More recently, OST (out of school time), another youth work genre, has organized itself as a 'field' of child and youth programs that occur during non-school hours. Attempts have been made for CYC and OST to join forces, so to speak, largely under the auspices of the National After-school Association. Such a merge would provide the largest venue for staff to come together as advocates for youth and youth-related programs, but could also be perceived as exclusionary to the large number of youth workers who associate with neither CYC or OST, e.g., work in recreation centers, churches, schools, health-care facilities, community agencies, reservations, libraries and museums.

Beyond this, is the colonization of youth work 'turf' by other professions and occupations. Such zoning violations are more than a substitution of one profession for youth work, but of course bring with it different ways of noticing, interpreting/naming, and working with young people, e.g. formal educationalists, counseling, probation workers, social workers, and the untrained too. This is how youth work as such can disappear, be changed, or just become a diminished presence in the human services/education, in the life-worlds of young people, and as advocates for better conditions for youth, locally to nationally to globally. Without strong national groups and international youth work organizations, global youth issues such as migration will be likely far less present on public agendas. And this too will lead to the increasing marginalization of the youth work field, from policy to direct practice.

Evidence-Based Practices

There is perhaps no topic that is getting more attention in funding circles than the need for evidence-based practice. If youth work could provide evidence of its worth, then it would be easier to leverage public (financial) support, so the logic goes. Youth work practitioners, researchers, advocates and activists have been elevating the trouble with this growing requirement for evidence as inherently problematic for the field (Matloff-Nieves et al., in press; Moore, 2013). The logic behind the mandate for evidence is couched in terms like quality, outcomes, and impacts: rendering any critique of the mandate utter foolishness. After all, who doesn't want youth work to be of strong quality with measureable outcomes and social impacts? Missed is the deeper interrogation of how predetermined mandates play out in the field and cause counter-effects to those expected: e.g., youth work practice that gets aimed at fewer social misbehaviors among teens in a community and is thus used for social control rather than transformative social conditions (e.g., Atkinson, Chico, & Horn, 2016). Many well-intentioned folks are caught in the wheel of thoughtless bureaucracy in efforts to find just the right mix of 'quality' interventions that will yield just the right kind of outcomes. Those able to put the 'science' behind their approach are rewarded as those with power and pocketbooks seem pleased in their compliance: and the mutual dance is reinforced. The future of youth work then might mean playing the evidence game while ensuring that doing so will not jeopardize the integrity of pro-youth/youth led/ youth centered praxis. Or, the future of youth work might mean abandoning the reliance of funding sources that come with strings and pursuing alternative revenues: private donations, fees, entrepreneurship, good old fashioned fundraisers and use of internet 'go fund me' sites. If we let the young people lead this effort, we are likely to be surprised with some creative solutions.

We have sketched but a few considerations in the futures of youth work in the US – all of which will also be heavily reliant on recent political ideologies that have swayed much of the country to the 'alt-right'. The specific policies of the 'new normal' are not yet known, but we can expect less government support and growing marketization of services across all sectors, including youth services – to say the least. To counter this we must reclaim a praxis that keeps the light focused on young people. We turn next to a vision for an actionable stance.

Envisioning the Future of Youth Work

A true and moral youth work should frame its purpose and direct its work at the realities of the everyday lives of young people. This frame would include the deep consideration of the social, economic, political, and cultural status of young people, and be directed by and with those groups, organizations, policies, programs, and services which both enhance, deflect, and retard their life-worlds, their lives, and their individual and collective statuses in community and society. From this assertion, it follows that the futures of youth work should ideally be coupled to the current and future realities of young people as a population group, as an age-cohort, as a life moment, as a social role, and the like. Field and practice should be driven by people, not primarily by policy, moral panic, budget, 'evidence', or other necessary but secondary facts, practices, ideologies, philosophies, or by 'the ways things have been done and thus must continue to be done' rhetoric.

Elsewhere, we have questioned the value of youth work as a profession (Fusco & Baizerman, 2013). While still a possible way forward, the support for this direction remains contested space. If we stepped outside of organizational and professional boundaries, how would we (adults) respond to youth as they present themselves to us in the here and now? In our respective roles as professors in youth work and non-youth work worlds, and through our interactions with students who come from a variety of occupational, cultural, learning and economic backgrounds, we approach the teaching of youth work, not as a bound set of professional rules, but as a 'stance' towards young people.

A stance is both a perspective and a posture. It is not 'a claim about the world, but a certain attitude of investigation' (Rowbottom & Bueno, 2011: 8). In the context of youth work, it is a way of approaching how we see and understand young people and young people in the world, as well as a posture towards that perspective or how we also approach action. Rowbottom and Bueno call this a mode of engagement. While the ontology of one's stance may be difficult to determine, e.g. is likely a complicated amalgam, Ratcliffe (2011) argues that the more popular 'empirical stance' must be subjected to scrutiny. One must 'bracket' an empirical stance and adopt a phenomenological one. That is, empiricism cannot understand itself. One must dwell in a place having the full rational-emotive-social experience to really understand it.

Rather than consolidating youth work knowledge within a profession and a role that limits itself to particular organizational life, we might ask: what does it mean to be a police officer who has a youth work stance? A teacher? A business owner? A policy maker? A politician? A grocery store clerk? What would schools look like that employed youth workers? Hospitals? Police precincts? Etc.

Conclusion

The future of youth work is a more complicated question than it at first seems, given the reticula of youth works in youth's lives. Given too that public and other funding is in competition with needs and wants of other aged populations and simply other groups, the increased availability and speed of public citizen voices, and the relatively sluggish governmental responses to all of this, youth work, surely publicly funded youth work, is rarely a simple service strategy, and is even more complex and tied like Gulliver in these reticula of policies' rules procedures, practices, and knowledge. To imagine reasonable and likely futures for youth work is no simple task.

We tried to direct such an inquiry towards the key narratives currently being sketched out in the field. As discussed, here there are inherent logics that play out: if youth work could evidence itself as a practice with strong youth outcomes, we could garner support; if youth work became a profession, we could stabilize organizations and practices; etc. We have no particular aim in disproving these. When we talk of futures, we can talk of a future like the one we have already; a future where youth work is a profession carved along exclusionary lines etc.; or a future where youth workers work alongside other youth practitioners. We can also, in addition to or instead of, talk of a future where to be a youth worker means to work with, for, and alongside of young people having a particular stance – a stance that informs a contextually grounded praxis of responses – ways of responding to young people's presence, wants, and needs, to their place in community, society, and nation; to pathways and off-the-road opportunities toward adult statuses as persons and citizens, workers, and students, and all the rest.

In the 'real world' youth work also, if not at all times, works on behalf of local communities, society, and the nation in its response to both youth and to wider worlds. At its best, it is a conservative strategy for the youth population, while it may be less so for individuals, some social groups, and subpopulations. Aware of the following reification, youth work's purpose is to enhance individual social development and well-being within and across age-graded (schools, e.g.) and larger social worlds (e.g. community): To facilitate, guide, and in other ways make possible for individuals, groups, and youth populations opportunities for learning, 'fitting-in' and for being active citizens. To us, youth work is not a radical or revolutionary strategy for this age-group. At times, economic and political changes are advocated, worked at, and trained to make youth lives and their potential achievements possible. Here the 'radical' shows itself in social structural, social system, and social institutional changes to invite and support changes in young people's lives and opportunities. And herein lies the stance: one that positions itself close enough to young people to hear and see, to respond, and to advocate – in whatever role, occupationally or socially, that one finds oneself in.

Where youth work might be heading, and/or where it is going now, does not mean that it will look like this or that later, nor does it tell us where it will be, and how it will work in three or thirty years. More important, we can shape youth work's futures. Whether, and how and when we take on shaping youth work's futures, are our powerful moral choices. In a most powerful way, the possible and likely futures of youth work as a formal institution and as moral praxis is an imagining of our values, beliefs, and goals. It is trite but truthful to write the following: Be part of bringing about futures for youth work that keep it in its variety – philosophically, politically, and structurally, a practice attached inextricably to the actual wants, needs, and conditions of young people, and their places to create in our worlds.

References

Abbott, P., & Meerabeau, L. (1998). *The sociology of the caring professions* (2nd ed.). London: UCL Press Limited.

Actforyouth. (2013). *U.S. teen demographics.* Retrieved from http://www.actforyouth.net/adolescence/demographics

Anderson, C., & Bushman, B. (2001). Effects of violent video games on aggressive behavior, aggressive cognition, aggressive affect, physiological arousal, and prosocial behavior: A meta-analytic review of the scientific literature. *Psychological Science, 12,* 353–359.

APA. (2015). *Resolution on violent video games*. Retrieved from http://www.apa.org/about/policy/violent-video-games.aspx

Atkinson, K., Chico, E., & Horn, S. S. (2016). Youth work for social change: Preparing individuals to work with youth in diverse urban contexts. In K. M. Pozzoboni & B. Kirshner (Eds.), *The changing landscape of youth work: Theory and practice for an evolving field* (pp. 229–248). Charlotte, NC: Information Age Publishing.

Fernandes-Alcantara, A. L. (2015). *Disconnected youth: A look at 16 to 24 year olds who are not working or in school* (CRS report). Washington, DC: Congressional Research Service.

Fusco, D. (2012). *Advancing youth work: Current trends, critical questions*. New York, NY: Routledge.

Fusco, D., & Baizerman, M. (2013). Professionalization in youth work? Opening and deepening circles of inquiry. *Child and Youth Services, 34*, 89–99.

Gladwell, M. (2006). *The tipping point: How little things can make a big difference*. Boston, MA: Little, Brown and Company.

Johnston Goodstar, K., & VeLure Roholt, R. (2013). Unintended consequences of professionalizing: Lessons from teaching and social work. *Child and Youth Services, 34*, 139–155.

Matloff-Nieves, S., Wiggins, T., Fuqua, J., Ragonese, M., Pullano, S., & Bender, G. (in press). *Returning to responsive youth work in New York City. The handbook of youth work practice*. London: Sage Publications.

Moore, D. (2013). Exploring the dynamics of power in professionalizing after school. *Child and Youth Services, 34*, 172–185.

National Coalition for the Homeless. (2008). *Homeless youth*. Retrieved from http://www.nationalhomeless.org/factsheets/youth.html

Pozzoboni, K., & Kirshner, B. (Eds.). (2016). *The changing landscape of youth work: Theory and practice for an evolving field*. Charlotte, NC: Information Age Publishing.

Ratcliffe, M. (2011). Stance, feeling and phenomenology. *Synthese, 178*, 121–130.

Rooks, J. P. (1999). *Midwifery and childbirth in America*. Philadelphia, PA: Temple University Press.

Rowbottom, D. P., & Bueno, O. (2011). How to change it: Modes of engagement, rationality, and stance voluntarism. *Stance and Rationality: A Perspective, 178*, 7–17.

USAID. (2012). *Youth in development: Realizing the demographic opportunity* (USAID policy report). Retrieved from https://www.usaid.gov/sites/default/files/documents/1870/Youth_in_Development_Policy_0.pdf

Vachon, W. (2013). Do not enter! What might we lose by gatekeeping youth work? *Child and Youth Services, 34*, 156–171.

Walker, J., & Walker, K. (2012). Establishing expertise in an emerging field. In D. Fusco (Ed.), *Advancing youth work: Current trends, critical questions* (pp. 39–51). New York, NY: Routledge.

CHAPTER 6

Future Prospects for Australasian Youth Work

Trudi Cooper and Rod Baxter

Introduction

This chapter will begin with a brief overview of the cultural and political context of youth work in New Zealand and Australia, including how colonial legacy and postcolonial histories have shaped contemporary youth work. The chapter will then present some vignettes of contemporary youth work practice in each country to illustrate its diversity. Youth agencies, adaptation to policy and funding changes will be analysed, and the current strengths, opportunities, weaknesses and threats facing youth work considered. The discussion will focus upon how practices have been shaped and changed over time. The chapter will conclude with suggestions about possible ways forward within the current socio-political framework, and suggest useful adjustments to existing structural arrangements, including what Australia can learn from New Zealand and vice versa.

It is important to discuss political context because contemporary youth work in Australia and New Zealand has been strongly influenced by neoliberal political ideologies that have demanded the monetisation of youth work's contribution. It is also important to examine how funding regimes influence provision and practice when discussing future prospects for youth work in Australasia and elsewhere. For example, in the mid-1990s in Australia there was a transition from recurrent funding to competitive tendering. This immediately increased competition between youth work agencies and ultimately most of the small community-managed agencies were displaced by large national and multinational corporate-style charities.

The colonial legacy is important because contemporary youth work in Australia and New Zealand has been influenced by the interplay between the legacy of British colonialism, and the post-colonial political and cultural histories of each country. Colonial influences on youth work can be found in the structure of some cultural and social institutions and in the origins and ethos of some contemporary Australian and New Zealand youth work organisations. The legacy of colonial influence has been maintained both formally and culturally. Formally, membership of the British Commonwealth means that the British Council sponsored Commonwealth Youth Programme has operated youth worker training programmes in Australia. Informally, the 'cultural cringe' has privileged the status of all things British over local equivalents, and was a factor in the employment of British academics during the 1980 and 1990s to teach youth work in Australian universities.

Postcolonial history is relevant because it has modified colonial influences and legacies. In Australasia, there has never been an English-style 'statutory youth service'. In Australia, the federated political structure means youth work varies considerably between states. Both New Zealand and Australia have diverged culturally from Britain and Europe because of their cultural connections to Pacific and South and East Asian countries, and because of their (different) relationships with the First Peoples in each country. This too, has changed youth work practice in ways not found in the United Kingdom or Europe, and will affect the future prospects for youth work in both countries.

Overview: Histories and Contexts

In countries like Australia and New Zealand, the historical, cultural and political context of youth work has been shaped by the colonial legacy and postcolonial history. The chapter begins with a discussion of how history and context have affected the development of contemporary youth work in each country. The territories that are now Australia and New Zealand were originally inhabited by First Peoples, Māori in New Zealand and in Australia population groups with over 200 distinct Aboriginal languages (Horton, 1996), now most commonly referred to collectively as Aboriginal and Torres Strait Islanders (ATSI). The term First Peoples is not used universally in Australasia, and may not be how some of these groups self-identify, but is used here because the term is common in the international literature. Australia was claimed as British territory in 1789 and New Zealand became a British colony in 1832. Some parts of Australia were a British penal colony until 1868 (Australian Government, 2016). The arrival of European settlers led to violent conflict with the First Peoples and the importation of disease into both countries led to high mortality amongst First Peoples.

In New Zealand, *Te Tiriti o Waitangi* (the Treaty signed at the northern town of Waitangi) interrupted colonial conflict in 1840 and laid a roadmap for a new national identity (King, 2003). This identity is founded on a bicultural relationship between *iwi* (Māori tribes) and Pākehā (non-Māori). Te Tiriti o Waitangi, like many relationships, has experienced an interesting journey. At times, Te Tiriti has divided the nation in New Zealand, and at other times it has been a source of pride, strength and success. Ultimately, a common commitment to Te Tiriti principles and a bicultural partnership has protected Māori rights and enabled participation in a fuller sense. Te Tiriti remains aspirational; both iwi and Pākehā are still exploring biculturalism and bilingualism together. The people of New Zealand increasingly refer to the country as *Aotearoa*, news reporters are celebrated for pronouncing Māori place names accurately (and berated for ignorance), and children are given names in *te reo Māori* (native language) rather than English translations. Youth work in Aotearoa New Zealand is staunchly committed to Māori ways of working with *tamariki* and *taiohi* (children and young people), and investigating traditional indigenous approaches that remain relevant in contemporary times (Baxter, Caddie, & Cameron, 2016).

In Australia, there was no treaty, and Indigenous Australians were harshly suppressed and denied basic rights (Chesterman & Galligan, 1997). It is estimated that as land was appropriated by the colonists, 95% of the ATSI population died from disease, dispossession, or massacre (Wilkinson, 2016). Aboriginal Australians were not counted in the population census until 1967 and could not vote on the same terms as white Australians until 1984 (Prentis, 2011: 218). The 19th century gold rushes in both countries hastened the arrival of European and Chinese migrants. In Australia, various racialized policies to maintain British supremacy developed in the 19th and 20th centuries, and persisted until the 1970s and 1980s. The intergenerational effects of institutional racism are felt today. Policies included the forced removal of Aboriginal children from their families (Human Rights and Equal Opportunity Commission, 1997). Removed children were brought up in church-run missions, and are referred to as 'stolen generations'. This policy formally ceased in the 1970s, but Indigenous children are still over-represented in the out-of-home care system. The 'white Australia' policy gave preferential immigration status to white migrants, and was only repealed in the 1970s (Richards, 2008). Apartheid-style residence and curfews were imposed upon Indigenous people that forced them to live outside towns and prevented them from entering after nightfall, (South West Aboriginal Land and Sea Council, 2015). Although these types of laws were voided by the Racial Discrimination Act 1975, housing segregation persists especially in rural areas because community ties and on-going exclusion and economic inequality mean that most population groups have stayed where they were. Since the Mabo and Wik land rights judgements in 1993 and 1996, some ATSI people have been able to regain rights over land taken from them (Prentis, 2011).

The British child migration scheme operated in Australia from 1901 until 1983 (Coldrey, 1999), in collaboration with various churches, the Christian Brothers and youth organisations including Barnardos, Fairbridge and the YMCA. Under this scheme white children from British institutions were permanently settled in Australian institutions, usually farm schools located in remote regions, sometimes without parental knowledge or consent. Both child migrants and the 'stolen generations' were subject to harsh treatment and abuse (Dow & Phillips, 2009; Human Rights and Equal Opportunity Commission, 1997). Many organisations still involved in Australian youth work were party to both child migration and stolen generation policies. The abuse of Indigenous and migrant children that occurred in residential institutions has been acknowledged. This prompted policy change away from institutional care of children and young people. In place of institutional care, since the 1980s, youth workers have been involved in operating youth refuges for homeless young people.

In Aotearoa New Zealand, Māori make up 14.9% of the population and a third of people of Māori descent are aged under 15 years (Statistics New Zealand, 2013). In Australia in 2006, ATSI people comprised 2.5% of the Australian population and 4.5% of the youth population (Australian Bureau of Statistics, 2011). In both countries, social indicators show that the First Peoples youth are over represented in the youth justice system, in youth homelessness (Australian Bureau of Statistics, 2011), in youth unemployment, youth suicide (Cooper et al., 2016a) and in other indicators of social disadvantage (White & Wyn, 2012). Both countries are constitutional monarchies, with the UK monarch as the head of state. Australia is a federation of states whereas New Zealand in a non-federated unitary country.

Colonial history as well as differences in postcolonial policy have shaped how contemporary youth work has evolved in each country, and also influences possibilities for future directions. In both countries a higher proportion of First Peoples youth engage with youth workers, primarily because youth work is targeted towards addressing social disadvantage.

Contemporary Practice in Australia

In Australia, youth work is funded through multiple government departments, at national and state levels, and by local government, with each funding scheme having its own policy guidelines for youth work and youth services (Cooper, 2018a). Federal funding for youth work comes through departments responsible for housing, health, community services and crime prevention. At state level, the departments responsible for welfare and child protection, housing, health, communities, multicultural interests, sport and recreation, arts, multicultural affairs, Indigenous affairs, and justice, provide some funding for youth work. For this reason, youth work differs between (and within) states, and therefore lacks uniformity. There is no 'Australian youth service' or singular approach to youth work (Cooper, 2018a). Although services that receive federal funding are similar in all states, state-based youth work programmes differ across Australia. Most examples here relate to Western Australia. Australian youth workers operate in various settings including youth accommodation, schools, and community centres. In this respect, the boundaries between youth work and youth social work differ from the UK, with youth workers in Australia more likely to be involved in youth welfare services than in the UK.

The large religious charities (Salvation Army, and charities affiliated to the main Christian denominations) have become major providers of youth work and youth services, competing with other international youth organisations like the YMCA and with non-government organisations, like Save the Children and World Vision. Some local government councils provide youth work either directly, or in conjunction with small local community-based organisations. The services described here have been selected to illustrate the diversity of practice and particular policy effects, especially the relationship between policy and youth work provision.

Youth accommodation is an important component of Australian youth work. Youth hostels staffed by youth workers provide emergency accommodation for homeless young people aged 15 years and over, and the same services provide support towards independent living for young people aged 16–21 years. Youth Futures WA is an example of a community-based agency that began as a small organisation that managed one hostel offering emergency accommodation to homeless young people. Over a period of 25 years, Youth Futures has expanded to provide more holistic integrated support, including, alternative education, drug education, support for young single mothers, family mediation, counselling and mentoring, life-skills support to enable young people to move into more permanent accommodation and support for young people leaving detention. In another instance a Foyer model is used by Anglicare WA, a large corporate charity affiliated to the Anglican Church. Under the Foyer model, youth workers also support young people to re-engage with education or employment, and address substance abuse issues. Youth accommodation is primarily funded through federal funding. Anglicare offers a range of other youth services including a detached youth work project, youth counselling, and employment services.

Youth workers are also involved in youth health initiatives including mental health, addictions, youth sexual health services and youth cancer support services. Youth health services are funded by a mix of state and federal funding. Examples of youth work involvement in mental health include Headspace, which is a federally-funded multi-professional initiative; the Perth Inner City Youth Services Pillar program, which is a community-based youth organisation, and ReachOut.com which is a not-for-profit online mental health and well-being initiative. A few youth workers are employed in other health promotion and support related roles, including sexual health, cancer support, health services for homeless young people, and in initiatives where they contribute to multi-disciplinary teams of practitioners, for example, the Drug and Alcohol Youth Service, which is a detox service, run by Mission Australia.

In Australia, local government councils can decide whether or not to fund youth work from rates revenue under their community services portfolio. If they decide to provide youth services, each council then decides whether to provide services directly, or to contract services out to other organisations. Some councils provide youth work directly and fund open youth work in the form of youth centres, detached youth work and sometimes 'Youth Advisory Councils' (YACS) to encourage youth participation in council policy. Other local government councils sub-contract youth services to local community-based agencies or national charities to provide recreation based services. Still other local government councils do not provide or fund any youth work. State government funds various cadet programmes including St John's Ambulance (The Order of St John), Red Cross, Surf Lifesaving, Emergency Services Cadets, Police Cadets, and also provides some funding to Guides and Scouts. There are a variety of youth-led activist and social enterprise organisations in Australia, supported by the Foundation for Young Australians, an organisation funded by a mix of government grants and philanthropic donations and partnerships (Foundation for Young Australians, 2016).

Some schools employ youth workers or chaplains (some of whom are youth work trained). The federal chaplaincy program was extended to youth workers by the federal Labor government, but when the Liberal/ National Coalition regained power they excluded youth workers from this programme and restricted it to chaplains only. Alternative education schools, for students who are not able to attend mainstream schools, often employ youth workers in support roles.

Crime prevention funding from federal government is used to fund a variety of youth work programmes, including recreational programmes. In some states these are operated by the Police as Police and Citizens' Youth Clubs. Although this arrangement is becoming less common, it persists especially in rural areas. More usually, crime prevention money funds recreation-based youth work operated by non-government organisations. In addition, youth night patrols are funded in some Indigenous communities (Cooper et al., 2016b). The role of the youth night patrol is to prevent young people becoming either victims or perpetrators of crime by building relationships with young people and providing them with safe transport home. Some patrols provide informal support and referral. These patrols operate mostly in regional and remote areas, and sometimes function as the only base for youth work in the locality. Some patrols are run and managed by Indigenous communities but many are managed by other organisations. There are competing models of youth night patrol (Cooper et al., 2016b) with some types of patrol operating in close collaboration with police and youth curfew legislation (Cooper & Love, 2017). This type of work raises questions about whether a voluntary relationship is a central component of practice.

There is some specialist youth work with ATSI young people; for example, the Wirrpanda Foundation. This is a charitable foundation linked to a major football club, which employs ATSI youth workers, is ATSI managed, and aims to improve life for ATSI young Australians. Programmes focus on the four 'pillars' of: health, employment, justice and education. In addition, there are some specialist youth work programmes for migrant young people. Some, like programs run by the Edmund Rice Catholic non-government organisation, support settlement, especially for young humanitarian migrants, other like the Catalyst programme run by the Youth Affairs Council of Western Australia (YACWA), help young migrants gain skills to politically lobby their elected representatives on issues of concern. In addition, there are LGBTQI advocacy and support youth services in many states, and in Western Australia The Freedom Centre is operated by the WA AIDS Council, which is a non-government peak body. Mentoring is used as a strategy across many different types of youth work agency (MacCallum, Beltman, Coffey, & Cooper, 2017) and is supported by resources developed by the Australian Youth Mentoring Network (2017).

State governments receive advice on youth policy and youth work from the 'Youth Peak' bodies in each state (for example, the Youth Affair Council of Western Australia (YACWA); the Youth Affairs Council of Victoria (YACvic); the Youth Affairs Network of Queensland (YANQ); Youth Action, in New South Wales; Youth Network of Tasmania (YNOT). These are state-based, community managed advisory bodies that receive small grants from state government. Each organisation is membership managed and operates only within the state where they are based. Their central role is policy advice. Other activities of the youth peak bodies vary between states. Youth peak bodies have been involved in providing information and policy advice for youth workers, and in partnering in research about youth work and youth issues, as well as providing advice to government and lobbying on youth issues. At various times there has been a national youth peak body 'Australian Youth Affairs Coalition' (AYAC). This body still exists, but is not currently funded, and operates on a voluntary basis. In addition, some states have Commissioners for Children and Young People. This role is informed by a rights perspective and is broadly defined.

The Commissioner can offer advice to government and politicians on youth policy, youth services or youth work, and can commission research. The institutional arrangements for accreditation of youth work are very different from those found in the UK (Cooper, 2013). There are national competency standards for sub-degree youth work courses. Degree courses are self-accredited by each university. Youth workers have established professional associations in three states (Western Australia, Victoria and South Australia), and these organisations are in the process of developing more comprehensive accreditation arrangements for all youth work qualifications, including youth work degrees.

Contemporary Practice in New Zealand

Youth work in Aotearoa New Zealand is funded through a vulnerable patchwork of fixed-term government contracts, philanthropy, emerging social enterprise and public donations. Central government has described this as a purchaser/ provider relationship whereby government 'purchases services' from 'providers' within a 'social investment' framework (Ministry of Youth Development -Te Manatū Whakahiato Taiohi, 2017; Ministry of Youth Development, 2017). This framework measures youth work primarily in terms of economic cost effectiveness. It is worth noting, that as this chapter was written, the right-wing National Government was replaced with a left-wing coalition, and this will likely see the demise of social investment practices.

Despite the competitive financial climate for youth work, there is sectoral unity, under the banner of 'youth development'. This is led by *Ara Taiohi*, Aotearoa's youth peak body. The goals of Ara Taiohi are to, (a) connect the sector, (b) raise standards of practice, (c) champion youth development and (d) promote sustainability (Ara Taiohi, 2017). It is now common to see youth workers collaborating beyond the confines of organisational structure. For example, faith-based youth ministry workers will team up with LGBTQI (known as 'Rainbow' in Aotearoa) youth leaders to collaboratively organise an event. Large, national uniformed groups, such as Scouts and New Zealand Red Cross, will work at local levels with independent community organisations and facilitate national meetings about 'collaboration for better service outcomes' that include young people directly in the conversation. Such partnerships with diverse, and at times, unexpected allies, are actively encouraged, mirroring the relational example of Te Tiriti o Waitangi.

Ara Taiohi has launched a national professional association for youth workers in Aotearoa, known as *Korowai Tupu*. The association includes members who describe their youth work practice within nine core competencies and who commit to ethical practice. A Code of Ethics for youth work (Ara Taiohi, 2011) was developed in Canterbury and adopted nationally in 2008 (Baxter & Satyanand, 2017). The Code of Ethics (Ara Taiohi, 2011) and youth work core competencies align with the principles of the Youth Development Strategy Aotearoa (Keelan, 2002; Ministry of Youth Affairs, 2002). The YDSA was developed after extensive consultation with young people and the youth development sector, which began in the late 1990s. The principles of the YDSA include:

1. Youth development is shaped by the big picture
2. Youth development is about young people being connected
3. Youth development is based on a consistent strengths-based approach
4. Youth development happens through quality relationships
5. Youth development is triggered when young people fully participate
6. Youth development needs good information.

The principles form a checklist for youth work programme development. The first two principles map the landscape and ecosystem young people exist within; the 'big picture' includes global forces and domestic influences, including Te Tiriti o Waitangi, whilst 'connectedness' considers young people's social domains. Social media has now been incorporated into practice, demonstrating the flexibility of the framework. The remaining four principles commit to strengths-based philosophies, building quality relationships, enabling youth participation, and accessing 'good information' by engaging in research, training and supervision. These principles inform youth worker training and youth work qualifications, including the Bachelor of Youth Development.

The Strategy remains relevant for youth workers, despite being ignored by most government departments since publication. An example of a service for young people that seems to ignore the YDSA is the 'Youth Service' (youthservice.govt.nz). This is a Ministry of Social Development government-funded NEET (Not in Education, Employment or Training) social welfare benefit service that works with a targeted cohort of 16–19 year olds. In most areas of Aotearoa, provision of this service is through local community organisations, after a competitive tendering process. Where no suitable providers are found, the Ministry operates the service directly.

Government policy has recently focused on the limitations of traditional responses to youth mental health (Shailer, Gammon, & Terte, 2013), and flexible funding has been offered to support innovative multi-professional responses. Many of these include youth work support, for example, the youth co-design initiatives facilitated by Lifehack (lifehackhq.co). Almost a dozen Youth One Stop Shops (YOSS) across Aotearoa focus on mental health and wellbeing. A typical YOSS includes free, confidential and highly accessible doctors, nurses, counsellors, youth workers and a range of other professionals in a multi-disciplinary practice. A decade ago, a typical YOSS would report most young people were presenting with sexual health concerns. More recently the focus of their work has changed to more complex mental health issues, and in some instances YOSSs are struggling to respond effectively. There are several specific services and programmes for queer-exploring and/or rainbow-identified young people (for example, Inside Out, Qtopia and Rainbow Youth), and youth workers in Aotearoa, almost regardless of the context, are committed to inclusive practices.

Another factor that has affected the wellbeing of young people is the disruption, anxiety and fear associated with natural disasters (Johnson & Ronan, 2014; O'Toole, 2017). The Canterbury region experienced a series of destructive earthquakes beginning in late 2010, registering 7.1 on the Richter scale, with the most severe event on 22 February 2011 at magnitude 6.3, devastating already weakened buildings and infrastructure. Millions of dollars have been donated through global humanitarian aid, most notably the Red Cross movement, for targeted disaster response and recovery programmes. Youth work has aimed to provide consistency and support for young people through the chaos and disruption, with services funded to expand, particularly through school-based mentoring. In parallel, youth worker self-care was also prioritised, with expanded provisions for professional supervision.

Mentoring in Aotearoa has become more common and the New Zealand Youth Mentoring Network (New Zealand Youth Mentoring Network, 2016) has published guidelines for mentoring programmes. As in Australia, many mentors are volunteers, supervised by paid youth workers. A common framework guiding youth mentoring is *Te Whare Tapa Whā* or holistic wellbeing from an indigenous perspective (Baxter & Jackson, 2016; Durie, 1998). *Te Whare Tapa Whā* encompasses physical, psychological, social and spiritual wellbeing, and students typically study *Te Whare Tapa Whā* in early adolescence, which means the approach is well-understood by young people when it is applied in a youth work context.

Discussion: Similarities and Challenges on Both Sides of the Tasman Sea

In Australia, a number of policy trends have affected recent developments in youth work, some of which have been unhelpful. Competitive tendering has increased competition between youth work agencies, resulting in reduced collaboration. Youth workers are sometimes under pressure to preferentially refer young people to services provided within their own organisation, even when services offered by other organisations may be more appropriate. Competitive tendering has also led to an increased domination of youth work by large national charities because they can afford to employ full-time staff to write tenders and to meet the acquittal requirements, and also because certain types of religiously affiliated organisations have taxation advantages. This has pushed out smaller community-managed secular youth work projects, and reduced local control and responsiveness in some youth services. Government policy for youth work and youth welfare policy has been ideologically driven, as illustrated by the 2013 policy to direct funding for school-based youth work into chaplaincy. Youth policy has also become more punitive over the last ten years, as illustrated by various policies, including proposals to restrict young people's access to income support, and place increasing compliance requirements on unemployed young people. Policy has also become more paternalistic toward Indigenous young people as illustrated by the Northern Territory Emergency Response. These trends have especially affected young people with the least family support, and made it more difficult for youth workers who have a welfare focus to offer a holistic response to young people that addresses both their material and informal educational needs.

More positively, there has been innovation in some of the youth mental health services, where models of inter-professional work have involved youth workers collaborating with other professionals to deliver youth-friendly services. This has contributed to a whole government approach to reducing youth suicide (Cooper et al., 2016a); however, this strategy has been least effective with the most marginalised youth populations, for example ATSI youth living in remote communities.

In Aotearoa, youth work has also been adversely affected by policy changes in the past decade, including funding reductions, forced organisational mergers (often prompted by funders) and urban migration from provincial areas. The NEET Youth Service has created competitive relationships in some communities that are already experiencing population decline. The organisation that successfully secures the NEET contract becomes the 'provider' and when delivering the service, may struggle to partner with other services that tendered unsuccessfully. The reduction of inter-agency collaboration inhibits positive outcomes for young people. The ideology that underpins the NEET programme is in tension with the ideology of other youth work premised on the principles and practices of the YDSA. There are only a few agencies that have managed these tensions well and retained their identity, whilst also effectively engaging young people labelled NEET. The ethical issues raised by Jeffs and Smith (2010) about the need to carefully scrutinise sources of youth work funding is pertinent in situations where some organisations adapt or abandon their core principles to secure funding.

The 1990s discourse about 'at-risk youth' (Brendro, Brokenleg, & van Bockern, 2002; Martin, 2002) has become less acceptable in Aotearoa, in favour of explicit strengths-based programmes. There is extensive international discussion about Positive Youth Development (PYD) and whether this is a deficit approach (Cooper, 2018a), but in Aotearoa, the principles of the YDSA mean that Positive Youth Development is applied through a strengths-based lens (Wayne Francis Charitable Trust Youth Advisory Group, 2011). As a bilingual country, New Zealand's youth workers are sensitive to how young people are described, and young people are no longer described as 'at-risk'. Instead language focuses on their talents, capabilities, and potential as assets to their communities. When the statutory care agency Child, Youth and Family was renamed as the 'Ministry for Vulnerable Children', the public outcry at the implied deficit prompted a request from Aotearoa's Children's Commissioner, Andrew Becroft to canvas an alternative secondary name. '*Oranga Tamariki*' (an overly simplistic translation is 'wellbeing of children') was supported, and the government adopted both names. Although, this does not entirely address the issue, it demonstrates benefits of a bilingual and bicultural response. In 2017, the newly elected coalition government immediately instructed the Ministry for Children to delete the word 'vulnerable'. Oranga Tamariki has excelled at hearing the voices of many young people in statutory care, and continues to do so in a meaningful way, largely through VOYCE – Whakarongo Mai! (voyce. org.nz).

The YDSA declared participation a key principle, and the Ministry of Youth Development published a series of useful resources for youth workers (Ministry of Youth Development, 2009). After a strong beginning in the first decade of the century, youth participation became less prominent in youth work practice, but re-emerged in youth activism. In response to the 2010/2011 Canterbury earthquakes, thousands of university students mobilised via Facebook as the Student Volunteer Army, and provided practical aid as an immediate response to the disaster.

In both countries and globally, there are many social changes that have implications for youth work in the future. One in particular is the rapid way in which digital technology has transformed everyday life including relationships with peers, institutions and work. There is not space to discuss all the future implications of these changes for youth work. However, we must discuss just one aspect: the implications of digital media for youth work and youth participation. An important youth work commitment is that young people should be involved in decisions that affect their lives. Youth work's role in relation to digitally-based youth-led initiatives is currently uneven, but in the UK Davies et al. (2011) have suggested how social media can be used by youth workers to promote youth participation. Digital technologies can be used either to strengthen or undermine inclusion, participation and democracy. We contend that youth workers in the future will need to become more aware of both possibilities. A challenge will be to develop youth work practice in ways that incorporate digital technologies to strengthen young people's social inclusion and democratic participation in decisions that affect their futures (Melvin, 2015, 2018, Chapter 10, this volume). This is becoming increasingly important as many contemporary social usages of digital media have become woven into the fabric of everyday life, but promote neither social inclusion nor democratic and responsive institutions. In the social sphere, social media can provide additional opportunities for social connection, but frequently strengthens existing power hierarchies of gender and race (through trolling, and 'fake news'). Online activist groups (for example GetUp! (getup.org.au) in Australia) provide opportunities for activism, which young people use to make their voices heard. At the same time, government and many commercial organisations use digital media (call centres and online contact) as gatekeeping mechanisms to distance themselves from the public and create barriers to gaining correct advice and redress when mistakes have been made. Youth workers will need to be aware of these trends and develop strategies to effectively resist the negative usages and embrace the positive possibilities of digital media to enhance their practice.

Future Prospects

In this final section, we conclude with suggestions about possible ways forward that would build on positive trends to strengthen future youth work, address current deficiencies, and respond to emerging social changes.

There are several positive trends within youth work. Youth workers have been active in both countries in cultural and gender diversity, and have worked in practical ways to support young people to obtain basic rights. In Australia youth workers have been active in supporting reconciliation between Indigenous and non-Indigenous Australians. In Aotearoa New Zealand, bicultural and bilingual whole-of-government approaches have shown formal respect for tikanga (Māori protocol); this has been embraced, and, often led, by youth workers. There have been interesting examples of innovative experimental youth work programmes in both countries (Reel Connections, Ballajura Connect Program), and programmes in the youth accommodation sector, youth health and youth mental health have responded to young people's needs. The 'youth peak' body system in both countries provides a genuine grassroots voice for young people and youth workers to speak to politicians and policy makers.

There are also some negative trends. Consistent policy and funding stability are necessary for long-term development of youth work strategy and services; this is a major problem currently being faced in both countries. This situation is partly a consequence of the neoliberal 'turn', embraced by both countries in the late 20th century, which led to competitive tendering and out-sourced short-term contracts for the provision of youth work. This political limitation will only be addressed when political parties withdraw their support for neo-liberal approaches to the provision of public services and infrastructure. In Australia, fragmented policy is a function of a federal system where responsibility for youth work is dispersed between multiple Departments at all three levels of government. This has some very clear disadvantages, but also means that some checks and balances are built into the system, especially when joint federal and state funding is provided. In New Zealand, funding instability is complicated by inadequate offerings from government, philanthropy and occasional sponsorship, ultimately reducing the autonomy of organisations and stifling any voice in advocacy on pertinent policy issues.

In both New Zealand and Australia, statistics for poverty, prison and social welfare show disproportionate representation of First Peoples and indicate that neither society has achieved cultural equality. Youth work can play a role in addressing this issue, but equality must be supported as part of a whole-of-government approach, where all services operate in the same direction to address issues of entrenched marginalisation.

There are some signs in both countries that the neoliberal political consensus is weakening; there is some recognition that competitive tendering does not provide better value for money or better services, and some acknowledge-ment of the wastefulness of competitive tendering processes. Accordingly, we contend that youth workers need to prepare for a post-neoliberal political environment, even though it is not yet clear what alternative values or fund-ing mechanisms will be proffered. On the left, there is a growing commitment to social equality, multiculturalism and diversity. This is reflected in Aotearoa New Zealand's new left-leaning coalition government including a pregnant Prime Minister, a Minister of Youth whom happens to be Māori, and a 23-year-old Member of Parliament, the youngest in almost 50 years. On the right, there is commitment to paternalism and socially conservative Christian values.

So, what is the way forward? To address the problems identified requires: (1) long-term commitment to a policy direction for youth work; (2) stable funding for youth work and youth services; (3) an articulation of how youth work contributes to broader social policy objectives (4) reinvention of youth work practices that affirm core principles whilst adapting to emerging social changes.

A long-term policy direction for youth work would require bipartisan political support. In the Australasian context, bi-partisan policy commitments are more achievable if they are based upon international treaty commitments. In Australia, some discussions of youth work draw upon a rights framework, for example the AYAC document defining youth work (Griffin & Lutterall, 2011). This framework tacitly assumes that there is a shared bipartisan political commitment to human rights. However, because political factions prioritise different rights, (civil, social or economic rights) an appeal to rights only works with left-leaning governments. The United Nations Sustainable Development Goals (2017) potentially provide a means to overcome this difficulty through commitment to a supranational policy framework, capable of supporting long-term whole of government goals, including gender equity, cultural inclusiveness, poverty eradication, social protection, sustainability and improved economic equality. The Sustainable Development Goals therefore provide a possible bipartisan framework for youth work within broader social and economic policy (Cooper, 2018b). Stable funding for youth work is even more difficult to achieve. This is particularly the case in Australia where responsibilities for youth work and youth policy lie across different layers and departments of government. The current (45th) federal government does not even have a Minister with responsibility for youth. As an alternative to competitive tendering for funding, government (at any level) could provide services directly, or enter into recurrent funding contracts with organisations, whereby long-term funding was assured, assuming services are provided satisfactorily. Philanthropic funding provides long-term support in a few instances, but cannot, and should not be a main source of finance.

To maintain future relevance, youth work must be able to respond to emerging social issues in ways that affirm its own core principles. This requires youth workers who have an appropriate understanding of both youth work and society. This has implications for youth workers' education and training, and, for on-going professional development. Degree-level professional qualifications in youth work need to provide both a strong understanding of the profession's core principles, and a recognition that youth work practice needs to be continually reinvented to address new opportunities and changing social conditions. Youth work degrees need to do much more than just prepare students for the present, they must ensure that students have sufficient skills in social, political and ethical analysis to enable them to reinvent their future practice with integrity.

Youth workers must also continue to engage proactively with government decision makers at all levels, educating governments about youth work. We must engage in discussion about the place of youth work in social policy, and the necessary conditions for successful youth work practice. It is ineffective to ask for more money, without placing youth work in a social policy context, in terms that policy makers and politicians understand. Likewise, governments need to ensure that policies in other portfolios do not inhibit or undermine the positive outcomes achieved through youth work. In both Aotearoa New Zealand and Australia, independent youth work professional associations are important contributors to this dialogue, assisted in Australia by a youth 'peak body' system at state level. This dialogue might also be further strengthened through youth workers taking a more active role in facilitating young people's participation in decision-making regarding issues that affect their lives. We would like to see the development of respectful partnerships between young people, youth workers and layers of government that reflect the profession's core commitments to social justice and inclusion. We learn from each other. This is reflected in the Māori word *ako*, which expresses the inseparability of learning and teaching. This reciprocity is integral to youth work, not only in in Aotearoa and Australia, but globally.

References

Ara Taiohi. (2011). *Code of ethics for youth work in Aotearoa New Zealand* (2nd ed.). Wellington: Ara Taiohi.

Ara Taiohi. (2017). *Our goals and strategies.*

Australian Bureau of Statistics. (2011). *Aboriginal and Torres Strait Islander wellbeing: A focus on children and youth.* Retrieved from http://www.abs.gov.au/ausstats/abs@.nsf/Lookup/4725.0Chapter110Apr%202011

Australian Government. (2016, January 20). *Convicts and the British colonies in Australia.* Retrieved from http://www.australia.gov.au/about-australia/australian-story/convicts-and-the-british-colonies

Australian Youth Mentoring Network. (2017). Retrieved from http://aymn.org.au/

Baxter, R., Caddie, M., & Cameron, G. B. (2016). Title. In D. Fusco & M. Heathfield (Eds.), *Youth and inequality in education: Global actions in youth work.* London: Routledge Ltd.

Baxter, R., & Jackson, M. (2016). Created to create: Balancing spiritual development in an indigenous holistic framework. In S. Devenish & P. Daughtry (Eds.), *Spirituality in youth work: New vocabularies, concepts and practices* (pp. 96–115). Newcastle upon Tyne: Cambridge Scholars Publishing.

Baxter, R., & Satyanand, A. (2017). *Kaiparahuarahi, 1*(1). Retrieved from http://www.arataiohi.org.nz

Brendro, L., Brokenleg, M., & van Bockern, S. (2002). *Reclaiming youth at risk: Our hope for the future* (Revised ed.). Bloomington, IN: Solution Tree.

Chesterman, J., & Galligan, B. (1997). *Citizens without rights : Aborigines and Australian citizenship*. Cambridge: Cambridge University Press.

Coldrey, B. (1999). *Good British stock: Child and youth migration to Australia*. Canberra: National Archives of Australia.

Cooper, T. (2013). Institutional context and youth work professionalization in post-welfare societies. *Child and Youth Services, 34*(2), 112–124. doi:10.1080/01459 35X.2013.785877

Cooper, T. (2018a). Defining youth work: Exploring the boundaries, continuity and diversity of youth work practice. In P. Alldred, F. Cullen, K. Edwards, & D. Fusco (Eds.), *Sage handbook of youth work practice*. London: Sage Publications.

Cooper, T. (2018b). *Sustainable development goals and Australian youth policy and participation*. Paper presented at the International Conference on Achieving Youth-Specific SDGs, Key Challenges and Policy Responses Rajiv Gandhi National Institute of Youth Development (RGNIYD), Sriperumbudur, Tamil Nadu, India.

Cooper, T., Ferguson, C., Chapman, B., & Cucow, S. (2016a). Success stories from youth suicide prevention in Australia: The youth work contribution. In D. Fusco & M. Heathfield (Eds.), *Youth and inequality in education: Global actions in youth work*. London: Routledge Ltd.

Cooper, T., & Love, T. (2017). A youth curfew: A retrospective view of the rise, fall and legacy of the northbridge policy. *Australian Journal of Social Issues, 52*(3), 204–221.

Cooper, T., Scott, J., Barclay, E., Sims, M., & Love, T. (2016b). Crime prevention and young people: Models and future direction for youth night patrols. *Crime Prevention and Community Safety, 18*(4), 226–283. doi:10.1057/s41300-016-0009-9

Davies, T., Bhullar, S., & Dowty, T. (2011). *Rethinking responses to children and young people's online lives*. Retrieved from https://eprints.soton.ac.uk/273226/1/Rethinkin g%2520Responses%2520to%2520Children%2520and%2520Young%2520Peoples %2520Online%2520Lives%2520-%2520Davies%252C%2520Bhullar%252C%2520 Dowty%2520-%2520EU%2520Kids%2520Online%2520ISSN%2520Copy.pdf

Dow, C., & Phillips, J. (2009). *'Forgotten Australians' and 'lost innocents': Child migrants and children in institutional care in Australia*. Retrieved from http://www.aph.gov.au/ About_Parliament/Parliamentary_Departments/Parliamentary_Library/pubs/ BN/0910/ChildMigrants

Durie, M. (1998). *Whaiora: Māori health development* (2nd ed.). Auckland: Oxford University Press.

Foundation for Young Australians. (2016). *2016 year in review*. Retrieved from http://fya.org.au/2016ayearinreview/

Griffin, R., & Lutterall, E. (2011). *Future focussed: Youth work in Australia: Reflections and aspirations*. Retrieved from http://www.ayac.org.au/index.php?mact=News,cntnt01, detail,0andcntnt01articleid=76andcntnt01returnid=67

Horton, D. R. (1996). *The AIATSIS map of Aboriginal Australia*. Retrieved from http://www.abc.net.au/indigenous/map/

Human Rights and Equal Opportunity Commission. (1997). *Bringing them home: Report of the national inquiry into the separation of Aboriginal and Torres Strait Islander children from their families.* Retrieved from https://www.humanrights.gov.au/ sites/default/files/content/pdf/social_justice/bringing_them_home_report.pdf

Jeffs, T., & Smith, M. (2010). Resourcing youth work: Dirty hands and tainted money. In S. Banks (Ed.), *Ethical issues in youth work* (2nd ed., Vol. 1, pp. 53–74). Oxon: Routledge.

Johnson, V. A., & Ronan, K. R. (2014). Classroom responses of New Zealand school teachers following the 2011 Christchurch earthquake. *Natural Hazards: Journal of the International Society for the Prevention and Mitigation of Natural Hazards, 72*(2), 1075–1092.

Keelan, J. T. (2002). *E Tipu E Rea: A framework for Taiohi Māori development.* Retrieved from http://www.arataiohi.org.nz/resource-centre/key-documents/e-tipu-e-rea-a-framework-for-taiohi-maaori-youth-development

King, M. (2003). *The Penguin history of New Zealand.* Auckland: Penguin Books.

MacCallum, J., Beltman, S., Coffey, A., & Cooper, T. (2017). Taking care of youth mentoring relationships: Red flags, repair, and respectful resolution. *Mentoring and Tutoring: Partnership in Learning, 25*(3), 250–271. doi:10.1080/13611267.2017.1364799

Martin, L. (2002). *The invisible table: Perspectives on youth and youthwork in New Zealand.* Palmerston North: Dunmore Press.

Ministry of Youth Affairs. (2002). *Youth development strategy Aotearoa.* Retrieved from http://www.myd.govt.nz/documents/resources-and-reports/publications/youth-development-strategy-aotearoa/ydsa.pdf

Ministry of Youth Development -Te Manatū Whakahiato Taiohi. (2017). *Funding.* Retrieved from http://www.myd.govt.nz/funding/

Ministry of Youth Development. (2009). *Keepin' it real: A resource for involving young people.* Retrieved from http://www.myd.govt.nz/documents/about-myd/ publications/keepin-it-real/keepin-it-real.pdf

Ministry of Youth Development. (2017). *Youth investment strategy.* Wellington: Ministry of Youth Development.

New Zealand Youth Mentoring Network. (2016). *Guide to effective and safe practice in youth mentoring, Aotearoa New Zealand* (2nd ed.). Auckland: New Zealand Youth Mentoring Network.

O'Toole, V. M. (2017). 'Fear would well up and it was just a luxury that you just didn't have time for': Teachers' emotion regulation strategies at school during the February 2011 Christchurch earthquake. *Social Psychology of Education: An International Journal, 20*(3), 513–542.

Prentis, M. (2011). *Concise companion to Aboriginal history.* Sydney: Rosenberg Pub.

Richards, E. (2008). *Destination Australia: Migration to Australia since 1901.* Sydney: University of New South Wales Press.

Shailer, J. L., Gammon, R. A., & Terte, I. (2013). Youth with serious mental health disorders: Wraparound as a promising intervention in New Zealand. *Australian and New Zealand Journal of Family Therapy, 34*(3), 186–213.

South West Aboriginal Land and Sea Council. (2015). *An introduction to Noongar history and culture.* Retrieved from https://www.noongarculture.org.au/wp-content/uploads/2013/07/IntroductiontoNoongarCultureforweb.pdf

Statistics New Zealand. (2013). *2013 census quickstats about Māori.* Retrieved from http://www.stats.govt.nz

Sustainable Development Goals. (2017). Retrieved from http://www.un.org/sustainabledevelopment/sustainable-development-goals/

Wayne Francis Charitable Trust Youth Advisory Group. (2011). *Positive youth development in Aotearoa: Weaving connections – Tuhonohono rangatahi.* Retrieved from https://www.wfct.org.nz/assets/Uploads/PYDA-2017.pdf

White, R. D., & Wyn, J. (2012). *Youth and society* (3rd ed.). South Melbourne: Oxford University Press.

Wilkinson, L. (2016). *Today we're alive : Generating performance in a cross-cultural context, an Australian experience.* Newcastle upon Tyne: Cambridge Scholars Publishing.

CHAPTER 7

Youth Work: Global Futures – Pictures from the Developing World

Stuart Wroe

> The majority world cannot simply be ignored or wished away.
> JOSEPH ET AL., 2002: 7

∴

Introduction

The ubiquity of the colloquial use of 'developing/developed' world, to indicate countries that fare relatively poorly or well in social and economic measures, implies a consensus about the definition, meaning and precision of this term that does not exist. The United Nations has no clear definition of 'the developing world', yet categorises as many as one hundred and fifty-nine countries in these terms, further highlighting those at the top of this list as the 'Least Developed Countries'. These groupings exclude Europe, Northern America, Japan, Australia and New Zealand which are classed as 'developed'. The presentation of 'least developed/developing/developed' implies a linear process wherein all other countries in the world are striving to emulate Europe, Northern America, Japan, Australia and New Zealand.

Yet, the World Bank no longer talks of 'the developing world'. From 2016, their World Development Indicators no longer distinguish between 'developed' and 'developing' countries (World Bank, n.d.). With no definition of 'the developing world', and with the World Bank considering it outdated, this Chapter will no longer use these pejorative, subjective and confusing classifications and will develop Chambers' (1995) reversals paradigm considering what and how countries that were classed as 'developed' (the dominant minority) can learn from youth development practice and practitioners in the majority world – not lecturing but 'handing over the stick'.

© KONINKLIJKE BRILL NV, LEIDEN, 2019 | DOI:10.1163/9789004396555_007

'Youth Work: Global Futures – A Picture from the Majority World'

Drawing on Joseph et al. (2002: 6), within a global context, this chapter uses the term 'majority' to refer to those people who either live or have their origins predominantly, but not exclusively, in 'the global South' – another subjective and confusing classification. The majority population 'share a common experience of being subjugated to global domination by Western (white) nations' (ibid.: 6), which continues through globalising processes. 'For people in the majority world, globalisation represents the imposition of a western global outlook and the displacement of traditional indigenous ways of life' (ibid.: 8). The use of the term 'majority' thus serves to highlight the marginalisation of the majority from global decision-making processes as well as the need for the world to listen to these other, majority, voices.

In 2002, the Development Education Association (now Think Global) recommended that NGOs, as well as youth work and community development organisations develop methodologies which draw from the experiences of the majority world, so that these perspectives become a natural component of the work at local, national and international levels (Joseph et al., 2002). However, with some notable exceptions from Global Youth Work (GYW), little seems to have substantially changed over the intervening years in mainstreaming majority world perspectives and methodologies in youth and community development practice in the UK.

This chapter considers an example of meaningful participative youth development practice from a majority world perspective. Dave Beck and Rod Purcell (2010: 154) in exploring both the theory and practice of a community development model for participative approaches in work with young people, emphasise 'the main rationale for participative methods is based on the belief that people themselves are best placed to know what their problems are and, with the right support, can develop the most appropriate solutions to those problems'. As Chambers (1995: 175) asks, 'Whose Reality Counts? The reality of the few in centres of power? Or ... of the many poor at the periphery?'

Before considering the example of the Afrika Youth Movement's (AYM) participative youth development practice, it is important to acknowledge that, as Joseph et al. (2002: 6) warn:

> The journey from the local to the global, and vice versa, is a dynamic learning process. To undertake a journey of this kind it is important to tread cautiously as language, professional terminology, values, beliefs or even life experiences that are taken for granted may well not be applicable

in other national or social environments. It is therefore important to acknowledge that our discourse, though drawn from different parts of the world, is heavily influenced by our life experiences in the UK.

In the process, we will reflect on this majority world practice drawing on key youth and community understandings from the UK, attempting to find and explore commonalities but also points of difference from which to learn.

The Afrika Youth Movement (AYM) is an action-oriented movement of young thinkers and visionaries that strives for the development, active participation and leadership of African young people in the fight for peace and social justice on the continent. It is a Pan-African grassroots community organising movement of young people, that works village by village, country by country. It recognises that the personal realities of young people's lives across the continent of Africa are 'local, complex, diverse, dynamic and unpredictable' (Chambers, 1997: 167) (or lcddu as he puts it), formed by, and within, complex and diverse histories and experiences of colonialisation and de-colonialisation. Resultantly, there is no one single youth narrative across the continent of Africa.

Neither is there one single indigenous youth leadership narrative. For individuals, leadership development, in the absence of a singular leadership narrative, has been about finding and forging, amongst competing influences, a leadership path that works for them (Bolden & Kirk, 2005). Moreover, it has been argued (Blunt & Jones, 1997; Wheatley, 2001; Jackson, 2004) that imposed minority world management and leadership theory (drawn predominantly from North American and European/Western experiences) represents a new form of colonialism; downplaying indigenous knowledge and values and enforcing, and reinforcing pejorative, subjective and confusing ways of thinking and acting. These are rooted in minority world ideologies and agendas driven from the vantage point of Washington or London, 'a reflection of arrogance and perceived superiority' (Joseph, 1996: 11), and 'an outdated monument to an immodest era' (Sachs, 1992: 12). Chambers' (1995) reversals paradigm calls for the norm to be stood on its head, for the majority (but seldom heard) world to express their reality, and to put that reality first.

> ... young people, start now serving your community so when you take on that critical leadership, you would still understand your position as serving not entitlement! And finally let's harness our energy, passion and creativity in bettering this motherland not destroying it. (ityafrica.net, 2015)

Africa is home to fifty-four recognised sovereign states and countries, four territories and 1.265 billion people. Africa is the youngest continent on the planet. In 2017, 41 percent of the population are children under the age of 15, and young people aged 15 to 24 an additional 19 percent (UN, 2017). This figure is expected to double by 2050 (Gyimah-Brempong & Kimenyi, 2013). The African Union's Youth Charter states that 'youth or young people shall refer to every person between the ages of 15 and 35 years', a legacy of the impact of centuries of colonialism – 'to redress the imbalances of the past' (Government of South Africa, 1996). The United Nations' *African Youth Report 2009* (UNECA, 2009) goes further and defines 'youth' as people between 15 and 39 years of age. There is a high incidence of poverty amongst the young people of Africa. The United Nations (2011) and World Bank (2009) estimated that in 2008 more than 70 percent of young people in Africa lived on less than $2 a day, and 46 percent lived on less than $1.25 a day.

The importance of youth participation and involvement in the development of the continent was enshrined in The African Union Constitutive Act (2000). The African Union developed a continental policy framework in the form of the African Youth Charter, which prescribes responsibilities to Member States for the development of young people, adopted at The Summit of Heads of State and Government in Banjul in July 2006:

> ... youth are partners, assets and a prerequisite for sustainable development and for the peace and prosperity of Africa with a unique contribution to make to the present and to future development. (UN, n.d.: 9)

In their *Youth Policy and the Future of African Development*, working paper (2013: 1) Gyimah-Brempong and Kimenyi declare, 'the size, energy, enthusiasm, innovation and dynamism of youth are assets that can be harnessed for Africa's development'.

To harness this size, energy, enthusiasm, innovation and dynamism, the AYM vision has been shaped through a participatory process of connecting African young people through social media, online spaces and opening critical conversational grassroots spaces for African youth (AYM, 2017). As Margaret Ledwith (n.d.) maintains, 'reclaiming the radical agenda begins by creating critical spaces for dialogue' to 'extraordinarily re-experience the ordinary' (Shor, 1992: 122). The AYM takes a strengths-based approach to young people. As a result of experiencing different 'local, complex, diverse, dynamic and unpredictable' ('lcddu') realities (Chambers, op. cit.), in different contexts, within complex and diverse histories and experiences of colonialisation and de-colonialisation, they develop different strengths and assets. These qualities are drivers for positive growth and change, recognising that 'young people themselves are the solution, rather than passive victims' (Stuart & Maynard, 2015: 239).

In the UK, we recognise that young people's voluntary participation is 'an important feature of youth work practice'. This, alongside 'the unstructured or partially structured nature of just 'being there' and of being able to be responsive in the moment' (Spence & Devanney, 2006: 82) are foundational to practice. Yet according to Connolly (2016: 2), in the UK,

> The harsh reality is that much, if not most, of the current, adult-led work in this area is tokenistic, does not lead to the political changes or changes in services/practice that children and young people require and is based on an understanding that their participation can be justified either as an end in itself, or as a convenient tool to promote their personal development.

Yet Max-Neef (1991) in identifying 'interdependent human needs', asserts participation is fundamental. Reason and Bradbury (2001: 8) contend participation is an 'ontological given' 'fundamental to the nature of our being', a 'transformative concept [...] a way of life, a way of seeing the world and a way of being in the world' – 'to be denied the capacity for potentially successful participation is to be denied one's humanity' (Doyal & Gough, 1991: 184).

Youth development from uniquely African perspectives is seen as part of wider Pan-Africanist ideologies, socio-political worldviews and processes – a belief that African peoples, both on the African continent and in the Diaspora, share not merely a common history, but a common destiny with a sense of interconnected pasts and futures (Makalani, n.d.). The AYM's Pan Africanism resonates at political, social and personal levels. Fanon (1967) advocated a process of meaning making, action and activity, of re-engaging and applying one's heritage to the present, as vital to sustaining identities. 'Simply looking back is not enough to take us forward' (Malik, 2006). Similarly Butters and Newell (1978),[1] in examining the 'cultural matrix' of the social education repertoire and its historical adjuncts, foresaw a radical youth development paradigm of 'self-emancipation', which 'insists that the great majority of young people can only fulfil their cultural potential if they join together in a struggle to overthrow the institutions and ideologies of the dominant classes' (ibid.: 43–44).

Tunisian blogger, award-winning activist and founder and chair of the AYM, Aya Chebbi describes herself as a 'full-time Pan-Africanist and feminist' leading a movement 'of young thinkers and visionaries, trying a different approach towards the realization of Africa's economic, social and political prosperity' (Ruano, 2015):

> I want to bring together and connect African youth who will be taking over
> the leadership of their nations in a few years, and restore indeed our values
> of African humanism, Ubuntu[2] and togetherness so that together we can
> develop Africa as a continent and not as separate nations. (Ruano, 2015)

Chebbi's vision is based on her activism in, and experience of, the 2011 Tunisian 'Revolution of Dignity' – as it was called in Tunisia:

> My inspiration is my commitment to change the narrative about Tunisia,
> Africa […] through people's stories […] to challenge the misrepresenta-
> tion and misinformation on the mainstream media that eventually shape
> the incomplete perceptions of others about these regions … to challenge
> that simply with real stories by offering another definition, logic, image
> or narrative. (ibid.)

To Chebbi, the 'Arab Spring' was and is a Western narrative – a type of miseducation reproducing the present by distorting or erasing the past (Giroux, 2015). Tunisia's revolution was different from Egypt's, Libya's, Syria's and other countries'.

> Putting all countries under one basket called the "Arab Spring" is not
> innocent […] There was even a book called The Arab Awakening. As if
> we were sleeping and suddenly startled awake! Undermining the entire
> social justice struggle in Tunisia […] every other conscious political revolt
> in North Africa and the Middle East. The Western media wants to write
> and recreate our own history in their own words creating a false public
> memory. All these names don't represent us and what we call it is not
> featured in the media. (Ruano, 2015)

Additionally, Chebbi contends a lingering struggle across Africa is the legacy of dependency on donor money from the institutions of the minority world. In the period following the 2011 Tunisian 'Revolution of Dignity', there was a 'boom' in new organisations being formed, funded by the United States with external institutions, rather than indigenous individuals, trying to guide the agenda, leadership (including youth leadership) and civil society – a new colonialism, a 'post-Washington' position firmly embedded in liberal capitalist ideology (Mohan, 2013).

> One cannot expect positive results from an educational or political action
> program which fails to respect the particular view of the world held by

the people. Such a program constitutes cultural invasion, good intentions notwithstanding. (Freire, 1972: 93)

It was at an intergenerational dialogue with African heads of states organised as part of the 50th Anniversary of the African Union, that Chebbi discovered that youth marginalisation in Africa is a real issue. Her vision is that in their 'otherness' and shared marginalisation, young Africans, could develop a sense of common leadership, social and political identity and a Freirean critical consciousness (*conscientização*) – of 'reading the world' – that would enable them to question the nature of their historical and social situation, and in turn challenge the status quo. Conscientização is a developmental process in which people develop a critical awareness of social structures. It is intrinsically an action-reflection methodology in which people come to see the reality of their own oppression through their own experience, and then act to transform that reality (Smith, 1976).

That is how AYM was born. Many inspiring young Africans availed themselves to working with me to make this vision a concrete reality. We shaped together our shared vision, values and objectives. (Ruano, 2015)

With over 10,000 activists from 40 countries (Diplomacy Opp, 2017), Chebbi seeks to 'disrupt the system and provide alternatives'.

In a ripple effect I want to radicalise all the youth of the continent, to develop their social and political identity, with radicalisation[3] as a place of belonging. (Chebbi, 2017, Skype interview, 18 August)

Chebbi continues, "The process is one of individual empowerment – enhancing the capacity of individual young people, strengthening the belief in their voice – as key to collective progress", especially as 'the young perceive that their right to say their own word has been stolen from them and that few things are more important than the struggle to win it back' (Shaull, 1996: 16)

The AYM reflects Chambers' (1997: 237) 'primacy of the personal' as a 'vision as practice' methodology to facilitate 'good change' flowing from 'personal decisions and action'. Young people and their organisations are empowered to realise their potential as transformative agents of global and community development, solving their own problems individually or through local organisations and networks (Korten, 1990; Thomas, 2000).

In Cameroon, supported by their villages, there are a thousand AYM activists organising in their communities. Each activist brings change – in themselves, their community, their country and across Africa. This process of youth mobilisation and community organising is in stark contrast to minority world approaches where numbers attending an event in one place are seen a measure of success. This process of youth mobilisation and grassroots community organising with people, with communities, village by village, country by country, Chebbi insists, is not seen in the minority world. It also highlights the distinct emphasis on individuals and their empowerment as key to collective progress. "How do we strengthen the capability of this person?" Chebbi asks. "It is through the strengthening of their belief in their voice" (Skype interview, 18 August, 2017).

> All development is ultimately about expanding human potential and enlarging human freedom. It is about people developing the capabilities that empower them to make choices and to lead lives that they value. (UNDP, 2007: 1)

The 'capabilities approach' as formulated by Sen (1992), and taken up in the UN's Human Development Report, develops the positive and negative freedoms of political theorist Isaiah Berlin. For Berlin (1969), negative freedom (freedom from) referred to the absence of obstacles, interference or coercion. Positive freedom (freedom to) on the other hand is about the possibility of acting in the world, to have agency. The AYM approach is based on positive freedoms, 'of conceiving goals and policies of my own and realizing them' (ibid.: 131).

In explaining the AYM's participatory process of connecting African young people through online and grassroots spaces, Chebbi asserts: Western organisations think of young people as participants but do not place them at the centre of decision making; that mainstream media have biases, and; that "what's documented is from the past". In an age of technology, online hangouts, forums and blogs "making every space youthful" facilitates "real participation" through spaces "created on our terms". This accelerates change through a transnational movement working together – "Our continent, our agenda". In effect the "thinking of youth is borderless" (Skype interview, 18 August, 2017).

Korten (1990) notes the possibilities offered by new communication technologies, and the networks they utilise and create, in activating social change. However, as the majority of Africans are offline, activism also relies on face to face meetings in communities. AYM have established hubs in all African countries to connect more with young Africans at the grassroots. Activists also "fight to be in the space" at the annual AYM Forum which is described as, "a method of disruption" (Chebbi, Skype interview, 18 August, 2017). Individual activists are often sponsored by their villages to attend. In Pan-Africanist socio-political worldviews and processes, there are no pre-determined people to be leader, all it takes is to give people space to be who they are.

AYM's leadership organise themselves so that they practice what they preach ... "This is your continent – determine your destiny". It is also significant that the leadership of the AYM – and the Pan-Africanist movement – is 'self-consciously' gendered with young women such as Chebbi and AYM Forum 2017 Chair and Advisory Board Member Marion Osieyo taking leading roles. Osieyo, who was born in Nairobi and raised in London, with a Masters in Global Governance and Diplomacy from Oxford, was selected in 2015 by the European Commission as a 'Future Leader' of International Co-operation and Development. The gendered leadership is cited as "another version of 'what power looks like'" (Chebbi, Skype interview, 18 August, 2017). These are 'stories of differently experienced power' (Ledwith, n.d.) – celebrating young women's voices, perspectives and energy, making the spaces feminist and youthful. Martha Nussbaum (2007) in *Women and Development: The Capabilities Approach* argues the approach can fairly claim to make a distinctive contribution to the practical pursuit of gender justice:

> The capabilities approach is the systematization and theorization of [...] thoughts and plans. It is plural because what women strive for contains a plurality of irreducibly distinct components. It is focused on capability or empowerment, even as the women's own thinking is focused on creating opportunities and choices, rather than imposing on any individual a required mode of functioning. (ibid.: 302)

As mentioned above, the uniquely African concept of *Ubuntu* is at the heart of the AYM process. Ubuntu is a Nguni/IsiZulu word often translated as 'I am because we are'. This is a philosophy of coexistence, whereby a person can only be conceived of in relation to others:

> Africans have this thing called UBUNTU. It is about the essence of being human, it is part of the gift that Africa will give the world. It embraces hospitality, caring about others, being able to go the extra mile for the sake of others. We believe that a person is a person through another person, that my humanity is caught up, bound up, inextricably, with yours [...] The solitary individual is a contradiction in terms and, therefore, you seek to work for the common good because your humanity comes into its own community, in belonging. (Desmond Tutu, 1999: 22)

'A person is a person through other people' resonates with UK youth and community development values, purposes and standards with its emphases on collective learning, objectives and action, political literacy (FCDL, 2015). Yet Ubuntu has deeper resonance with Ledwith and Springett's (2010) 'transformative practice':

> We are inextricably connected by the web of common humanity, but more than this, we are woven into all forms of life on earth. The concept of life as an ecosystem, held in fragile balance, helps us to understand that by harming anyone or anything we are violating this interdependence, and so endangering the well-being of the whole [...] the essence of a world that runs counter to the top down, competitive values of the western worldview [...] seeing our world in a more connected and cooperative way influences how we act. For these reasons, participatory practice begins in lived reality, in our being in the world. And it is questioning this everyday experience that leads to changed understanding. (Ledwith & Springett, 2010: 13)

Ubuntu represents the power of community. Research has indicated that leadership in African contexts begins with accepting and taking up one's role within a community or social context – the concept of 'self in community' is rooted in the concept of Ubuntu (Bolden & Kirk, 2005).

However, as opposed to the minority world emphasis on outcomes – Chebbi suggests, open any North American and European organisation's website and the focus is on numbers (Skype interview, 18 August, 2017) – there are no set outcomes in the AYM's activism. Within a 'participatory worldview – one which is founded on co-operation and true democracy rather than competition and free market politics' (Ledwith, n.d.), the focus is on process, moving with the changing times, and on stories of social change. It is a place to nurture change makers. It is Chebbi's (2017) vision that another definition, logic, image or narrative is offered "through people's [...] real stories". Citing Freire (1972), Margaret Ledwith (2005: 177) believes firmly in 'the stories of everyday life as the beginning of a process of progressive social change' with consciousness at its heart. Transformative practice, Ledwith and Springett (2010) insist, arises from practical theory generated from the narratives contained in these stories and this is seen as the best way to inform both policy and practice.

Participatory practice is a tool for examining this knowledge. It allows practitioners to consider the way they view the world, and to situate their local practice within bigger social issues (ibid.) – 'to exist, humanly, is to name the world, to change it. [...] Men [sic] are not built in silence, but in word, in work, in action-reflection' (Freire, 1972: 61). '... little stories become collective narratives that change the way we see the world' and 'seeing the world differently changes the world' (Ledwith, n.d.).

> As we attempt to analyse dialogue as a human phenomenon, we discover something which is the essence of dialogue itself: the word ... Within the word we find two dimensions, reflection and action, in such radical interaction that if one is sacrificed — even in part — the other immediately suffers. There is no true word which is not at the same time a praxis. Thus, to speak a true word is to transform the world. (Freire, 1972: 60)

Beset with challenges (many externally imposed) Bolden and Kirk (2005: 13) insist the only credible response for the continent of Africa is 'one of collective effort whereby the masses are encouraged and supported to take up their leadership roles', rooted in the concept of Ubuntu in 'accepting and taking up one's role within a community (or social) context. The concept of 'self in community' becomes the essential building block of shared or distributed leadership'.

Chebbi concludes by placing AYM's activism within frameworks of 'global citizenship', a commonalities perspective and global activism:

> ... belonging to a community of global diversity from around the world without borders. The more you meet and connect with people from other parts of the world, the more you realize how similar you are, how much in common you have, how many common struggles you share and how much you can do together and learn from each other. Global citizenship for me also comes with shared responsibility. If we are to belong to a global community, then we need to act together for the protection and betterment of that community. (Ruano, 2015)

Korten (1995: 187) argues that in the context of interconnected globalising processes, peoples' organisations, the building blocks of a 'just, sustainable and inclusive society', need to be 'global as well as local' forming coalitions and alliances to build a 'global movement for change'. Alliance building, locally and globally (externally to the majority world) and addressing issues of equality and justice, are critical features of the Black perspective of global youth work developed by Joseph et al. (2002), 'from colonial and hierarchical relationships of the past to democratic partnerships of the future' (ibid.: 15). This perspective recognises that the world's communities are locked into 'interdependent' relationships and that alliances not only need to be developed within the majority world, but between the majority and minority worlds too. It is also essential that strategic relationships are developed with movements for equality such as those concerning gender, age, disability, sexuality, 'race', environment, economic exploitation and so on which cut across both the majority and minority worlds (Joseph et al., 2002).

Yet much development education in the UK is still seen as value-laden, based on British, middle class beliefs (Pardinaz-Solis, 2006), 'a form of middle-class self-gratification ... another location for guilt rather than action' (Baker, 2006:1). Pardinaz-Solis (2006: 4), a Mexican educator working in Britain observes:

> in practice, in general, development education in Britain is still driven by fixed black and white binaries of us [North, rich, more developed, educated with lots of answers] and them [South, poor, less developed, uneducated, in need of help].

However, as Tinker (2007) and I would argue, 'The North-South lens is blurred, cracked, and warped'. Instead of looking for differences between marginalised young people, countries and cultures, global youth work views marginalised young people through a 'commonalities lens'. It focusses on shared experiences, 'creating solidarity and the space to learn from one another as equals' (ibid.). Conversely, as with the colloquial use of 'developing' and 'developed' worlds, the North-South lens divides and alienates.

A Commonalities Lens Guides Global Youth Work Practice

> Global youth work is informal education which starts from young people's everyday experiences, seeks to develop their understanding of the local and the global influences on their lives, and encourages positive action for change. (Burke, 2015: 7)

A developing educational process within youth work practice in the UK and Ireland, global youth work is an approach that starts from the perspective of a young person's personal life and their community, then embraces a global dimension – exploring the similarities, differences and links between that young person's life and young people's lives in other communities. Located right in the middle of minority-majority world processes and debates (Andreotti, 2006), the primary basis of global youth work is that of education for social change, working towards making change in individuals, nations and global society.

Looking to the future, there are many analogies between the AYM's activism and Butters and Newell's (1978: 40) youth development paradigm of radical practice – 'self-emancipation' 'which has yet to become established'. In this paradigm, youth work is about politically educating young people so that they can challenge the dominant cultural and social order – and then establish one of their own. It is about personal and political emancipation, about leading groups and communities in campaigns, struggles, militancy and non-acceptance of the dominant order. The minority world can learn from the AYM's 'peer-group situations where young people can seek to understand and to theorise from their experiences of struggle against established powers, and to recognise and realise their true interests, [a]t the same time [...] building up parallel youth organisations' (Butters & Newell, 1978: 44).

Self in Community to Self-Emancipation

In the minority world, could the AYM model of youth leadership help us achieve realisation of Butters' radical conceptualisation of the youth work process as the 'sponsorship of peer-group support by helping sub-cultural groups enquire into their political history' (Butters & Newell, 1978: 39)? Could Ubuntu's sense of self in community lead to young people's self-emancipation?

Butters and Newell (1978: 38) call for an epistemic break – to escape the 'cultural control institutions of policing, schooling and welfaring' found within the Social Education Repertoire (SER), and handed down to youth work 'by the dominant interests in society' in 'maintaining the infrastructures – social and ideological – of a capitalist society' (ibid.: 46). Traversing this 'critical breaking frontier' (ibid.: 44) would release a youth work process which resonates with the AYM's – 'a peer-group pedagogy [...] helping sub-cultural groups enquire into their political history and geography' (ibid.: 39).

Just as the personal realities of young people's lives across the continent of Africa are formed by and within complex and diverse histories and experiences of colonialisation and de-colonialisation, the realities of the many marginalised and disadvantaged young people in the minority world are similarly 'local, complex, diverse, dynamic and unpredictable' (Chambers, 1997: 167). Just as Chebbi seeks to radicalise all of Africa's young people "to develop their social and political identity, with radicalisation ... a place of belonging [which] disrupt[s] the system and provide[s] alternatives" (Chebbi, Skype interview, 18 August, 2017), Giroux (2015) urges the revival of radical imaginaries as the basis for new forms of collective struggle – a critical pedagogy of risk taking, dangerous thinking and critical challenge – through which young people come to understand and critically interpret their own experiences of struggle with collective power, and work to redefine and agentically realise their own interests (Butters & Newell, 1978).

In moving forward, we need to develop methodologies that draw on the wisdom and experiences of the majority world. AYM's activism frames world-changing in participatory global citizenship. The primary basis of Global Youth Work is education for social change – in individuals, nations and global society. It strives for democratic partnerships that will bring about global transformations by addressing issues of equality and justice. The world's communities are locked into 'interdependent' relationships; alliances need to be developed within the majority world, and also between the majority and minority worlds. It is essential therefore that strategic *global* relationships are developed with movements for equality such as those concerning gender, age, disability, sexuality, 'race', environment, and economic exploitation. The power of Global Youth Work is its potential to enable young people to understand 'self in community', and in challenging them to take up their role within the wider global community.

Notes

1   Butters and Newell's (1978) work is built on Peter Leonard's (1975) exploration of radical social work grounded in individual and collective conscientisation, originating in Freire's (1972) *Pedagogy of the Oppressed*.
2   Discussion of this idea follows later in the chapter.
3   A source of contemporary confusion, if radical serves the purpose of indicating a relative position on a continuum of organised opinion, 'radicalise' and 'radicalisation' then indicates movement on that continuum. This begs the question on what continuum? Sedgwick (2010: 481) emphasises the 'relative' nature of the concept of 'radical' and the location of it and what is seen as 'moderate' on a continuum. He stresses the care need to be taken in specifying 'both the continuum being referred to and the location of what is seen as "moderate" on that continuum'. Without this location, radical or radicalisation in effect becomes an 'absolute' term. This happens when the line between moderate and radical is presumed to be self-evident, and the continuum is also presumed to be self-evident – as in the dominant UK discourse, the 'political shibboleth' (Schmid, 2013: iv), that terrorism is caused by the presence of extremist ideology in opposition to 'British values', however loosely defined, or understood. Schmid proposes radicalism (as opposed to extremism) 'While both stand at some distance from mainstream political thinking, the first tends to be open-minded, while the second manifests a closed

mind ...' (Schmid, 2013: iv). Additionally, Navarro (2015: 2) notes radical 'principles and demands often provide the backbone of tomorrow's mainstream thought and attitudes'.

References

Andreotti, V. (2006). Theory without practice is idle, practice without theory is blind: The potential contributions of post-colonial theory to development education. *Development Education Journal, 12*(3), 7–10.

AYM. (2017). *History* [Online]. Retrieved September 13, 2017, from http://afrikayouthmovement.org/history/

Baker, J. (2006). Development education and Black and minority ethnic people. *Development Education Journal, 12*(3), 1–3.

Beck, D., & Purcell, R. (2010). Developing generative themes for community action. In S. Curran, R. Harrison, & D. Mackinnon (Eds.), *Working with young people* (2nd ed., pp. 154–163). London: Sage Publications.

Berlin, I. (1969). Two concepts of liberty. In N. Warburton (Ed.), *Philosophy: Basic readings*. Abingdon: Routledge.

Blunt, P., & Jones, M. (1997). Exploring the limits of Western leadership theory in East Asia and Africa. *Personnel Review, 26*(1–2), 6–23.

Bolden, R., & Kirk, P. (2005, December 12–13). *Leadership in Africa: Meanings, impacts and identities*. Paper presented at Studying Leadership: Future Agendas, 4th International Conference on Leadership Research, Lancaster University Management School.

Burke, T. (2005). *Strengthening and sustaining: An analysis of Y Care International's global youth work provision*. London: Y Care International.

Butters, S., & Newell, R. (1978). *The realities of training*. Leicester: National Youth Bureau.

Chambers, R. (1995). Poverty and livelihoods: Whose reality counts? *Environment and Urbanization, 7*(1), 175–200.

Chambers, R. (1997). *Whose reality counts*. London: ITDG.

Chebbi, A. (2017, August 18). *Meaningful participative youth development practice from a majority world perspective* (interviewed by Wroe, S.). Skype.

Connolly, D. (2017, July 5–7). *Establishing a centre for children and young people's rights in the north of the UK, October 2016*. Paper presented at Professional Association of Lecturers in Youth and Community Work Annual Conference, University of Hull, Hull. Retrieved February 15, 2018, from http://www.tagpalycw.org/Conference%20 2017%20Hull/2.5%20Dialogue%20and%20Change%20(Dan%20Connolly).pdf

Diplomacy Opp. (2017). *Afrika youth movement statement on protests in Togo | Diplomacy opportunities* [Online]. Retrieved November 15, 2017, from https://diplomacyopp.com/2017/09/27/afrika-youth-movement-statement-on-protests-in-togo-diplomacy-opportunities/

Doyal, L., & Gough, I. (1991). *A theory of human need.* New York, NY: Guildford Press.

FCDL. (2015). *Community development national occupational standards* [Online]. Retrieved October 20, 2017, from https://www.fcdl.org.uk/app/download/18739655/CDNOS+mar2015.pdf

Freire, P. (1972). *Pedagogy of the oppressed.* Harmondsworth: Penguin Books.

Giroux, H. (2015). *Dangerous thinking in the age of the new authoritarianism (Critical interventions: Politics, culture, and the promise of democracy).* New York, NY: Routledge.

Government of South Africa. (1996). *National youth commision act.*

Gyimah-Brempong, K., & Kimenyi, S. (2013). *Youth policy and the future of African development.* Washington, DC: Brookings Institution.

ITY Africa. (2015). *INTERVIEW: Aya Chebbi on her agenda for African youth!* [Online]. Retrieved June 27, 2017, from http://www.ityafrica.net/2015/10/interview-aya-chebbi-on-her-agenda-for.html

Jackson, T. (2004). *Management and change in Africa: A cross-cultural perspective.* London: Routledge.

Joseph, J. (1996). Global youth work: Reconceptualising development education? *Development Education Journal, 5.*

Joseph, J., Akpokavi, K. B., Chauhan, V., & Cummins, V. (2002). *Towards global democracy: An exploration of Black perspectives in global youth work.* London: DEA.

Korten, D. (1990). *Getting to the 21st century: Voluntary action and the global agenda.* Hartford, CT: Kumarian Press.

Korten, D. (1995). Steps toward people centred development: Vision and strategies. In N. Heyzer, J. V. Riker, & A. B. Quizon (Eds.), *Government-NGO relations in Asia: Prospects and challenges for people-centred development* (pp. 165–189). London: Palgrave Macmillan.

Gyimah-Brempong, K., & Kimenyi, M. S. (2013). *Youth policy and the future of African development.* Washington, DC: Brookings Institution.

Ledwith, M. (2005). *Community development: A critical approach.* Bristol: Policy Press.

Ledwith, M. (n.d.). *Community development & human flourishing: Be the change!* [Online]. Retrieved October 20, 2017, from https://www.cdhn.org/sites/default/files/oldwebsite/Community%20Development%20and%20Human%20Flourishing%20Be%20the%20Change%21%20Professor%20Margaret%20Ledwith.pdf

Ledwith, M., & Springett, J. (2010). *Participatory practice: Community-based action for transformative change.* Bristol: Policy Press.

Leonard, P. (1975). Towards a paradigm for radical practice. In R. Bailey & M. Brake (Eds.), *Radical social work* (pp. 46–61). New York, NY: Pantheon.

Makalani. (n.d.). *Pan–Africanism* [Online]. Retrieved September 13, 2017, from http://exhibitions.nypl.org/africanaage/essay-Pan-Africanism.html

Malik, R. (2006). British or Muslim: Creating a context for dialogue: The discursive construction and racialisation of Muslim identities. *Youth and Policy, 92*, 91–106.

Max-Neef, M. A. (1991). *Human scale development: Conception, application and further reflections.* New York, NY: Apex Press.

Mohan, G. (2013). Rising powers. In T. Papaioannou & M. Butcher (Eds.), *International development in a changing world.* London: Bloomsbury Academic.

Nussbaum, M. (2000). *Women and development: The capabilities approach.* Cambridge: Cambridge University Press.

Pardinaz-Solis, R. (2006). A single voice from the South in the turbulent waters of the North. *Development Education Journal, 12*(3), 4–7.

Reason, P., & Bradbury, H. (Eds.). (2001). *Handbook of action research: Participative inquiry and practice.* London: Sage Publications.

Ruano, J. (2015). *Interview with Aya Chebbi, African youth movement founder* [Online]. Retrieved October 11, 2017, from http://www.globaleducationmagazine.com/interview-aya-chebbi-african-youth-movement-founder/

Sachs, W. (1992). Development: A guide to the ruins. *New Internationalist, 232*, 2–8.

Sen, A. (1992). *Inequality reexamined.* Oxford: Clarendon Press.

Shaull, R. (1996). *Foreword.* In P. Freire (Ed.), *Pedagogy of the oppressed 30th anniversary edition.* New York, NY: Continuum.

Shor, I. (1992). *Empowering education: Critical teaching for social change.* London: University of Chicago Press.

Smith, W. A. (1976). *The meaning of Conscientizaçao: The goal of Paulo Freire's pedagogy.* Amherst, MA: Center for International Education.

Spence, J., & Devanney, C. (2006). Every day is different. In S. Curran, R. Harrison, & D. Mackinnon (Eds.), *Working with young people* (2nd ed., pp. 73–86). London: Sage Publications.

Stuart, K., & Maynard, L. (2015). Non-formal youth development and its impact on young people's lives: Case study – Brathay trust, UK. *Italian Journal of Sociology of Education, 7*(1), 231–262.

Thomas, A. (2000). Development as practice in a liberal capitalist world. *Journal of International Development, 12*(6), 773–787.

Tinker, J. (2007). *Should we dump the North-South lens?* [Online]. Retrieved July 24, 2007, from http://www.comminit.com/drum_beat_401.html

Tutu, D. (1999). *No future without forgiveness: A personal overview of South Africa's truth and reconciliation commission.* London: Doubleday.

UNECA. (2009). *African youth report 2009: Expanding opportunities for and with young people in Africa.* Addis Ababa: UNECA (UN Economic Commission for Africa).

United Nations. (2011). *Population below national poverty lines: Millennium development goals database, UN statistics division.* New York, NY: United Nations.

United Nations. (n.d.). *African youth charter* [Online]. Retrieved October 20, 2017, from http://www.un.org/en/africa/osaa/pdf/au/african_youth_charter_2006.pdf

United Nations, Department of Economic and Social Affairs, Population Division. (2017). *World population prospects: The 2017 revision.* New York, NY: United Nations.

United Nations Development Programme (UNDP). (2007). *Fighting climate change: Human solidarity in a divided world. Human development report 2007/2008.* New York, NY: United Nations.

Wheatley, M. (2001). *Restoring hope to the future through critical education of leaders. Vimukt Shiksha, a bulletin of Shikshantar.* Udaipur, Rajasthan: The People's Institute for Rethinking Education and Development.

World Bank. (2009). *Poverty headcount ratio at $1.25 a day, 2009.* World Bank Research Group.

World Bank. (n.d.). *World Bank country and lending groups* [Online]. Retrieved June 27, 2017, from https://datahelpdesk.worldbank.org/knowledgebase/articles/906519-world-bank-country-and-lending-groups

CHAPTER 8

Dichotomous Voluntary Futures

Ilona Buchroth and Dan Connolly

> The issue that we need to address ... is how we can use our skills and experience of resisting dominant discourses and empowering youth work practice to collectivize and voice the compromised positions in which voluntary organisations find themselves.
>
> BUCHROTH & HUSBAND, 2015: 119

∴

Introduction

This chapter builds on the work that has already been done to describe the dilemmas facing the voluntary youth sector in relation to New Public Management (NPM), neoliberalism, austerity and new legal measures in curtailing the voice of charities who attempt to challenge government policy. On the one hand, the chapter presents scenarios where the demands of neoliberalism are fully embraced and interventions are made via a competitive process that are aimed at the level of the individual in order to assuage a pathologised interpretation of the causes of inequality and disadvantage. The chapter describes how these demands impact on young people, staff, organisational relationships, governance and the sector more widely – resulting in a comprehensive constraint young people's voices.

We argue that this silencing is achieved by the interlocking pressures of external measures that constrain voice from the top down, including changes to charity law, combined with internal, 'bottom-up' measures such as reducing workers to the role of technician rather than responsive professional. This approach affronts the core values, principles and very definitions of Community and Youth Work expressed in terms of its commitments to democracy, challenging structural inequalities, promoting social justice and championing young people's right to be heard, and their voices taken into account.

The interests of those who seek to constrain and curtail the emancipatory work done by the voluntary youth sector are well served if those who work in

© KONINKLIJKE BRILL NV, LEIDEN, 2019 | DOI:10.1163/9789004396555_008

the sector are either unaware that alternative paths are available, or if they display the 'apathetic cynicism which so conveniences those who presume power' (Bright, 2015: 246).

Taking up Bright's challenge to expose 'alternatives paths', the chapter presents scenarios where the Sector has been able to successfully 'reassert its distinctiveness through collectivism, democratic determination and civil courage' (Buchroth & Husband, 2015: 119). In these scenarios, existing skills and experiences are brought powerfully into play to promote an alternative future for the Sector that places understandings of, and challenges to, structural oppression at the heart of practice. In this way, the active voice of young people is liberated to become a driving force – shaping the future of the Sector at every level of practice, measurement and governance.

Loss of Control and De-Professionalisation

One of neoliberalism's main features is its capacity to shift the locus of control of work with young people onto external bodies and away from those who govern, run and use services (Bunyan & Ord, 2012). This has a marginalising, de-professionalising and disempowering effect, which draws the voluntary sector further away from its core value base.

It is increasingly common that youth organisations rely on a diffuse portfolio of funding sources, which require compliance with an equally wide range of monitoring systems and performance indicators (Duffy, 2018). The resulting managerial demands can take a heavy toll on organisations. Not only is compliance with a range of different systems labour intensive, the complexities associated with the expectation of New Pubic Management (NPM) can go beyond the scope, skills and confidence levels of voluntary committees and boards which are required to undertake increasingly demanding roles (Rochester, 2014).

As a result, boards tend to become 'professionalised' in different ways. Either organisations report that they become more dependent on their paid staff (Scott & Russell, 2001), or they specifically recruit board members with clearly identified skill sets, often from other sectors and especially from business and commerce. This approach is both encouraged, and may be explicitly demanded by some funders (Malone & Okwonga, 2011). It is this 'imported' expertise that is then seen as lending organisations their sense of professionalism, rather than the primary 'youth work business' of organisations or their responsiveness to the voices and interests of the communities with whom they work. These trends create democratic deficits and mitigate against the meaningful involvement of young people in determining their own affairs. These narrow and politically loaded interpretations of professionalism also risk becoming internalised and normalised by youth workers themselves:

> I think to have so many lay people on the management committee who don't have the necessary set of skills. ... I think it's valuable to have some there to offer the perspective of the community but definitely not to have an over-emphasis on community members. (Youth Work Practitioner)

Describing the reality of how control has been ceded however, is a necessary starting point in the process of reclaiming it. Canella and Lincoln's analysis of Foucault's contribution to understanding how neoliberalism can be resisted is encouraging:

> Many have decried the work of Foucault as depressing and as if eliminating possibilities for human agency. However ... his very conceptualisations of power as non-existent without resistance, as exercised/infused rather than hierarchical, provide prospects for critical actions that would counter and even deterritorialise neoliberalism. (Thompson, 2003, cited in Canella & Lincoln, 2015: 60)

From this starting point, it becomes easier to re-formulate the issue of control and to build a compelling case to rethink how power might be configured *internally* in line with voluntary sector values, rather than *externally* in assuaging the false logic of neoliberal ideologues who claim that the rules of commercial markets must apply equally to the public and voluntary sectors.

In relation to the 'professionalisation' of voluntary youth organisations' boards, this means re-thinking 'professionalism' as contextual and asking 'Whose voices need to determine how we run this organisation?'. This is not to say that accountants and those with business experience do not have a role to play in supporting and advising organisations in the voluntary youth sector. But the duty of voluntary organisations is not to be 'business-like'. It is to be 'voluntary-like'. This means ensuring that the business and direction of voluntary organisations are shaped and controlled by the voices of those with the greatest expertise, investment and experience in whichever field the organisation is engaged. Thus for voluntary youth organisations, this must be young people themselves together with those trained and qualified to work with them. These ideals need to be reflected in the structure of organisations, as the Director of a young people's rights' organisation in the North East of England explains:

The CIC (Community Interest Company) structure and the decision to be limited by guarantee rather than shares enabled us to maintain local, democratic accountability in a number of ways once we left the Local Authority. It ensured that young people would continue to share the power of decision-making alongside adults at all levels of the project's operation and governance. So one of the current directors lists her occupation as 'Sixth Form Student' on the Companies House website which I think says it all really. The Head of Children's Services from the County Council has continued to chair the Board as she did under the previous structure and the local NHS remains a key partner with board-level representation. Also project staff are represented on the governing board on a rolling basis and the three most senior roles were re-shaped to become co-directors. ... We have access to accountancy services and external advice around social enterprise of course – *but these people advise the organisation – they don't run it.*

At the same time as seeking to 'professionalise' (i.e. commercialise) voluntary sector boards, neoliberal influence has overtly 'deprofessionalised' youth workers. Top down models arising from external target setting and outcomes-led practice affect youth workers' roles, perceptions of 'professionalism' and professional autonomy. It also serves to constrain young people's power in shaping the world around them.

Grundy (1987) drawing on Habermas' (1987) knowledge constitutive interests, outlines how a curriculum that works to an external set of outcomes reduces practitioners to 'technicians', thus resulting in 'the technocratic assault that has become the modus operandi of professional and social control' (Bright, 2015: 245). The work of a technician is essentially reactive to plans and programmes that are conceived and determined outside of the actual experience and interaction with participants/young people. The success of workers' interventions is therefore judged by how closely they resemble or fulfil the externally set plan they are working *to*, rather than by their capacity to respond to the voices, interests and rights of the young people they are working *with*.

The reality is that what most funders require is pre-set outcomes that deliver against an adult-driven or Government-led agenda. They expect us to tell them what will change before we've even spoken to children and young people about what needs to change! (Project Fundraiser)

A prominent example of this within the neoliberal context is the objectification and categorisation of young people purely in relation to their proximity to (or distance from) the employment market i.e. 'NEET' (Not in Employment, Education or Training) (ONS, 2015).

> ... constructing practices that define individual human beings in relation to forms of measurement and capital, rather than as always valued affirmations of life, nature, and complex connections. (Cannella & Lincoln, 2015: 57–58)

In this context, the worker's role is reduced to that of an employment technician, with the value of the work judged solely by the numbers of young people entering employment and training.

This raises particular concerns regarding professional values, and autonomy, and the distribution of power in practice. Professional autonomy in Community and Youth Work is closely related to the concept of phroensis, or 'practical wisdom'. Smith, drawing on Aristotle, defines this as being guided by workers' understanding of what 'makes for human wellbeing' (Smith, 1994: 76). Targeted work with young people leaves little room for workers to exercise the professional discretion about what constitutes 'human wellbeing', or to work collaboratively with young people to determine what issues are of concern to them.

In relation to this crucial link between understanding and professionalism, it is worth noting that the 2017 consultation on the development of standards for the employer-led 'Degree Apprenticeships' in Youth Work in the UK demanded that:

> Each apprenticeship standard has to be expressed as the knowledge, skills and *behaviours* required for an occupation. (Professional Association of Lecturers in Youth and Community Work, 2017, emphasis added)

This stands in contrast to the assessment of trainee Community and Youth Work professionals undertaking traditional degree qualification routes, where the emphasis is primarily on on knowledge, skills, values and *understanding*, rather than pre-set, competency based 'behaviours' (see National Youth Agency, n.d.; National Occupational Standards for Youth Work).

The relative unpredictability of outcomes arising from interactions with young people that would truly put them in charge of defining their own needs and determining the agenda for change is therefore fundamentally at odds with the neoliberal-positivist paradigm in which young people are either regarded as consumers of services or recipients of interventions. In the same vein, the value of practitioners is determined by their skill to implement these pre-determined interventions, rather than their understanding and capacity for critical phroensis. This is mirrored in the way some employers define the potential value of staff and prioritise the focus of their training:

> The last thing we want is workers who have been trained to come in and challenge things. (Employer involved in design of national youth work training programme)

This statement stands in contrast to the commonly-held view amongst youth work educators and academics that professionalism is partly defined by practitioners' capacity to challenge the status quo, and, as a result, generate change in favour of young people and communities. This is closely linked to the notion of youth workers as 'critical practitioners' (Bamber & Murphy, 1999; Tyler, 2009).

Cooper (2012) takes the link between professionalism and challenge further, arguing that a failure to engage in critical practice would not merely result in vital opportunities being missed, but actually risks workers becoming a source of harm to young people. Drawing on Bourdieu's (1992) concept of 'symbolic violence', Cooper argues that the failure to challenge perpetuates violent acts of cultural domination.

Voice

Key to challenging the imposition of top-down targets and to retrieving workers' sense of professionalism, is the need to create spaces for young people to shape the direction of the work, and thus reset agendas for change from the bottom-up.

This places an expectation on workers in the voluntary youth sector to engage young people in genuine conversations about what matters to them, and to be willing to work alongside them as partners in bringing about change. In contrast to the perspective of the employer quoted earlier, this will inevitably require that workers 'challenge things' – in particular to stand by young people when they seek to challenge those who wield power over them and deny them their rights. This approach matches Grundy's (1987: 99ff) concept of 'curriculum as praxis' where learning about the social world is a shared endeavour (between teachers and students or between workers and young people) that overtly acknowledges the ways in which power and inequalities are manifest, and directly seeks to redress these through shared emancipatory activity:

So neither fundamental orientations towards technical nor practical reasoning will ensure that the even more fundamental interest in autonomy
and responsibility will be served. There must be an interest in freeing
persons from the coercion of the technical and the possible deceit of the
practical. This is the interest in emancipation. (ibid.: 17)

Drawing on Habermas' (1992) theories of dialogue and communicative action,
this approach is operationalised by the young people's rights organisation
referred to above. When approached by service providers (schools, hospitals
etc.), the first step is always to place power in the hands of children and young
people. Once a potential group of children and/or young people has been
identified by the service provider, the Agenda Day™ process ensures that it is
children and young people who decide – via democratic discussion and collective debate in an adult-free environment – what the focus for change will
be. Sometimes the young people's agenda for change matches with that of
the adults commissioning the work – and sometimes it does not. The process
of achieving change from this point onwards, as the young people form their
own 'project groups', can be highly complex and subject to extended delays.
It often involves elements of conflict (between young people and service providers), and inevitably requires workers to draw constantly on their 'practical
wisdom' and discretion in making difficult judgements about potential ways
forward.

In this model, outcomes are created as each project group moves forward,
rather than being set before the work even starts. Difficulties (including failure
in reaching desired outcomes) are faced jointly by the project group and workers as part of a collaborative enterprise. In contrast to top-down models, young
people are valued not as recipients of services, but as co-creators of outcomes,
and as experts in their own lives. The workers are valued not for their technical
ability to merely replicate pre-set and externally determined outcomes, but
for their professional expertise in autonomously applying what they understand about the social world to each new and unique circumstance which they
encounter alongside young people.[1]

A further way in which neoliberalism attempts to place the market as the
sole arbiter of value is in relation to how voluntary sector projects are measured and evaluated. This is described in stark terms by Doug Nicholls in his
extensive analysis of the impact of neoliberalism on the youth work profession:

It is the mentality of the market that assumes that processes designed to
foster human relationships can be quantified and weighed on the grocer's scales. (Nicholls, 2012: 159)

As an alternative to the grocer's scales, Social Accounting and Audit (SAA) provides a potentially useful tool through which the Sector can meet the challenge of measurement in a way that is more congruently alligned with its values. Social auditing takes direct responsibility for the fact that all organisations benefit from implementing mechanisms that rigorously and regularly measure their capacity to meet the goals they have set for themselves. The difference, again lies in the contrast between internally established measures based on core values and externally imposed measures based on marketisation, political ideology, surveillance and control.[2]

Voice – of the Sector

Young people-led/'Youth voice' organisations have also been collectively silenced by the way in which the wider voluntary sector has been corralled into increasingly narrow political spaces. The restrictions arising from targeted funding regimes, commissioning contract cultures and ever-closer relationships with the state are well documented, and highlight the impact on the independence and telos of the voluntary youth sector.

A vibrant and thriving voluntary sector is essential in creating a healthy and democratic society. Organisational and sectoral independence is central to this aim. Voluntary activity acts as a critical counterbalance to the power of both the state and the corporate sector, enabling diverse needs, perspectives and aspirations to be expressed and reflected in public policy and services, in supporting the creation of a social environment in which everyone can flourish. Independence of purpose, voice and action – the three aspects of independence set out in the Voluntary Sector's 'Barometer of Independence' – each underpin this role (Civil Exchange, 2016: 4).

Following on from annual reports by the Baring Foundation on the state of the voluntary sector, the most recent report by the Civil Exchange (2016) concluded that the sector's independence had hit a five year low and is now near crisis point.

Most notable in the changing nature of the voluntary sector is that in addition to the indirect restrictions arising from conditions imposed by funding sources, there is now also a formal curtailment of the Sector's role and function. This is in sharp contrast to the 'social compact' of the early New Labour years which formally acknowledged the Sector's right to 'campaign, to comment on government policy and to challenge that policy' (Home Office, 1998, cited in Bunyan & Ord, 2012: 25). Instead, the Sector now has to contend with 'no advocacy' clauses in all taxpayer-funded grants as well as the 'Lobbying

Act' (Transparency of Lobbying, Non-party Campaigning and Trade Union Administration Act, 2014) that forbids charities to speak out on issues a year ahead of elections. As a result, the Sector has moved away from its remit of being a potential 'critic of the state' to becoming an 'arm of the state' (Buchroth, 2012).

Fortunately, there are counter examples emerging that reveal the Sector's courage in continuing to speak out against injustice, despite structural attempts to curtail and constrain its critical voice. At a very local level, where arguably the Sector might feel more vulnerable in comparison with large and relatively powerful, national voluntary organisations, one community based organisation in the North East of England has worked consistently to retain its focus on raising public awareness around issues that concern the local community. Actively resisting the self-censorship that has become commonplace (Civil Exchange, 2016), they are adopting an openly confident stance by publicly declaring that the project's role must be to reverse trends of 'hopeless inactivity'. As one of the project staff put it:

> People have been told for so long that they can't do things, they have forgotten what they can do – they need community leadership to encourage them to ... you need to employ people to make relationships with people. ... Where the community gives each other permission, then things grow.

This worker's response reinforces the argument that it is practice, not policy that matters (Davies, 2010), that the 'meaning of youth work depends on what practitioners do' (Cooper, 2012: 55). With a clear focus on local issues, the project sees its remit both to actively and collectively raise local concerns whilst simultaneously problematising the constraints that are revealed in these processes.

One example of the project's reaction to identified local issues is illustrated by the launch of a campaign in response to sub-standard housing in the area, and the damaging impact of absentee landlords. Using a community organising approach, the project supported a group of local people to engage with residents who were leaving sub-standard properties, encouraging them to put stickers on the properties as they left saying: 'Don't rent here' and listing the respective faults of that property. What emerges from this example is an opportunity to '[make] small gains in local situations whilst all the while working to towards the abolition of oppressive conditions in general' (Bamber & Murphy, 1999: 240).

This example also exemplifies Bamber and Murphy's point that it is advisable:

> to make 'realistic and prudent decisions ... to act in such a way [so as not] to unnecessarily trigger the forces of reaction so that the incipient action is crushed before it has the chance to establish itself ... issues need to be taken up in such a way that it is difficult to demonize or stereotype the activists. (ibid.: 241)

Competition

Another feature of the neoliberal context that youth organisations need to negotiate, is how competition rather than exchange has become the root principle of the 'market' (Brown, 2015). Traditional liberal perspectives regarded exchange (e.g. of goods, services and capital) to be the central feature of market-based economics. For this to work effectively, 'partners' to exchange required various forms of protection and oversight. As Canella and Lincoln (2015) point out, neoliberalism replaces exchange with open competition. It thus becomes: 'a form of embodiment that no longer functions to protect the various partners engaged through exchange' (ibid.: 54).

In order to survive in this competitive environment, many organisations now have a clear focus on how to improve their market standing and position and are encouraged to borrow heavily from the systems, language and practices of the private sector (Tyler, 2009).

> It's now commonplace for the third sector to justify its importance in terms of its turnover and the numbers of people it employs, rather than through its connection to diverse communities, its expert knowledge, its independent voice. (Baring Foundation, 2016)

One youth worker in the North East of England reflected on this in respect of their experience of 'organisational branding':

> ... I went to this presentation of ... rebranding a piece of work. And they spent £1.5 million to pay a company to research their national brand identity. What does that say to you? To me it reeks of how NIKE would behave, or Adidas or some other. ... And this presentation was so convincing. At the end I was clapping and hooting ... because it was the most in-depth

> analysis, so clever ... what it means to be having a shared identity across
> all platforms ....

The positive presentation of organisations' work has become an essential element in enhancing competitive positioning and added value in market metrics (Brown, 2015). Many organisations now use a wide spectrum of outlets
(reports, presentations, websites and social media) to 'sell themselves'. There
is, of course, a reasonable expectation that all organisations, regardless of
whether they are 'for-profit' or otherwise, will put resources into describing
what they do and achieve, and that they make this information accessible
in creative ways to different audiences. Potential funders, for instance, may
require information to be presented in particular ways, and young people and
parents in others. In this sense, it is clear that voluntary organisations do need
to 'advertise' themselves effectively.

   Yet the sector has a responsibility to pay attention to ends as well as means.
Being distinctive and diverse is important to voluntary youth organisations
because the needs, interests and aspirations of young people and communities
are complex, distinctive and diverse. This diversity, if it is to be respected and
valued as integral to a democratic society and to human flourishing, requires
the availability of a similarly diverse range of opportunities and support –
especially to those most marginalised and requiring additional resources.

   Advertising that aims to creatively and imaginatively distinguish one organisation from another and that helps, via collaboration, to establish a comprehensive, co-operative network of coherent provision (thus avoiding wasteful
duplication) is clearly congruent with the democratic values of inclusivity and
diversity that lie at the heart of the Sector's identity. Advertising that aims to
achieve geographical and practice dominance *at the cost of other agencies*, and,
which in doing so, marks them as 'competitors' is clearly not. Sector leaders
have a responsibility to know the difference, and to recognise 'the extent to
which parts of the voluntary sector have been colonised by neoliberal thinking' (Murray, 2015: 1).

   The pervasive ideology of competition also impacts negatively on the voluntary sector in other ways. Organisations are encouraged, and indeed expected
to compete with similar agencies, with bigger organisations appearing to fare
much better in this scenario:

> It also reveals a system that routinely discriminates against small charities
> on the basis of their size, preventing them from competing fairly, leaving
> them deprived of funding or at the mercy of larger providers, many of
> which can behave unscrupulously. (Lloyds Bank Foundation, 2016)

According to surveys undertaken by the Third Sector Research Centre, the allocation of government funding rises proportionally to the annual income of organisations (Clifford & Backus, 2010). Many smaller organisations have shrunk in size, and resultantly so has their capacity to attract government funding. This situation has been exacerbated by the unequal distribution of spending cuts: on average, between 2009 and 2012 for example, smaller organisations lost between 20–25% of their income, whilst larger organisations only had 1.6% of statutory funding cuts to accommodate (Baring Foundation, 2016). The survival of smaller organisations increasingly depends on being subcontracted to bigger organisations that might well have the infrastructure to bid for contracts, but not necessarily the local knowledge and links to deliver them.

Strengthening local knowledge was cited by one community-based project in the North East of England as vital to its success and survival:

> Unlike some organisations whose strategy has been to grow 'bigger' [expand geographically] we have decided to 'go deeper', i.e. we have become 'hyper-local'. I think the idea that bigger is better is going down. (Project Worker)

It is important to note in this context that the project was not portraying its local knowledge as a marketable commodity, but that its deep-rooted connections with local concerns provided internal strength and solidity that other (external) organisations would be unable to replicate, infiltrate or challenge.

Competition has also been allowed to invade the policy and practice of 'partnership working' – arguably the natural approach for youth organisations committed to working in solidarity with each other. This facet of practice traditionally distinguished the Sector from both its private and public counterparts.

Partnership working, supported by the rhetoric of 'joined up' thinking, met with significant policy support during the New Labour Years. However, as Bunyan and Ord (2012) point out, the dominance of commisioning and market competition came to usurp cooperation. Competetive logic has now become firmly and structurally embedded in a number of funding regimes; this includes some local authorities explicitly prohibiting the discussion of tenders with other groups (Benson, 2014; Cannella & Lincoln, 2015).

The resulting climate of distrust, secrecy and, at times, underhand tactics undermines the development of a collective voice, and further constrains the Sector's professional commitment to social justice, solidarity, equality and democratic praxis. The market-focused, neoliberal environment thus succeeds in undermining many of the central features of the critical, social and educational perspectives that underpin the Profession's radically transformative traditions.

The opportunity to collaborate rather than compete presented itself to the voluntary youth sector in one region of North East England in 2015. The region was targeted for the development of an 'Onside Youth Zone', centre-based provision costing 'in the order of £6million' (Onside), to be funded mainly by locally-sourced private and public sector monies. The proposed project raised a number of concerns within the local Voluntary Youth and Community Sector. These focused around un-necessary duplication of services; additional threats to already fragile funding (as the local authority would be limiting its funding to the Youth Zone once existing contracts timed-out); poor access to the Youth Zone for young people from outlying areas, and, perhaps most significantly, the imposition of a 'one-size fits all' approach to service provision which contrasted with the more organic, neighbourhood-based and responsive approaches that had been developed across the area over many years.

Whilst Sector networks existed at the time, the perceived threat from Onside gave these networks new energy and focus. The Sector formed a new consortium and began to collaborate and communicate in new ways:

> For the first time in a long time we were all in the same room together – and with a common goal. From that we started to talk about being together even more. We brought in other members so that we could take some action. (Senior Youth Worker)

Discussions with the external representatives attempting to implement the Youth Zone left the Sector emboldened, and with a renewed sense of their own professionalism and collective value. This was partly in response to comments from the external representatives that were interpreted by some members of the local voluntary sector as attempts to 'belittle' them, e.g. by suggesting that there were significant potential funders that were beyond the access of smaller, local projects. The local representatives responded by simply asking: 'Why?'. A sense of renewed, collaborative purpose also emerged as they recognised for themselves the significance of their individual and combined contributions to the area:

> We are now working much better together. More as a collective of 'natural neighbours'. We recognise that we are all so unique, so different. (Senior Youth Worker)

With support from a regional charitable trust, relationships within the consortium have continued to strengthen. The power of their refreshed collective voice has begun to bear fruit beyond the decision by the local authority not to proceed with a Youth Zone:

> Some of us were chosen (by the consortium) to be representatives at a meeting about the Youth Investment Fund. When we brought the information back to the full consortium it took us no more than an hour to come up with a plan to decide how the money could be allocated between us. We're now working together as a collective. We've got three lead organisations and we've split the area into three so we can reflect local need. Because we've come together and trusted each other we've now been able to fund open-access youth work. ... I'm really excited about the future. I think we're going to become a force for good. (Senior Youth Worker)

Winners, Losers and Precariatisation

Competition, by its very nature creates winners and losers, and inherently promotes and legitimises inequality. The competitive organisational environment therefore mirrors and parallels the neoliberal entrepreneurialism that shapes perspectives on the nature *and causes* of disadvantage. The ideology of competition is reflected in the need for individuals to take responsibility for what are public and socio-structural issues. In this environment, it is individuals' 'lack of entrepreneurial spirit' or self-improvement, (their inability, or presumed unwillingness to acquire the requisite skills and attributes to survive in the competitive market), rather than structural inequalities, that are to blame for, precariatisation (Standing, 2016). These discourses of deficit and responsbilisation, which mirror popular assumptions, are increasingly reflected in targets and prescriptive outcomes.

Drawing on the British Social Attitudes Survey (2015), Volmert et al. (2016), outline how public perceptions of poverty are shaped by popular models that attribute poverty either to individuals' inadequate effort, poor motivation and choices, or to assumptions of shared community norms and values, such as 'cultures of worklessness'. The latter in particular underpins the trend to rebrand welfare recipients as 'scroungers', 'fakers' or 'shirkers' and to create groups of 'revolting subjects', in generating a 'disgust consensus' (Tyler, 2013: 23), in the production of objects of ridicule, whose 'human struggles become forms of entertainment' (Burnett, 2017: 217) – people who have to 'undergo a number of degrading rituals in their struggle to survive' (Bond & Hallsworth, 2017: 75).

The 2013 Church Action on Poverty report 'The Blame Game Must Stop' reveals how the Voluntary Sector is able to effectively counter such stigmatising discourses by enabling the voices of those who find themselves caught up in poverty to be heard. Such work encourages attention to be paid to published facts, and acts as a counter-discourse to inaccurate, yet popular and damaging myths. The report cites for example research that contrasts the difference between the actual amount of the welfare budget spent on benefits to unemployed people (3%) with the figure that people popularly think it to be (41%) (McCarron & Purcell, 2013).

Despite the multiple impacts of competition in terms of survival, partnership working and the pathologising of poverty as outlined above, alternative paths continue to be explored and implemented within the voluntary youth sector.

In an area of the North East of England that has been, like many others, severely impacted by austerity, local voluntary agencies, with the support of the local authority, have established a 'Youth Foundation'. In a brave attempt to collaborate their way through to a more promising future, and in the very best traditions of the Sector, the agencies involved have publicly committed themselves to the following expectations for the Foundation:

- Draw together grassroots services to be able to bid for larger funding, contracts, corporate sponsorship and philanthropic opportunities in a way that would be unfeasible for small independent organisations.
- Bring together the skills within the sector that already exist in an organised way to build capacity.
- Make the best use of the considerable resources already available through a 'venue bank'.
- Offer open membership.
- Support and develop the wider youth sector to limit the impact of funding reductions.
- Provide an 'equal voice for all' with an 'equal balance of power'.
- Provide an independent support network for fundraising to address issues around co-working and trust with no lead from a delivery agent to negate power imbalances in partnerships.
- Reduce duplication enabling more young people to access services and participate in bringing together a cross-section of providers.
- Provide a structure which gives a space for the voices of young people to be heard in terms of service needs and priorities (Wharton Trust).

This example of principled, local and determined action sits alongside the others in this chapter in demonstrating that where the voluntary youth sector is clear about its unique, democratic contribution – especially in relation to issues of voice and power – it is able to work alongside local communities in a way that is meaningful and purposeful whilst remaining congruent with its traditional, collaborative and non-competitive value base.

Conclusion

This chapter has exposed a number of the challenges facing the voluntary youth sector as it responds to the pervasive impact of more than thirty years of neoliberal cultures and regimes that persist in trying to shape the sector in the image and interests of the market.

This exposition has been undertaken not to further depress or disappoint those working in the Sector, but rather to inspire resistance by revealing how individuals and organisations have met challenges 'head-on' in ways that stand in bold contrast to the prevailing discourse and its associated practices:

> ..one of the tasks of the progressive educator through a serious correct political analysis is to unveil opportunities for hope whatever the obstacles may be. (Freire, 1992: 3)

There is tremendous pressure on the sector to submit to externalised control, commercialised governance; market-led evaluation and technocratic interpretations of what it means to be professional. In short, to help maintain a status quo that 'so conveniences those who presume power' (Bright, 2015: 246).

Yet, the examples provided reveal how some voluntary organisations are demonstrating that it remains possible to walk a different path. They retain values-led control of their own destiny, give young people genuine power at board level; enable young voices to determine the agenda for change; measure themselves against progress made towards a fairer society, and support staff in using their understanding to respond as professional, challenging and critical practitioners. They also maintain and celebrate the power of their independent status and voice:

> You have got to retain the ability to say "no". You only get this by acting collectively. (Project Worker)

The pressure on organisations to compete is equally invidious. Pressure to 'sell' themselves and their 'brand'; to mark other voluntary agencies as competitors rather than partners; to then 'beat' these same agencies to the money, regardless of the impact this will have on the diversity, coherence or relevance of local provision; to be silent and secret when tendering for contracts, and to collude with the prevailing 'disgust consensus' (Tyler, 2013, op. cit.) in order to secure work that serves to further stigmatise individuals and groups already pushed to the edges of society by ugly and inaccurate myths about their lives and motivations.

Yet not all organisations succumb to this pressure. Some are able to successfully advertise their distinctiveness in order to help create cohesive, 'hyper-local' networks of diverse provision that directly address inequality and injustice; to go 'deeper' rather than bigger; to promote transparency, trust and solidarity between sector partners when considering applying for funding; to collaborate in strengthening the power of their collective voice and to amplify the voices of those whose real stories need to be heard and believed.

There is some evidence to suggest that public attitudes towards the idea that the rules of commercial markets should apply to the public and voluntary sectors is beginning to shift, particularly as more large-scale 'contracted out' services collapse and fail under private sector management. At the same time, it is unrealistic to assume that significant change is just around the corner. Drawing on Mathieson (1980), Bamber and Murphy (1999) point out however that there remain dangers in some critical practitioners falling into damaging inertia traps: disempowered on the one hand by the absence of revolutionary change to external systems and processes, yet dismissive at the same time of the 'small gains in local situations' (Bamber & Murphy, 1999: 240) that can be made whilst working towards the abolition of oppressive conditions more generally.

It is precisely these 'small gains', these 'opportunities for hope' that this chapter has attempted to show can make a difference in resisting dominant, neoliberal discourses, and, which potentially point the way to future paths for the wider Sector that will enable it to collectively negotiate ways around the obstacles it faces.

Notes

1   Examples of this approach in action can be accessed via the "Investing in Children" website. See "Further Reading" at the end of this chapter.

2   A case study describing how social auditing can be used in the voluntary and community sector can be accessed via the SAA website. See "Further Reading" at the end of this chapter.

Further Reading

http://investinginchildren.weebly.com/our-work.html
http://www.socialauditnetwork.org.uk/files/1614/5251/1553/SAN_Case_Study_-_ASAN_FINAL.pdf

References

Bamber, J., & Murphy, H. (1999). Youth work: The possibilities for critical practice. *Journal of Youth Work Studies, 2*(2), 227–242.

Baring Foundation. (2016). *Independence in question; the voluntary sector in 2016.* Retrieved February 26, 2018, from http://baringfoundation.org.uk/wp-content/uploads/2016/03/Independence-in-question.pdf

Benson, A. (2014). *"The devil that has come amongst us" the impact of commissioning and procurement practice NCIA inquiry into the future of voluntary services* (Working Paper 6). Retrieved October 9, 2017, from http://www.independentaction.net/wp-content/uploads/sites/8/2014/06/Commissioning-and-procurement-final.pdf

Bond, E., & Hallsworth, S. (2017). The degradation and humiliation of young people. In V. Cooper & D. Whyte (Eds.), *The violence of austerity.* London: Pluto Press.

Bourdieu, P. (1992). *Language and symbolic power.* Cambridge, MA: Polity Press.

Bright, G. (2015). In search of soul. In G. Bright (Ed.), *Youth work histories policy and contexts.* London: Palgrave.

British Social Attitudes Survey. (2015). Retrieved April 12, 2018, from http://www.bsa.natcen.ac.uk/

Brown, W. (2015). *Undoing the demos: Neoliberalism's stealth revolution.* New York, NY: Zone Books.

Buchroth, I. (2012). Managing in the voluntary sector: The particular challenges of managerialism. In J. Ord (Ed.), *Critical issues in youth work management.* London: Routledge.

Buchroth, I., & Husband, M. (2015). Youth work in the voluntary sector. In G. Bright (Ed.), *Youth work histories policy and contexts.* London: Palgrave.

Bunyan, P., & Ord, J. (2012). The neo-liberal policy context. In J. Ord (Ed.), *Critical issues in youth work management.* London: Routledge.

Burnett, J. (2017). Austerity and the production of hate. In V. Cooper & D. Whyte (Eds.), *The violence of austerity.* London: Pluto Press.

Canella, G. S., & Lincoln, Y. S. (2015). Critical qualitative research in global neoliberalism – Foucault, inquiry and transformative possibilities. In N. K. Denzin & M. D. Giardina (Eds.), *Qualitative inquiry and the politics of research* (pp. 51–74). London: Routledge.

Civil Exchange. (2016). *Independence in question; the voluntary sector*. Retrieved February 26, 2018, from https://baringfoundation.org.uk/wp-content/uploads/2016/03/Independence-in-question.pdf

Clifford, D., & Backus, P. (2010). *Are big charities becoming increasingly dominant? Third Sector Research Centre (TSRC)* (Working Paper 38). Birmingham: TSRC.

Cooper, C. (2012). Imagining 'radical' youth work possibilities – Challenging the 'symbolic violence' within the mainstream tradition in contemporary state-led youth work practice in England. *Journal of Youth Studies, 15*(1), 53–71.

Davies, B. (2010). Policy analysis: The first and vital skill of practice. In J. Batsleer & B. Davies (Eds.), *What is youth work*. Exeter: Learning Matters.

Dean, J. (2015). Volunteering, the market, and neoliberalism. *People Place and Policy, 9*(2), 139–148. Retrieved December 27, 2017, from https://extra.shu.ac.uk/ppp-online/volunteering-the-market-and-neoliberalism/

Duffy, D. N. (2018). *Evaluation and governing in the 21st century: Disciplinary measures, transformative possibilities*. London: Palgrave Macmillan.

Foucault, M. (2008). *The birth of biopolitics: Lectures at the Colleges de France 1978–1979*. New York, NY: Palgrave Macmillan.

Freire, P. (1992). *Pedagogy of hope; Reliving pedagogy of the oppressed*. London: Continuum.

Grundy, S. (1987). *Curriculum: Product or praxis*. Lewis: Falmer.

Habermas, J. (1987). *Knowledge and human interests*. Oxford: Polity Press.

Habermas, J. (1992). *The theory of communicative action*. Boston, MA: Beacon Press.

Home Office. (1998). *Compact on relations between government and the voluntary and community sector in England*. Retrieved November 20, 2017, from http://www.compactvoice.org.uk/sites/default/files/compact_1998.pdf

Lloyds Bank Foundation. (2016). *Broken commissioning threatens survival of small charities* (Online news article). Retrieved December 27, 2017, from https://www.lloydsbankfoundation.org.uk/news/news/2016/12/07/commissioning-in-crisis-report/

Malone, D., & Okwonga, M. (2011). *The state of UK charity boards: A quantitative analysis*. London: Institute for Philanthropy.

Mathiesen, T. (1980). *Law, society and political action – Towards a strategy under late capitalism*. London: Academic Press.

McCarron, A., & Purcell, L. (2013). *The blame game must stop: Challenging the stigmatisation of people experiencing poverty*. Church Action on Poverty.

Murray, U. (2013, July 10–12). *The boundaries between the voluntary sector and neo-liberalism*. Paper presented to the 8th International Critical Management Conference: Extending the limits of neo-liberal capitalism, University of Manchester, Manchester. Retrieved December 27, 2017, from http://www.independentaction.net/wp-content/uploads/2013/09/Voluntary-Sector-Neo-Liberal-thinking-Ursula-Murray.pdf

National Youth Agency. (n.d.). *National occupational standards for youth work.* Retrieved April 15, 2018, from http://www.nya.org.uk/wp-content/uploads/2014/06/National-Occupation-Standards-for-Youth-Work.pdf

Nicholls, D. (2012). *For youth workers and youth work. Speaking out for a better future.* Bristol: Policy Press.

ONS (Office for National Statistics). (2015, May 21). Young people Not in Education, Employment or Training (NEET). *Statistical Bulletin.* Retrieved December 24, 2017, from https://www.ons.gov.uk/employmentandlabourmarket/peoplenotinwork/unemployment/bulletins/youngpeoplenotineducationemploymentortrainingneet/2015-05-21

Onside. (n.d.). Retrieved December 24, 2017, from http://www.onsideyouthzones.org/what-we-do/funding-a-youth-zone/

Pusey, M. (1987). *Jurgen Habermas.* London: Tavistock.

Rochester, C. (2014). *The impact of commissioning and contracting on volunteers and volunteering in voluntary services groups* (Working Paper 8).

Scott, D., & Russell, L. (2001). Contracting: The experience of service delivery agencies. In H. Harris & C. Rochester (Eds.), *Voluntary organisations and policy in Britain: Perspective on change and choice* (pp. 49–63). Basingstoke: Palgrave.

Slocock, C. (2016). *Independence in question: The voluntary sector in 2016.* Retrieved November 30, 2017, from http://baringfoundation.org.uk/blog/independence-in-question-the-voluntary-sector-in-2016/

Smith, M. K. (1994). *Local education: Community, conversation, praxis.* Buckingham: Open University Press.

Social Audit Network. (n.d.). Retrieved January 14, 2018, from http://www.socialauditnetwork.org.uk/

Standing, G. (2016). *The precariat: The new dangerous class.* London: Bloomsbury Academic.

TAG (The Professional Association of Lecturers in Community and Youth Work). (2017). Email consultation from the national youth agency on proposed apprenticeship standards for youth work. *Members Bulletin Issue 8: 2017–2018* (Unpublished).

Tyler, I. (2013). *Revolting subjects, social abjection and resistance in neo-liberal Britain.* London: Zed Books.

Tyler, M. (2009). Managing the tensions. In J. Wood & J. Hine (Eds.), *Working with young people, theory and policy for practice.* London: Sage Publications.

Volmert, A., Pineau, M., & Kendall-Taylor, N. (2016). *Talking about poverty: How experts and the public understand UK poverty.* Washington, DC: Joseph Rowntree Foundation/FrameWorks Institute, The National Children's Bureau.

Wharton Trust. (n.d.). *Hartlepool Young People's Foundation (HYPF) briefing.* Retrieved January 14, 2018, from http://www.whartontrust.org.uk/docs/HYPFCEOBriefing.pdf

CHAPTER 9

Where Is Faith-Based Youth Work Heading?

Naomi Thompson

Introduction

Since the global financial crash of the early twenty-first century, youth and community work has seen a decrease in funding alongside an increase in need. The effect of the dominantly right-wing response to the fiscal crisis on Western economies has seen both a reduction in state funding for work with young people and communities, as well as a decrease in resources and increase in burden on the charities sector. This has severely impacted on youth work, both in contexts where state funding was previously available, and in other contexts where the provision of services for young people relies solely on the voluntary, community and charities sectors.

The years of austerity politics that have followed the financial crisis in the UK have led to severe cuts to state-funded youth work with budgets no longer ring-fenced at national level, and youth services set to be the first public service to completely disappear (Jeffs, 2015). Much youth work has been commissioned out with lower budgets and/or taken on by the struggling charities sector. Possibly the most consistently funded youth work over recent years has been that undertaken by faith groups. Whilst these faith groups have often operated rather separately from secular youth work providers (and even from each other), it is argued that times of challenge also bring opportunities for creative practice (Coburn & Gormally, 2017).

As funding for youth services has declined over recent years in the UK, there has been an increase in partnerships between secular and faith-based providers. These partnerships take various forms including faith-based projects employing non-religious staff or volunteers, local authorities or other funders commissioning work out to faith-based providers, as well as a range of more mutually negotiated, equal partnerships between secular and faith-based providers. Whilst statutory and other secular youth services have been subject to a neoliberal 'targets and outcomes' culture over recent decades, faith-based youth work has largely avoided this (Jeffs, 2015).

This chapter explores what the future of faith-based youth work might look like. In particular, it considers the recent growth in partnership working between faith-based and secular youth work, and the need for this to continue

© KONINKLIJKE BRILL NV, LEIDEN, 2019 | DOI:10.1163/9789004396555_009

as public services face an uncertain future. It examines how these partnerships increase the capacity for faith-based youth work to contribute to civil society and continue to grow in prominence as a key player in the provision of youth and community services. It also identifies the increasing challenges presented to faith-based youth work by the right-wing ideologies that have gained in prominence in the UK and beyond. These include not just the austerity agenda but also a discourse of surveillance and suspicion. In the UK, this is seen particularly through recent counter-extremism legislation and calls for faith-based youth work providers to be registered, monitored and inspected (Home Office, 2015). Such ideologies of suspicion and surveillance have gained a platform on a global level, perhaps most clearly illustrated by the movements which drove the Brexit vote and the election of Donald Trump as President of the USA. This backdrop of suspicion makes the increase in partnership working all the more pertinent and crucial in breaking down misunderstandings.

The discussion in this chapter draws on research conducted with 15 youth workers involved in partnership working between Christian and secular organisations. The research brings out the positive and negative experiences of the youth workers and the shared values held between the partners. Whilst this research focused on Christian-secular partnerships in the UK, the discussion connects the findings to some wider contexts, albeit to a limited extent.

The chapter concludes that the future of faith-based youth work is in the continuation and expansion of such partnerships between the secular and faith-based sectors. These partnerships have a clear role to play in plugging gaps in provision and enabling workers and organisations to support each other in a climate where they are stretched and under-resourced. The discussion draws on the concept of 'progressive localism' (Featherstone et al., 2011) to argue that these partnerships need to go further to form an active resistance to right-wing ideologies. Both secular and faith-based youth work contain strands and traditions of radical practice that have a role to play in actively and collaboratively resisting neoliberal culture, and standing up for those who are most affected by growing inequalities (de St Croix, 2010; Pimlott, 2015a).

What Do We Mean by Faith-Based Youth Work?

There have been debates within faith-based youth work as to what actually constitutes *youth work* and whether more confessional or proselytising forms of practice fit the definition. In Christian youth work, this has manifested in a debate as to what is youth work and what is youth ministry (Thompson, 2017). Whilst Brierley (2003) suggests that youth ministry is a specialist branch of youth work that focuses on Christian faith transmission, Collins-Mayo et al. (2010) distinguish clearly between them as practices with different values and philosophies. Similarly, in Muslim youth work, Hamid (2006) distinguishes between Muslim youth work and Islamic youth work with the former focusing on social education and the latter on teaching Islam. For the purposes of this chapter, an interpretation of faith-based youth *work* in its non-confessional form is adopted. Thus, this chapter is not concerned with those forms of youth *ministry* which are focused primarily on faith transmission or that emerge as evangelical or proselytising endeavours directed at non-adherents. Instead, the focus is on the forms of faith-based youth work centrally concerned with engaging with civil society, promoting human flourishing and pursuing the common good, which draw from the well of accepted youth work values, of which there are many manifestations within the faith sector (Bright et al., 2018; Jeffs, 2015; Pimlott, 2015a, 2015b).

Right-Wing Politics and Rolling Back State Provision

Recent years have seen a rise in extreme right politics in various countries. For example, both Brexit and President Trump have emerged from the same right-wing values and rhetoric. This is a political rhetoric that creates divisions and discourages state 'hand-outs'. In the US and the UK, a significant rolling back of the state is underway. This is being implemented in a systematic dismantling of state provision that will not be easily reversed. We can see this through health-care systems where significant structural changes, such as the attempts to abolish 'Obamacare' in the US and the restructuring of the NHS to allow more contracts to profit-making providers in the UK, are reforming both the systems and structures themselves, as well as the values and cultures that underpin them. However, growing inequality in these contexts is not just a by-product of right-wing austerity, it is a direct outcome of right-wing policy discourses of 'othering' (see, for example, Pihlaja & Thompson, 2017, on how policy exacerbates the exclusion of young Muslims). Both the Brexit and Trump campaigns catalysed and drew on far-right rhetoric that created division and fear between groups of people, and was, at times, explicitly racist. At an institutional level, forms of civic religion (particularly within Christianity) have been drawn on to support these campaigns. Yet, faith groups are also involved in the resisting these, as some of the examples in this chapter demonstrate.

Youth work has never had a statutory footing in the US although there is a well-developed youth development and after-school sector, and, to an extent, a shared academic body of literature with the UK. Recent years have seen discussions of professionalisation and standardised competency frameworks for youth work in the US, but these have, as yet, not emerged, and any hopes for increased state sponsorship for such work seem to be waning. Whilst some of the well-established national organisations delivering youth work are faith-based (see, for example, Young Life and the YMCA movement), there is a history of separation of secular and faith-based practice in both the USA and the UK (Bright et al., 2018; Thompson, 2017).

In the UK, statutory youth services have been closed down in some localities, stripped back to the bare bones in others, and have all but disappeared. The non-statutory UK youth work sector spans small and large charities and organisations, with the emergence of social enterprises and even some entirely private profit-making businesses in recent years. Faith-based providers are one of various stakeholders in the current landscape, and arguably one of the least precarious. Since the early twenty-first century, faith groups have been reported as holding the largest share of youth work provision, even before statutory decline (Brierley, 2003; Green, 2006; Stanton, 2013).

Over recent years, UK youth work theorists, Mark K. Smith and Tony Jeffs appear to have shown little sympathy for the decline of the statutory sector, and, have even at times championed what they perceive to be the thriving faith-based sector (see for example, Smith, 2015; Jeffs, 2015). In fact, Jeffs and Smith predicted as early as the 1980s that youth work's professionalised 'local authority' era in the UK would come to an end (see Jeffs, 1982; Jeffs & Smith, 1987, 1990, 1993, 2006; Jeffs & Spence, 2008). However, they also recognise that this does not mean the end of grassroots youth work, largely because youth work is alive and well in the faith-based sector, particularly in Christian practice (Smith, 2015; Jeffs, 2015). Jeffs, in particular, states that 'whenever discussion of "a youth work crisis" occurs it is important to recall the "crisis" relates almost exclusively to secular units' (Jeffs, 2015: 11). He frames the distinction between secular and faith-based youth work in relation to the presence of shared values:

> Secular and statutory youth work clearly has much to learn from both the faith-based and uniformed sectors ... Faith-based youth work is doing so much better, by comparison, primarily because it operates according to a set of shared internal beliefs – educational and spiritual. Beliefs that mean it has ambitions both for itself and those it seeks to serve. By way of comparison one encounters only a void at the heart of secular and statutory funded youth work. (Jeffs, 2015: 14)

Jeffs' analysis of the decline of secular youth work is largely related to its distortion by the neoliberal culture of recent decades with its emphasis on targets and outcomes in youth work. He suggests national voluntary sector organisations have been 'hollowed out' in the same way as state-funded organisations:

> Frankly the latter now needs a reason to exist; a justification over and above a self-serving wish to pay their wage-bills. Until better reasons to flourish are articulated the national organisations will continue to 'hollow-out' and clubs and units carry on vanishing. Not least because individuals will not freely give of their time to 'dance to the tune of others' nor will young people in any number seek to affiliate to organisations that ultimately only need them to meet targets and secure funding. (Jeffs, 2015: 14)

This is a view supported by the *In Defence of Youth Work* campaign in the UK, which was formed in 2009 before austerity kicked in, in critique of the increasing prevalence of market values in youth work (IDYW, 2009).

Plugging the Gaps?

The faith-based and secular youth work sectors have typically been very separate from each other. However, the faith-based sector has regained prominence in the field over recent decades. This is due to a combination of factors including cutbacks to secular services, alongside relative stability in the faith-based sector, as well as some youth workers actively bridging the divide to form secular-faith partnerships. Separation between the sectors has arguably been exacerbated by mutual suspicion from both sides, although suspicion of faith-based youth work by the wider field has been more widely reported (Clayton & Stanton, 2008; Hart, 2016). Anecdotally, at the national level in the UK, it is possible to find both recent examples of separation and of reaching out. For example, the former National Council for Voluntary Youth Services (NCVYS) did not appear to make any significant attempt to include the faith-based sector in its networks. The *In Defence of Youth Work* campaign however made bringing together the secular and faith-based sectors the theme of its 2015 national conference, recognising a shared resistance to neoliberalism. The largest part of the UK faith sector is Christian (indeed, it is the largest youth work sector overall); they have largely tended to organise their own conferences and training programmes even while laying claim to youth work standards and frameworks developed in the wider field.

Whilst it could be tempting in a dominantly secular text to simply consider the role of faith groups in plugging gaps left by the state and other cutbacks to youth work provision, it is instead important to emphasise that faith-based youth work has a long history that precedes state and secular funding:

The origins of faith-based youth work, and indeed youth work more generally, lie in the Sunday School movements of the UK and America and in
Jewish youth work, which were developed as lay movements in response
to social need (Jeffs & Spence, 2011; Lynn & Wright, 1971; Pimlott, 2015b;
Stanton, 2011). The largest sector of the UK youth work field (Brierley, 2003;
Green, 2006; Stanton, 2013), and a significant player in community-based
provision in other contexts such as Australia and the USA, faith-based practice has had an influential role in youth work's history and development ...
it remains important to recognise its significance across time and place,
rather than as a 'poor relation' to the wider field. (Bright et al., 2018: 198)

In the UK in the late 1700s and in the US in the early 1800s, the early Sunday
Schools emerged before any form of statutory education existed to teach young
people to read and write on their only day off from work (Thompson, 2017).
The national voluntary sector network, UK Youth (previously the National
Association of Girls' Clubs) was borne, in part, out of the Jewish Girls' Work
movement in the UK (Jeffs & Spence, 2011). As such, faith-based youth work
existed long before the welfare state in the UK and did not emerge in response
to its decline. Arguably though, much faith-based youth work may have developed in recognition of state absence, particularly in the international context
where state-sponsored youth work is a rarity.

Faith-based practice has arguably played a role in both colluding with and
challenging the austerity agenda in the UK. When the Church of England
was reported to be receiving £5m of 'Big Society' funding, the National Secular Society accused them of 'colluding in the destruction of the welfare state'
(National Secular Society, 2010). By contrast, faith-based organisations such
as The Trussell Trust have both provided for those affected by welfare reform
and challenged the political discourse underpinning it (The Trussell Trust,
2017). At the local level, faith-based organisations have continued to provide
services for their local communities, and many children and young people
in the UK will have, for example, attended some form of activity in a church
hall; whether play groups, after-school clubs, holiday clubs, youth clubs, or
uniformed groups. These local services are not new initiatives developed in
times of austerity, but have long existed as part of children's and youth provision in local communities. Such forms of faith-based provision have, however,
potentially become more visible, particularly where faith-based and secular
partnerships have emerged, whether through contracts from local authorities
looking to commission out services previously delivered in-house, or as part of
local partnerships looking to provide joined-up services in areas where other
provision has declined or ceased.

Progressive Localism – The Way Forward?

It is through collaborative partnerships, rather than through relying on one benevolent, paternal funder, that the youth work sector is likely to sustain itself in any of the world's economies. The austerity climate might even be a catalyst for such work in some contexts. In the UK, austerity has been tied up in policy discourses that emphasise communities sustaining themselves through the mantras of 'Big Society' and 'Localism' introduced under David Cameron's Coalition Government (2010–2015). Its youth statement, Positive for Youth (2011) draws on these philosophies of rolling back the state, and local and community organisations sustaining what was previously protected through statutory funding.

It was in this climate of austerity, localism and of state residualism, that Featherstone et al. (2011) introduced the concept of 'progressive localism' as a possible way forward. It is worth emphasising here that David Featherstone and his colleagues are deeply critical of 'austerity localism' and frame it as the latest implementation of a form of politically driven neoliberalism that imposes market values on public services in order to justify the reduction of welfare provision. As such, 'progressive localism' is not a collusion with neoliberalism (as in the receipt of 'Big Society' funding to simply replace what was previously state-provided but with less money), but involves active resistance to it (as in the campaigning against the damaging effects of the erosion of welfare). Featherstone et al.'s (2011) 'progressive localism' is politically active rather than politically compliant; it opposes austerity and resists neoliberalism.

Arguably, therefore, forming genuinely collaborative partnerships in a marketized culture of competitiveness could subvert neoliberal values. However, for organisations committed to social justice, there is a need to go beyond simply resisting the values of the market to explicitly challenge the division and inequality created by right-wing discourses of austerity and fear. A recent example of such a manifestation of radical 'progressive localism' can be seen in the response to the Grenfell Tower fire in London in 2017. The fire in a social housing apartment block caused at least 70 deaths (although at the time of writing the exact number remains unconfirmed) and made many more people homeless. In response, local community organisations including mosques and churches came together, to provide shelter and food, and to act as donation centres. The response has also included locally-led campaigns to raise awareness of the inadequacy and unsafe nature of the housing being provided for Britain's poorest. The Christian-founded Trussell Trust is another UK example of 'progressive localism'; it partners with local organisations including churches and other community buildings to house and staff food banks. Alongside this local provision, it campaigns against austerity and poverty, raising awareness of poverty and hunger at local and national levels.

Models of Partnership

The different forms of partnership that emerge to support local youth work appear to have varying levels of potential to achieve the aim of 'progressive localism'. The primary qualitative research outlined below took place with 15 youth workers working in Christian-secular partnerships of some form. The discussion explores the various models of partnership as well as the values and tensions that emerge from the youth workers' experiences. Of the 15 youth workers who shared their experiences of partnership working, all but one were the Christian partner; therefore, the narratives explored below represent primarily the perspectives of the Christian youth workers in such partnerships. Three dominant models of partnership emerged from the research:

Model 1: Christian organisations employing non-Christian staff and volunteers

One of the forms of partnership that emerged was where the church or Christian organisation employed non-Christian staff or volunteers. This was most prevalent in relation to the employment of non-Christian volunteers to help out with church-based youth work where there was a shortage of willing volunteers from within the congregation. However, some examples of purposefully employing staff or volunteers from wider backgrounds also exist. One youth worker running a youth club in a cathedral explained how he employed volunteers from among the older young people most of whom were not Christians themselves: "I run a nominally Christian youth group for the Cathedral, but I have very few Christian volunteers. Most of the volunteers are young people themselves and have little or no church background". This youth worker saw this as part of an empowering and grassroots practice where volunteers emerge from within the existing community rather than being recruited into it. As many of the volunteers were older young people nurtured through the youth group, he viewed it as a key facet of his practice. He felt that it facilitated an 'ethos of inclusivity' within the church stating that: "The fact that our volunteers are mostly not Christian sends a message about inclusivity and acceptance to the young people. We are a church, but all are welcome, and invited to contribute". On a practical level, this youth worker also explained that it meant he was able to employ volunteers based on their ability to engage with young people, rather than simply their 'creedal agreement'.

Model 2: Secular funding commissioned to Christian providers

Another dominant model of partnership between the Christian and secular sectors involves churches or Christian organisations receiving funding from local authorities or other secular commissioners to deliver youth work provision in a local area. In the youth workers' experiences, these partnerships were, in some cases, based on collaborative relationships with the funder. However, in others, it was felt that no real relationship existed between the partners:

> The project simply received funding from the local authority. Records were kept to show how much work was taking place and occasionally there would be a monitoring visit. Other than fulfilling their contractual obligation with the local authority there really wasn't much in terms of collaboration.

It is arguable that in contractual relationships with 'the state' such as this one, that it is particularly difficult to actively challenge neoliberal agendas, and that these forms of partnership might even be interpreted as colluding with politically-driven austerity localism, however well-intentioned the workers. The youth workers recognised some of the challenges that receiving secular funding threw up, such as their work feeling disjointed, or having to adapt it to the changing priorities of the funder.

There were examples where the receipt of such funding was based on more collaborative principles. One youth worker explained how an ongoing relationship of trust had been built with the local council through the church's delivery of community-based youth work for several years before receiving funding to do so. He stated: "The local councils were brave enough to "hire" a church to run their youth provision despite a number of reservations. I was told by one councillor that "despite all the God stuff, the church has earned our respect". In such examples where trust and respect has been built over time, there is more potential for faith-based partners to resist neoliberal cultures and to shape the work around more holistic values than those of the market. The same youth worker stated that: "We were also able to do it in our own way – avoiding any pre-defined outcomes such as targets or accreditation". This suggests there is potential through such partnerships to resist the neoliberal 'targets and outcomes' culture that has been imposed on youth work in recent decades.

Model 3: Equal partnerships

The most positively discussed model of joint working was that based on equal partnerships between Christian and secular organisations. These partnerships were motivated by a shared desire for social justice, and to engage with, and respond to the needs of the local community. The forms of work delivered through these partnerships were varied and included youth clubs, youth forums, detached youth work, schools work, drop-in sessions and advice, guidance and support services for young people. One youth worker explained how local youth workers had formed a collaborative network to ensure they were working together in meeting the needs of their community. In this case, the network was formed and led by the church-employed youth worker:

> We run a local activity network of all local interested groups in providing positive activities for children, young people and families. We meet every six weeks, give updates on work, identify gaps in provision, and then collaborate to fill those gaps. Sometimes this includes fundraising, sometimes just creative working. It has led to holiday clubs, lunch clubs, trips, residentials, play days and targeted work. For example, we realised that at Halloween there was often a spike in anti-social behaviour, so we collaborated between four agencies and took twenty of the most likely offenders away for the night. This was a great trip, and it reduced anti-social behaviour on the estate at home.

By collaborating to fund and deliver their work, rather than compete against each other, partnerships such as these go some way to resisting neoliberal culture. However, it isn't clear how far they go beyond 'filling gaps' to actively resist or campaign against austerity in the ways suggested by 'progressive localism'.

Shared Values – Towards the Common Good

The youth workers in the study identified a number of shared values they had in common with their partners. These included: believing in young people; contributing to their wellbeing; having fun; providing safe spaces; offering support; respecting young people and each other; working together; and building community. A unique feature of the partnerships was that collaboration between secular and faith-based providers allows for a holistic understanding of young people's wellbeing that includes their spiritual development. The only non-Christian youth worker in the sample related a positive experience of working with Christian youth workers, suggesting that the work was richer for their input and expertise:

> From a secular point of view, the Church has never asked that we make religion a part of our provision. Young people have naturally brought

discussions about their faith to us and we have had the resources to discuss and answer. The Church workers have never been worried about discussing other faiths and have always approached the topic with honesty and respect.

The youth workers also felt that working in partnership meant that the local offer available to young people was enhanced and the overall quality of youth work in the area improved:

Doing things together builds relationships between partners. This then improves collaboration, shared values, referrals between projects, joined-up working ... Working together creates additional capacity, avoids duplicating things, and means that resources go further. It also stops people feeling isolated, and it puts a check on whether other people think your work is helpful ... Working together eventually builds a better place for everyone. That's what I hope anyway.

This understanding of working together to build 'a better place for everyone' goes beyond simply plugging gaps in provision to a shared pursuit of the common good. The youth workers also understood the partnerships as having a role in reducing divisions between people, particularly through bringing both youth workers and young people from different backgrounds together:

We ran a residential for young people from all over the district. This meant that while I was able to support other youth workers, funded by the parish councils, I was also able to take young people from the church along. While there, they got the opportunity to work with and get to know other young people from all over the area. This opportunity wouldn't have come about had I not been a part of the secular team as well.

This suggests that such partnerships may, implicitly at least, be challenging right-wing discourses of division and fear, and subverting neoliberalism by resisting the 'targets and outcomes' culture. However, explicit examples of partnerships being used to actively resist or campaign against poverty, austerity and inequality did not emerge in the narratives of the youth workers involved with the research. There were, however, signs of and clear potential for 'progressive localism' to be catalysed through these partnerships, and in the values the youth workers professed to underpin them.

Partnerships in Tension

The youth workers' experiences of partnership working were largely positive. When directly asked about tensions, however, some did emerge. The
most common issue that respondents identified as causing some tension
was where suspicion existed between partners. Significantly though, several
of the youth workers reported that suspicion is reduced and understanding
increased by the process of working together and building relationships with
each other.

There were some examples of negative experiences that related to bad practice on the part of both the Christian and secular partners in certain situations.
One Christian youth worker expressed his discomfort at the way his former
employing organisation had misled funders about the work they were delivering, describing them as "two-faced":

> Privately the Christian [organisation] was vehemently evangelical in its
> outlook. It would only employ Christian youth workers. There was a clear
> agenda of wanting to evangelise to the young people. However, this was
> never articulated in the contractual agreement to deliver open access
> youth work on behalf of the local authority.

Other tensions emerged where one partner felt exploited by the other. One
Christian youth worker said he felt his organisation was 'used' by the secular
partner:

> We enabled them to hit all their funders' targets, because we had done
> the hard graft of building the relationships, whilst they had more fund-
> ing, were better paid and would not have succeeded without us, but this
> was not reflected in any contribution to our costs.

It was also stated that the vision of the work could be compromised by working together or receiving funding from secular partners, perhaps reflecting the
imposition of neoliberal values on state-funded youth work:

> Our vision and our ability to change and react to circumstances has
> felt very restricted by the money. Because they want a certain style
> and amount of work, we weren't always free to use our time and
> resources to best help the young people. This is partly because our
> understanding of helping young people does not necessarily line up
> with the Council's.

It should be noted here, that for the Christian youth workers, it was not always the secular partner that they were in tension with in such cases. The church-employed youth workers also reported that it was sometimes the church that created tensions when a youth worker attempted to work with external partners, where the wider church did not share the vision or see value in such work.

The youth workers' experiences of partnership working were generally positive, and they could all identify shared values between the Christian and secular partners in the overall pursuit of the common good. However, a key tension that appeared to exist in some of the partnerships is whether there was shared agreement, implicit or explicit, on whether they were resisting or complying with neoliberalism and austerity politics. Where partnerships were focused primarily on funding or on meeting targets, it could be suggested that the ability for either partner to be actively resistant to neoliberalism was greatly inhibited.

Wider Contexts

The primary research discussed in this chapter is limited to a small sample of youth workers engaged in Christian-secular partnerships in the UK. There are clearly many more contexts in which faith-based youth workers from various traditions and in various countries actively contribute to civil society through their work with young people. Whilst there is not space here to give recognition to them all, it is worth identifying some recent examples.

Recent UK research (Bright et al., 2018; Thompson et al., forthcoming) outlines the experiences of youth workers from various faith groups who are engaging with their wider communities and resisting the right-wing discourses of division and austerity, both implicitly and explicitly. One of their research participants, for example, was a Sikh youth work volunteer who established a youth led committee in his Gurdwara in Scotland. He was also working both within his local community, and bringing them into the Gurdwara to foster inclusion and understanding between Sikh and non-Sikh community members. Bright et al. also interviewed a Christian youth worker and Muslim youth worker both working for the same Christian-run project that encourages inter-faith dialogue between young people, demonstrating a purposeful example of partnership in a faith-based organisation employing people not from the particular faith tradition in order to foster inclusivity. Also encouraging inter-faith dialogue, a Jewish youth worker in the research was fostering conversations with Muslim young people, and the leader of a Muslim Scout group was working in partnership with local Sikh and Christian Scout groups to run joint events, and visit each other's places of worship.

In his research with young British Sikhs, Singh (2015) found that these young people were keen to engage with their wider communities and joined in with local community efforts including the responses to the major floods in the south of England in 2014. Young Sikhs were also involved in langar, which is the sharing of food that typically takes place in the Gurdwara. In recent years, the number of non-Sikhs attending Gurdwaras to share langar has grown significantly, and they have become an active movement in feeding the homeless. Singh outlines how this is happening on a global level, with the UK's 250 Gurdwaras alone serving an estimated 5000 meals to non-Sikhs each week. Singh also identifies how some young Sikhs have been involved in taking langar out of the Gurdwara into their wider communities to operate as food banks feeding those living in poverty. He identifies examples of this in the UK, Canada, and the USA.

There are however very real challenges to fostering these forms of practice. The neoliberal climate often pits different groups against each other in competing for funding, establishing who owns certain 'outcomes' and identifying whose work is having most impact or 'return'. Alongside this, divisive policy such as counter-extremism legislation exacerbates tensions between different groups. Khan (2013) outlines how the Preventing Violent Extremism legislation in the UK creates suspicion and stigma and isolates Muslim young people and communities in particular. This climate of suspicion and fear also impacts on other groups. Recent media reporting in the UK, Canada and elsewhere suggests Sikh communities have faced a similar backlash to Muslim groups. Inspection and monitoring of all faith-based providers working with children and young people is promised by the UK's Counter-extremism Strategy (Home Office, 2015). These tensions, however, only make partnerships and shared understandings more crucial to subverting the climate of fear, fostering dialogue and understanding, and breaking down divisions. In this regard, faith-based youth work has a distinct role to play in engaging with civil society, working towards the common good and challenging inequalities (Pimlott, 2015a, 2015b).

Conclusion

Faith-based youth work has a long history of contributing to civil society, and recent years have seen an increase in faith groups working in partnership with other stakeholders in the pursuit of the common good (Pimlott, 2015b). Featherstone et al.'s (2011) concept of 'progressive localism' offers a useful framework for understanding the potential of such partnerships to resist inequality and effect change. It is a concept that fits most closely with the examples of the more mutually negotiated, equal partnerships explored here, that go some way to subverting neoliberalism by prioritising collaboration over competition. The potential impact of such progressive partnerships lies in how far they move beyond a passive plugging of gaps in provision, towards an active resistance and subversion of neoliberal culture.

Although the Christian youth workers in the study explored here were perhaps less focused on outcomes and targets than their secular partners, they did, at times, speak the language of neoliberalism when discussing their partnership work. They recognised where partners were "more interested in profile, money, targets, etcetera" and how they contribute to this. There was a sense among some of the Christian youth workers of being used for such outcomes at times. However, when discussing the shared values of the work, they did not draw on bureaucratic or neoliberal language such as 'funders' targets', but on positive, asset-focused ideas and concepts that fit with the idea of working for the common good, such as 'believing in young people' and 'creating community'.

These partnerships are, arguably, the future of progressive faith-based youth work that engages civil society and supports the wider youth work sector. Moving into the future, more integrated models of training and practice would support the development of these progressive partnerships as a mainstream approach to youth work. This is a new and innovative area of practice that has real potential to develop into a framework for a more integrated approach to youth work where colleagues from different traditions and backgrounds can support each other, break down division and intolerance and work holistically with diverse groups of young people. Secular and faith-based youth workers have historically worked and trained separately, with even inter-faith work not engaging with non-religious partners.

As such partnerships continue to increase, they need to develop an ongoing resilience to the neoliberal climate which often encourages competitiveness over collaboration. They need to foster genuine collaboration, mutual support and the pursuit of shared values for the good of young people. This was present in the youth workers' narratives in this research through their identification of shared values such as working together and building community. Youth work has a history of political and radical practice, both in the secular and faith-based sectors (de St Croix, 2010; Pimlott, 2015a). As such, albeit not without tensions, these progressive partnerships have the potential to move into the future as active agents in the subversion of neoliberalism, the championing of social justice, and in the fight against growing inequality.

Acknowledgement

The primary research data outlined in this chapter was originally used in a shorter article entitled 'The friends you never call' published in the Christian youth work magazine, *Youthwork,* in April 2016.

References

Brierley, D. (2003). *Joined up: An introduction to youthwork and ministry.* Carlisle: Spring Harvest Publishing/Authentic Lifestyle.

Bright, G., Thompson, N., Hart, P., & Hayden, B. (2018). Faith-based youth work: Education, engagement and ethics. In P. Alldred, F. Cullen, K. Edwards, & D. Fusco (Eds.), *The Sage handbook of youth work practice.* London: Sage Publications.

Clayton, M.-A., & Stanton, N. (2008). The changing world's view of Christian youthwork. *Youth & Policy, 100,* 109–128.

Coburn, A., & Gormally, S. (2017). Beyond brexit: The impact of leaving the EU on the youth work sector. *Youth and Policy.* Retrieved from http://www.youthandpolicy.org/articles/beyond-brexit-the-impact-of-leaving-the-eu-on-the-youth-work-sector/

Collins-Mayo, S., Mayo, B., Nash, S., & Cocksworth, C. (2010). *The faith of generation Y.* London: Church House Publishing.

de St Croix, T. (2010). Taking sides: Dilemmas and possibilities for radical youth work. In B. Belton (Ed.), *Radical youth work.* Lyme Regis: Russell House.

Featherstone, D., Ince, A., MacKinnon, D., Strauss, K., & Cumbers, A. (2011). Progressive localism and the construction of political alternatives. *Transactions of the Institute of British Geographers, 37,* 177–182.

Green, M. (2006). *A journey of discovery: Spirituality and spiritual development in youth work.* Leicester: The National Youth Agency.

Hamid, S. (2006). Models of Muslim youthwork: Between reform and empowerment. *Youth and Policy, 92,* 81–89.

Hart, P. (2016). Attitudes towards working 'out-of-hours' with young people: Christian and secular perspectives. *Youth and Policy, 115,* 43–62.

HM Government. (2011). *Positive for youth.* London: Crown copyright.

Home Office. (2015). *Counter-extremism strategy.* London: Crown copyright.

In Defence of Youth Work. (2009). *The open letter.* Retrieved from https://indefenceofyouthwork.com/the-in-defence-of-youth-work-letter-2/

Jeffs, T. (1982). Youth and community service and the cuts. *Youth and Policy, 1,* 19–27.

Jeffs, T. (2015). What sort of future? In N. Stanton (Ed.), *Innovation in youth work.* London: YMCA George Williams College.

Jeffs, T., & Smith, M. K. (1987). What future for initial training? *Youth and Policy, 20,* 7–14.

Jeffs, T., & Smith, M. K. (1990). Youth work, youth service and the next few years. *Youth and Policy, 31*, 21–29.

Jeffs, T., & Smith, M. K. (1993). Getting the job done: Training for youth work – Past, present and future. *Youth and Policy, 40*, 10–32.

Jeffs, T., & Smith, M. K. (2006). Where is youth matters taking us? *Youth and Policy, 91*, 23–40.

Jeffs, T., & Spence, J. (2008). Farewell to all that? The uncertain future of youth and community work education. *Youth and Policy, 97/98*, 135–166.

Jeffs, T., & Spence, J. (2011). The development of youth work with girls and young women in the nineteenth century. In R. Gilchrist, T. Hodgson, T. Jeffs, J. Spence, N. Stanton, & J. Walker (Eds.), *Reflecting on the past: Essays in the history of youth and community work*. Lyme Regis: Russell House.

Khan, M. G. (2013). *Young Muslims, pedagogy and Islam*. Bristol: Policy Press.

Lynn, R. W., & Wright, E. (1971). *The big little school: Two hundred years of the sunday school*. New York, NY: Harper and Row.

National Secular Society. (2010). *Church of England gets £5 million government hand-out for 'Big Society' promotion*. Retrieved August 6, 2010, from http://www.secularism.org.uk/church-of-england-gets-gbp5-mill.html

Pihlaja, S., & Thompson, N. (2017). *Young Muslims and exclusion – Experiences of 'othering'*. Retrieved from http://www.youthandpolicy.org/articles/young-muslims-and-exclusion/

Pimlott, N. (2015a). *Embracing the passion: Christian youth work and politics*. Birmingham: FYT.

Pimlott, N. (2015b). Faith-based youth work and civil society. In M. K. Smith, N. Stanton, & T. Wylie (Eds.), *Youth work and faith: Debates, delights and dilemmas*. Lyme Regis: Russell House Publishing.

Singh, J. (2015, July 22). From the temple to the street: How Sikh kitchens are becoming the new foodbanks. *The Conversation*. Retrieved from https://theconversation.com/from-the-temple-to-the-street-how-sikh-kitchens-are-becoming-the-new-food-banks-44611

Smith, M. K. (2015, February 6). Presentation to YRESEARCH Conference, YMCA George Williams College, London.

Stanton, N. (2011). From raikes' revolution to rigid institution: Sunday schools in twentieth century England. In R. Gilchrist, T. Hodgson, T. Jeffs, J. Spence, N. Stanton, & J. Walker (Eds.), *Reflecting on the past: Essays in the history of youth and community work*. Lyme Regis: Russell House Publishing.

Stanton, N. (2013). Faith-based Youth Work – Lessons from the Christian sector. In S. Curran, R. Harrison, & D. Mackinnon (Eds.), *Working with young people* (2nd ed.). London: Sage Publications.

The Trussell Trust. (2017). *Research and advocacy*. Retrieved from
　https://www.trusselltrust.org/what-we-do/research-advocacy/

Thompson, N. (2016, April). The friends you never call. *Youthwork*. Retrieved from
　https://www.youthandchildrens.work/Youthwork-past-issues/2016/April-2016/
　The-friends-you-never-call

Thompson, N. (2017). *Young people and church since 1900: Engagement and exclusion*.
　London: Routledge.

Thompson, N., Bright, G., & Hart, P. (forthcoming). Faith-based community develop-
　ment and youth work in Britain. In A. Dinham (Ed.), *Faith and community develop-
　ment in international perspective*. Bristol: Policy Press.

CHAPTER 10

The Future of Online Youth Work

Jane Melvin

We're living in topsy-turvy times, and I think that what causes the topsy-turvy feeling is inadequacy of old forms of thought to deal with new experiences. I've heard it said that the only real learning results from hang-ups, where instead of expanding the branches of what you already know, you have to stop and drift laterally for a while until you come across something that allows you to expand the roots of what you already know.

PIRSIG, 1974: 170

∴

Introduction

The aim of this chapter is to discuss the future of online youth work. From the outset, I would like to suggest that there is no future for online youth work: rather, the future lies in youth workers' ability to work with young people to manage and develop their online and digital lives, and for young people to contribute to decisions about which digital tools, spaces and places to use.

The notion of online youth work, where youth workers 'meet' young people solely within a virtual context, is potentially fraught with ethical, moral and structural complications. Based on recent research into the role of digital tools, spaces and places as mediators of youth work practice (Melvin, 2018), it is also likely to be less successful than interventions with young people that are already known to youth workers. From a Finnish perspective, Kivinienmi and Kriauciunas (2016: 5) state that 'digital youth work is not a separate form of youth work, but rather a new way realizing the core competencies of youth work', and it is from this position that this chapter is written.

One of the defining features of youth work is that it is person-centred, with youth workers claiming expertise in 'making sense of the experiences of youth and in being able to work with young people' (Jeffs, 2001: 156). The current landscape of UK youth work today is unrecognisable compared to 20 years ago. Youth work organisations and youth services, particularly in the English context, have been decimated (Wenham, 2015), due to the impact of governmental austerity measures '... which fell disproportionately ... on youth work everywhere' (Wylie, 2015: 45).

In the recent 2017 UK general election manifestos, whilst the Labour Party pledged to end the cuts to services for young people, only the Green Party stated an aim to invest in youth services (National Youth Agency, 2017). Additionally, in terms of national and political drivers for digital engagement, only the Labour and Conservative Parties recognised young people's digital learning needs (ibid.), although little indication was given as to how these needs were to be met. In the past three years, numerous reports[1] focusing on important aspects of young people's learning and development needs in a digital world have been published, but these focus predominantly on the role of schools and colleges. Such reports prompt questions as to whether formal education establishments on their own, have the capacity to truly achieve the stated outcomes, and how the potential of youth work approaches might be promoted in addressing these aims.

The current UK government's Digital Strategy document talks of:
- ensuring that we continue to tackle the root causes of digital exclusion and that everyone can increase their digital capability to make the most of the digital world;
- developing the full range of digital skills that individuals and companies across the country need in an increasingly digital economy, and supporting people to up-skill and re-skill throughout their working lives;
- strong collaboration between the public, private and third sector to tackle the digital skills gap in a coordinated and coherent way, so the sum is greater than the parts and everyone everywhere has better access to the training they want (Department for Digital Culture Media and Sport, 2017).

Young people are not specifically identified within these aspirations, but youth workers are well-placed to play a role in challenging the causes of digital exclusion and to narrow the digital skills gap. Yet, the landscape of disappearing services, underfunded organisations, and deficit-based models which problematize young people in our society, mean that whilst youth workers should be able to fulfil such roles, many of those who remain may not be adequately trained or given the appropriate resources to do so.

Youth work's response to the ever-evolving digital world is being debated across Europe (Harvey, 2016; Kivinienmi & Kriauciunas, 2016; Youth Working Party, 2017), but there is lesser evidence of a critical discourse within UK contexts as to how the digital learning needs of the 'always on' generation (Baron, 2010) can be met informally. And yet, the ubiquitous smartphone or mobile device are familiar parts of everyday life. Almost everyone has one, and young people would rather give up their bed and shelter for the night, than give up their mobile device (The Prince's Trust, 2013).

The Case for Meeting Young People's Digital Learning Needs

When describing the knowledge, skills and values that young people need to navigate the digital world, there are a number of terms used. Digital literacy is a common term and is used widely throughout documentation for educators, for example, within the national curriculum for English schools (Department for Education, 2013) and the Digital Strategy for Scotland (Digital Scotland, 2017). Jisc defines digital literacy as 'the capabilities which fit someone for living, learning and working in a digital society' (2018).

Wenmoth (2013) observes that educators are still testing out the terminology needed to describe this skill-set, and suggests that the term digital literacy can be defined as:

> ... the ability to use the various tools and applications, but rather in an individual's capacity to effectively and critically navigate, evaluate and create information using a range of digital technologies. This includes the ability to read and interpret media, to reproduce data and images through digital manipulation and to evaluate and apply new knowledge gained from digital environments.

However, he adds that this is not enough, suggesting that alongside digital literacy, a sense of digital citizenship is needed in terms of developing a sensibility to digital rights and responsibilities (ibid.). As a contrast, Rheingold's five digital literacies are identified as 'digital know-how' and encompass '... infotention ... crap detection ... participation power ... social digital know-how ... and collaboration' (2012: 9–11), thus incorporating elements of digital citizenship and literacies.

Bartlett and Miller group digital learning needs into three areas which they name as the ability to be 'digitally fluent'; these are: 'net-savviness' or knowing how the internet works, 'critical evaluative techniques' for checking the accuracy and worth of online information, and 'diversity', which is about the extent to which internet usage is '... broad, varied, and diverse' (2011: 19). Spencer (2015) argues that the term 'digital fluency' is broader than 'digital literacy', in that:

> Being *fluent* requires competencies and capabilities that go beyond the skill level. Someone who is digitally fluent not only selects tools and knows what to do with them, but can explain why they work in the way they do and how they might adapt what they do if the context were to change.

The difference between digital literacy and digital fluency can be explained by the following example. If a young person is digitally literate, they can follow guidance about using a specific application, platform or programme and can use it effectively. If they are fluent, they can seek, find and select an appropriate application, platform or programme from a range of tools, and can use it effectively, but can also navigate and share the outcomes collaboratively, confidently, appropriately, and safely, with others. Based on the definition above, the terms 'digitally fluent' or 'digital fluency' will be used from this point to describe young people's digital learning needs, in that the 'outcome of being digitally fluent relates to issues of responsibility, equity and access' (ibid.).

The UK Council for Child Internet Safety's (UKCCIS) framework 'Education for a Connected World' is aimed at '... anyone who works with children and young people ...', and talks of developing a skill-set which fits the definition of a digitally fluent user, and that is '... empowering, builds resilience and effects positive culture change ...' (UK Council for Child Internet Safety, n.d.). This focuses on eight areas:
- Self-image and Identity;
- Online relationships;
- Online reputation;
- Online bullying;
- Managing online information;
- Health, wellbeing and lifestyle;
- Privacy and security;
- Copyright and ownership.

In parallel to this, Leaton-Gray (2017) advocates for a new digital curriculum for schools that goes beyond:

... the current limited diet of online safety and computer coding, and which instead embraces topics such as:
- Privacy, information and education rights;
- Management of time and space;
- The provision, maintenance and protection of digital infrastructure;
- The role of technology within relationships;
- Digital criminology;
- Digital citizenship;
- Digital consumption;
- Respect, consent and empathy with others;
- Legislative protections;
- The role of media as an information source and influencer.

In terms of supporting young people to manage and develop their online and digital lives in the context of the lists above, discussion about youth work's response to digital tools, spaces and places is pertinent. Alongside the absence of specific policy aimed at supporting young people's digital fluencies and/or literacies through youth work interventions, and the seeming lack of recognition of the role that youth workers could play, there is also an paucity of discourse within the profession itself as to how digital technologies are fundamentally changing how young people socialise, communicate, study, and access information (Oblinger, 2012; Melvin, 2016). Itō, suggests that young people's engagement in the digital world should encourage educators to think about new ways to view the role of education in order to exploit potential learning opportunities, with particular focus on young people's '... participation in public life in general ...' (2009: 3), an aim that fits well within the principles and practices of youth work.

Youth workers involved in research projects between 2010 and 2012, identified the outcomes that can be achieved through the use of digital tools, spaces and places, as described in Figure 10.1 (Melvin, 2018). This model describes how digital tools were being used at that time, with enabling young people's access to wi-fi and the internet being cited as the most common intervention. Awareness in relation to digital literacy skills and safety concerns came next, followed by the facilitation of skills connected to agency in the form of campaigning and the contribution to democratic processes. The use of digital tools aimed at promoting young people's voice were also identified, but this type of work occurred much less frequently than work aimed at access and awareness at the lower levels of the triangle.

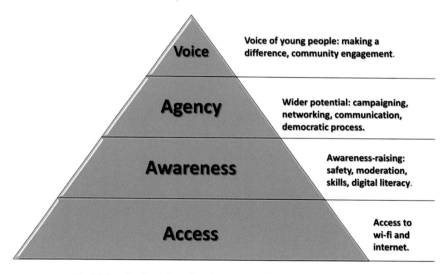

FIGURE 10.1   Model showing how digital tools can contribute to young people's digital learning needs (Melvin, 2018: 20)

In terms of examples of how and why youth workers should be interested in supporting young people to be digitally fluent, research into the notion of digital resilience found that many young people ranked their digital networks and the importance of being connected over other concerns (Young Minds and Ecorys, 2016). Such networks not only represent communication with friends and wider contexts for young people, they also represent opportunities to collaborate, share, and to stay connected, particularly if needing support. Bradford states that:

> ... young people are becoming increasingly accomplished in the occupation and use of these different spaces: they make friends online, sustain those friendships in a variety of ways *and* build friendships in school, on the street and in the youth club .... (2012: 146)

Aligned to this, is '... heightened anxiety arising from the need to be constantly reachable ...' (ibid.: 7). Any youth worker having to manage learning experiences with young people where Wi-Fi is not available, or the use of mobile devices is inappropriate, will have had experience of the fretfulness caused, and the associated conflict that can arise between staff and young people. Thus, in creating a response that describes how youth work as a profession can respond to what is undoubtedly a facet of young people's learning and development, it may not be sufficient to rely solely on more traditional notions of youth work principles and practice.

Rethinking the Pedagogy of Youth Work: Working towards a Digital Hybrid Pedagogy

Bright (2015) suggests that understanding the history, traditions and culture of a profession aids critical reflection about the direction of policy and practice in the future. Recognising the cultural historicity of youth work practice gives '... a better understanding of what we do and why we do it ...' (Gilchrist et al., 2001: 2). These are key factors when responding to changes, or implementing new practices. Merton and Wylie suggest that traditional youth work practice is underpinned by a pedagogy based on 'learning by doing ... people tackling real life problems and finding real life situations' (2002: 10), but it is possible that in the context of working in response to young people's digital learning needs, the pedagogy of youth work might need to be redefined.

Pedagogy, defined as the '... study of the methods and activities of teaching ...' (Cambridge Dictionary, n.d.), is a term that is used by youth work educators because of its roots in education and learning, but Curran and Golding (2013) suggest that many youth workers do not fit neatly into this definition because of the variety of contexts in which practice is now found. It is perhaps more useful therefore to consider the ideas of a hybrid pedagogy (Curran & Golding, 2013), which draws on the skills associated with a number of educational approaches, and which is linked to the idea of border pedagogies which can straddle the boundaries between formal, non-formal, informal (ibid.; Coburn, 2010), and digital learning contexts. This includes ideas of andragogy (defined as the study of the methods, processes and activities used to teach adults, but also concerned with intrinsic motivation, maturity and independence), and heutagogy (the study of the processes involved in facilitating self-directed learning).

Canning (2010) describes hybrid pedagogy as a sequence from pedagogy to andragogy to heutagogy, that facilitates learners in developing maturity and self-sufficiency. However, youth work is a much less linear process in that it circulates through, and within these concepts, in accordance with the social, emotional, cultural, moral, spiritual and physical developmental needs of the young people with whom we work (Smith, 2012). In terms of specific youth work interventions mediated by digital tools, spaces and places, it perhaps useful to consider the idea of a digital hybrid pedagogy based on the following definition:

> Digital [Hybrid] Pedagogy is precisely not about using digital technologies for teaching and, rather, about approaching those tools from a critical pedagogical perspective. So, it is as much about using digital tools thoughtfully as it is about deciding when not to use digital tools, and about paying attention to the impact of digital tools on learning. (Hybrid Pedagogy, n.d.)

In this context, Stommel proposes that it is not always easy, possible or appropriate to separate out a young person's digital ego from the rest of their identity. This therefore necessitates '... new and innovative ways to engage students in the practice of learning ...' (2012). He proposes the term 'digital hybrid pedagogue' (ibid.) as a way of describing educators who respond to young people's digital fluency needs, with a fusion or amalgam of methods, opportunities and experiences (ibid.), in the recognition that '... all [digital] learning is necessarily hybrid ...' (ibid.). This requires approaches that can engage with young people's '... digital selves ... [as well as their] ... physical selves ...' (ibid.). Thus, the digital hybrid pedagogue in a youth work context uses a combination of non-formal, informal, and experiential approaches, and has a holistic attitude to digital tools, spaces and places. The approach prioritises developing creative and responsive praxes which understand and meet young people's needs over adherence to targets and strict curricula.

Morris' (2013) ideas of digital hybrid pedagogy advocates that practice should begin '... with inquiry ... It reminds us that the new landscape of learning is mysterious and worth exploring ...'. This mirrors notions of youth work practice where learning outcomes can be unexpected and not necessarily predicted (Ord, 2016). McCarthy and Witmer (2016) promote '... community and collaboration ... in open and networked environments ...'. This aims to empower learners to find new ways to use digital tools, spaces and places, to enhance their learning and to create new ways to communicate, engage and share in wider cultural and political contexts, as well as '... an education that empowers them in that sphere, teaches them that language, and offers new opportunities of human connectivity (Rorabaugh, 2012).

In this context, Davies (2011) advocates for youth workers to have the skills to work in a variety of spaces and places, whether digital or not , commending practitioners to think about '... awareness ... use ... [and] outreach ...' (ibid.: 18–19) as a way of checking that the digital space or place is an appropriate one to be working in. Stommel suggests that the prime role of the digital hybrid pedagogue is to enable young people to reflect critically on the tools and platforms that they are using, and to '... reimagine the ways that communication and collaboration happen across cultural and political boundaries ...' (Stommel, 2014). Loveless and Williamson propose drivers to guide the development of young people's digital learning identities which focus on '... agency ... tools ... context ... and improvisation ...' (2013: 2402–2408). These can be used to inform a digital hybrid pedagogy; in this context, Wenger et al. (2009: 3698) discuss the need for educators to find a balance between 'conservative stability ... and runaway adoption'; an approach they call 'technology stewardship', which they describe as both a 'perspective and a practice' (ibid.: 819), so that youth workers become both sensitive and responsive to the digital fluency needs of young people.

Guiding Youth Work in Digital Contexts

Youth work curricula and policies often describe the use of a wide variety of experiences, tools and settings; yet whilst working in digital spaces and places is not precluded, it is difficult to find specific mention of the '... use of digital technologies to support communication, dialogue and collaboration, and to provide peer support ...' (Curran & Golding, 2012: 5) in current documentation.

Davies (2011: 2) suggests that this might be due to '... risk-averse UK public services ...', banning employees from using social media, resulting in strict policies that prevent youth workers using digital technologies as learning tools, as well as a lack of up-to-date equipment and free Wi-Fi networks in buildings that young people access (Melvin, 2012). Whilst Voluntary Community and Social Enterprise (VCSE) sector organisations might be driven more by their values and the attainment of 'social goals' rather than financial gain (National Audit Office, n.d.), and therefore have more control over the creation their policies, tendencies to risk aversion may also impact on them; moreover, a reduction in sources of grant aid to the charitable sector means that keeping up with hardware requirements and the pace of change can be difficult.

During research conducted between 2010 and 2012 (Melvin, 2011b; Melvin, 2012; Melvin, 2018), a number of youth workers reported choosing not to engage with young people using digital tools, spaces and places because they felt that young people had more skills and awareness than they did. However, a Prince's Trust report in 2016 found that it should not be assumed that digital capabilities amongst all young people are commonplace:

> Disadvantaged young people are likely to have lower quality access and lower levels of digital skills which impede their ability to take up education and employment opportunities. ... NEETs and those with a history of economic disadvantage lack traditional offline literacy skills, like problem solving and live in less digitally rich environments which are all related to having lower levels of digital skills. These inequalities express themselves mostly in the softer, social communication-related skills. (Helsper, 2016: 8)

This report draws on the Tech Partnership's Basic Digital Skills Framework (2015) as a means of increasing digital fluency amongst young people, but particularly those who are digitally disadvantaged, in the pursuit of achieving learning and development aimed at '... economic, employment and learning outcomes ... cultural outcomes ... social outcomes ... personal well-being ...' (Helsper, 2016: 84).

McCarthy and Witmer (2016) propose a values-based model, based on communication, collaboration, production and openness (the CCPO model); this mirrors notions of digital fluency. McClurken states that the use of any such model to scaffold practice should promote experimentation and experiential learning, since they play a key role in the formation of digital fluencies and the ability to '... think critically and strategically ...' (2008) about which digital tools, spaces or places will best serve the aims of a particular project. Critical thinking, collaboration, openness and production are all familiar terms within youth work practice, resulting in a framework that would work well alongside more traditional principles.

5 Rights, an organisation whose mission is: '... enabling children and young people to access the digital world creatively, knowledgeably and fearlessly ...' (2016a) models digital fluencies from a rights-based stance, suggesting that the following could serve as a starting point for practice:

- *The right to remove:* every child and young person under the age of 18 should have the right to easily edit or delete any and all content they themselves have created.
- *The right to know:* children and young people have the right to know who is holding and profiting from their information, what their information is being used for and whether it is being copied, sold or traded.
- *The right to safety and support:* children and young people should be confident that they will be protected from illegal practices, and supported if confronted by troubling or upsetting scenarios online.
- *The right to make informed and conscious choices (agency):* children and young people should be free to reach into creative and participatory places online, using digital technologies as tools, but at the same time have the capacity to disengage at will.
- *The right to digital literacy:* to access the knowledge that the internet can deliver, children and young people need to be taught the skills to use and critique digital technologies effectively, and given the tools to negotiate emerging social norms (5Rights, 2016b).

The Children's Commissioner for England adopts this approach throughout the 'Growing Up Digital' report, which describes children and young people gaining '... digital resilience ... [being] digitally informed ... [and having] digital power ...' (Growing Up Digital Taskforce, 2017: 3). However, the report focuses only on the role of teachers and schools, stopping short of exploring the potential that non-formal and informal educators, including VCSE sector organisations, have in promoting these competencies and behaviours.

Being a digital hybrid pedagogue implies being able to combine and apply different knowledge, approaches and skills, from different disciplines, to facilitate learning. There are echoes here of Engestrom and Young's (2001) notion of practitioners as boundary crossers, since straddling learning borders invariably requires the skills of the hybrid pedagogue in working on both or all sides of borders, and negotiating and bringing together differences in skill-sets, values and experience.

The very language of border crossing implies spaces and places bounded by recognisable structures; however, in the digital world, such borders and boundaries are less apparent. The idea of a digital hybrid pedagogy hints at:

> ... deeper resonances, suggesting not just that the *place* of learning is changed but that a hybrid pedagogy fundamentally rethinks our *conception of place*. (Stommel, 2012)

Hybridity implies a number of styles that are merged in order to work together. In terms of situating learning based on digital needs, Stommel talks of educators recognising that it is not just a case of mixing traditional approaches with a digital dimension, but of ensuring that the type of learning gained by young people in physical spaces and places is reflected and complemented by the types of learning that can occur digitally (ibid.). This is where the traditional principles and values of youth work practice might direct youth workers towards an approach and context that needs to be more hybrid, in order to meet young people's digital fluency needs.

A Model for Working in Digital Spaces and Places

Drawn from research with English youth workers between 2013–2017, and methodologically underpinned by Cultural Historical Activity Theory (CHAT) and Developmental Work Research techniques (DWR), a model to guide youth workers using digital tools, spaces and places as mediators of youth work practice has been formulated (Melvin, 2018). This is not a model designed to support online youth work: rather it is a model to support youth workers to work with young people using digital tools, spaces and places to mediate youth work interventions, thereby promoting digital fluency. Two further principles apply; firstly, that the use of digital tools, spaces and places as mediators of youth work practice is most effective as an extension to existing face-to-face youth work, where relationships between young people and youth workers have already been formed. Secondly, that a youth worker's choice of digital tool, space or place needs to be based on the needs and input of young people, not on the youth worker's choice of platform, app or device. This requires youth workers to develop the skills of the digital hybrid pedagogue.

Based conceptually on holistic models of youth work practice and McCarthy and Witmer's (2016) CCPO model, four 'spaces' named as safety, production, information and communication have been identified as central to practice, and are defined as follows:

- *Safety* – safe or unsafe digital practices, duty to safeguard and educate about the safe use of digital technologies;
- *Production* – digital literacy skills and behaviours, digital footprint, production of artefacts (campaigns, video, photo, blog, podcast etc.);
- *Information* – critical consumers of the internet, and broader information, advice and guidance needs;
- *Communication* – marketing and publicising of youth work, generic digital communication skills, self-promotion, digital footprint.

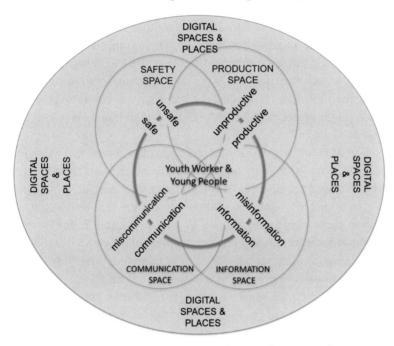

FIGURE 10.2   Youth work in digital spaces and places (Melvin, 2018: 158)

These were identified from the data as contexts for digital youth work and are underpinned by traditional notions of youth work curricula and the principles and practice of informal and experiential education. They are also influenced by ideas of digital hybrid pedagogy, in that youth workers need to be able to draw on a broad skill-set to facilitate digital fluency, both face-to-face and within digital spaces and places. This is supported by Whelan's (2015) suggestion that one facet of youth work is its ability to explore alternative, innovative or experiential approaches.

Within these above headings, issues related to young people's digital learning needs as well as youth work principles and practice can be represented by four continuum-based representations:
– safe–unsafe
– productive–unproductive
– information–misinformation
– communication–miscommunication
By using a continuum-based representation, it is not the intention to portray 'good' or 'bad' aspects of the digital world. For example, when working with young people on the safe-unsafe continuum, strategies for staying safe online can be located at one end, with preventative or harm minimisation work aimed at risk reduction strategies, located at the other end. Equally, in terms of professional practice, organisations can support youth workers to stay professionally safe online through policy (safe end), which might contain details of best practice, as well as explaining how other practices, for example, youth workers using their own personal social media accounts to communicate with young people, might present a risk to both individual staff and their organisations (unsafe end).

These different continuums can be placed into the model in Figure 10.2 which is set contextually in digital spaces and places, and can be defined as milieus where many young people 'meet' and 'socialise' mediated by digital tools. However, these spaces and places also represent the 'real-world' contexts where youth workers meet young people, as work promoting young people's digital fluency does not necessarily have to happen online: youth workers can still have face-to-face conversations about aspects of young people's experience in the digital world. Connected to the continuums described previously, are the safety, production, information and communication spaces which are represented as interconnected circles. The continuums are also represented as inter-related and inter-connected, as some issues, for example, the impact of a young person's digital footprint or digital tattoo (Think U Know, n.d.), occur throughout. The continuums can also be approached from two perspectives; that of curriculum-based interventions with young people, and as principles to guide and support professional youth work practice.

As previously proposed, interventions mediated by digital tools, spaces and places are likely to be more effective if carried out with young people with whom face-to-face relationships are established (Melvin, 2018), and within this context, the model can be used to scaffold practice that promotes digital fluency and digital resilience. A variety of tools: online, offline, digital, non-digital or hybrid approaches incorporating these in combination, can support both face-to-face work and online practice in digital spaces and places such as Facebook, Twitter or WhatsApp. Interventions do not necessarily need to be mediated by digital tools, spaces and places; face-to-face conversation and critical dialogue with young people are core elements of the youth worker's toolbox, and conversations might be sufficient. As a way of illustrating how the model works, an example relating to working with young people to raise their awareness of issues related to extremism and radicalisation, will be used. In describing each space separately, it is important to recognise that in reality, a digital hybrid approach would require youth workers and young people to be interacting with many elements at once, as shown by the overlapping circles in Figure 10.2.

Within the model's safe space, youth workers can develop young people's digital fluency and awareness in relation to both safe and unsafe practices, particularly in relation to how extremist groups groom young people online (Ranstorp, 2016; Von Behr et al., 2013), and how they might report their own concerns or those relating to their friends. Professionally, transparency is integral; youth workers engaging in such interventions must have access to effective managerial supervision. They must also operate under professional profiles that conform to organisational social media policies, and be clear about their presence and role online by using disclaimers, as operating out-side of such parameters is both ethically and educationally questionable, as well as risky.

The production space might consider what constitutes unproductive behav-iour; for example, how a young person's digital footprint/tattoo is impacted by liking certain pages, or sharing photos or posts relating to radicalised or extremist ideas on social media sites. Young people could also be facilitated in producing artefacts that promote positive images of youth, for example, how a group is working to challenge extremist views, such as those of the far right, or, to promote online projects such as the Austrian youth work intervention 'Jamal' in Vienna (Verdegaal & Haanstra, 2017). The digital footprint/tattoo of a youth worker's professional profile is also of relevance. It can serve to posi-tively promote the work of the wider organisation, as well as the individual practitioner, and contribute to measuring outcomes.

The information space enables the development of digital fluency skills: creating critical digital consumers, supporting young people to question what they encounter online, for example, the ability to identify and question propa-ganda, as well as encouraging young people to critically interrogate some of the implicit assumptions within 'Prevent-esque' agendas. This space might also include training to support youth workers to engage with young people who are at risk of being radicalised (both online and offline), and information regarding reporting processes, online resources and specialist organisations.

In the communication space, youth workers can enable young people to explore how extremist views are communicated, and how targeted individuals can be tracked and contacted, not only by extremist groups, but also by organisations like the FBI if their digital footprint/tattoo becomes of concern. Young people can also learn about how to communicate positively in ways that promote their positive engagement in their local communities, and, to challenge extremism of all kinds. Professionally, youth workers need support in developing communication with young people in digital spaces and places, particularly in promoting critical dialogue in challenging views outside of face-to-face practice.

Ethical and Boundaried Contact

As a final thought, some youth workers researched between 2010–2016 (Melvin, 2011a, 2011b, 2012, 2018), did not agree with youth work in digital spaces and places, and used arguments about ethical practice as the rationale for not working with young people in this way. Some queried the ethics of youth workers being present in young people's social media spaces, and some queried the need. This was due to concerns about young people's privacy, and that if privacy settings are not set appropriately, becoming a social media 'friend' of a young person, might allow a youth worker to access information regarding other young people through that young person's profile.

There are five elements that can support youth workers to work ethically with young people in digital spaces and places. These concerns can be managed and supervised in the same way that detached youth workers working on the streets, in parks and around shopping centres, manage being present in young people's physical spaces and places. These elements can be summarised as follows:
– Professional profiles supported through supervision;
– Negotiated;
– Transparent;
– Training and awareness;
– Supported by policy and guidance.
Youth workers working in digital spaces and places should have professional profiles and accounts that are connected to, and supported by, their organisations through policy. In this context accounts, passwords and usage can be monitored and discussed through managerial supervision in parallel with other aspects of a youth worker's face-to-face work. Working in this way needs to be negotiated with young people in relation to what digital tools, spaces and

places are used, and transparent so that young people can choose whether to engage digitally with a youth worker or not. Best practice demands that youth workers follow young people's leads; for example, if young people suggest a WhatsApp group or blog site as a way of extending a face-to-face project, then the youth worker needs to be supported in responding accordingly. Working with known young people, using closed groups and group pages, is a way to manage many of the concerns, and disclaimers. Moreover, 'sticky notes' can be used to make sure that young people understand the purpose of a youth worker's presence, the hours that they are likely to be online, and the code of conduct they should adhere to.

If youth workers are to engage effectively and ethically with young people online, it is vital that education and training, address these issues. The purpose, pros and cons of adopting an online approach that seeks to support the learning and development of young people should be clearly articulated. Organisations employing workers adopting these approaches need to ensure that they are clear about what represents good practice, and that policy and guidelines support this. Professional education should support practitioners in developing the skills to critically reflect upon the application of principles and values that extend across online and real world environments.

Conclusion

In the future, youth work must do more to support young people to develop the skills of digital fluency in order to navigate their lives both online and offline. This practice needs to build on established non-formal/informal face-to-face relationships, and be able to extend these interactions into digital spaces and places. To equip workers to do this, the pedagogy of youth work needs to be revisited to include a digital hybrid approach. This chapter suggests a model to scaffold practice in digital spaces and places in order to promote digital fluency in the areas of safety, production, information and communication, which hopes to support critical reflection on the development of policy and practice.

Note

1   Samples of reports:
     · Life in Likes (Children's Commissioner for England, 2018)
     · Digital Friendships Report (UK Safer Internet Centre, 2018)

- Growing Up Digital (Growing Up Digital Taskforce, 2017)
- Digital Reach: Digital Skills for the Hardest-to-Reach Young People (The Tech Partnership, 2015)
- Resilience for a Digital World (Young Minds and Ecorys, 2016)
- Connected Generation (Get Connected, 2015)
- Enabling Children and Young People to Access the Digital World Creatively, Knowledgably and Fearlessly (iRights, 2015)
- Basic Digital Skills Framework: addressing the 5 areas of digital capability. (The Tech Partnership, 2015)

References

5rights. (2016a). *Home page* [Online]. Retrieved October 8, 2017, from http://5rightsframework.com; http://5rightsframework.com/

5rights. (2016b). *The 5rights framework* [Online]. Retrieved October 8, 2017, from http://d1qmdf3vop2lo7.cloudfront.net/eggplant-cherry.cloudvent.net/compressed/2 f9a3db14b3477988c2355653d6b999d.pdf; http://d1qmdf3vop2lo7.cloudfront.net/egg-plant-cherry.cloudvent.net/compressed/2f9a3db14b3477988c2355653d6b999d.pdf

Baron, N. (2010). *Always on: Language in an online and mobile world*. New York, NY: Oxford University Press.

Bartlett, J., & Miller, C. (2011). *Truth, lies and the internet*. London: DEMOS.

Bradford, S. (2012). *Sociology, youth, and youth work practice*. New York, NY: Palgrave Macmillan.

Bright, G. (2015). *Youth work: Histories, policy and contexts*. London: Palgrave Macmillan.

Canning, N. (2010) Playing with heutagogy: Exploring strategies to empower mature learners in higher education. *Journal of Further and Higher Education, 34*(1), 59–71.

Cambridge Dictionary. (n.d.). *Pedagogy* [Online]. Retrieved July 14, 2017, from http://dictionary.cambridge.org/dictionary/english/pedagogy

Coburn, A. (2010). Youth work as border pedagogy. In J. Batsleer & B. Davies (Eds.), *What is youth work?* (Kindle ed.). Exeter: Learning Matters.

Curran, S., & Golding, T. (2012). *Moving from the periphery to the centre: Promoting conversation and developing communities of practice in online environments*. Proceedings of Renewing the Tradition: Sustaining and Sustainable Communities Through Informal Education, Brathay Hall, Cumbria.

Curran, S., & Golding, T. (2013). Crossing the boundaries? Working informally in formal settings. In S. Curran, R. Harrison, & D. Mackinnon (Eds.), *Working with young people*. London: Sage Publications.

Davies, T. (2011). Connected generation. *Freedom from Fear*. UNICRI Max Plank Institute, Basel Institute on Governance.

Department for Digital Culture Media and Sport. (2017). *Digital skills and inclusion – Giving everyone access to the digital skills they need* [Online]. Retrieved September 3, 2017, from https://www.gov.uk/government/publications/uk-digital-strategy/2-digital-skills-and-inclusion-giving-everyone-access-to-the-digital-skills-they-need

Department for Education. (2013). *National curriculum in England: Computing programmes of study* [Online]. Retrieved April 24, 2018, from https://www.gov.uk/government/publications/national-curriculum-in-england-computing-programmes-of-study/national-curriculum-in-england-computing-programmes-of-study

Digital Scotland. (2017). *Realising Scotland's full potential in a digital world: A digital strategy for Scotland*. Retrieved from http://www.gov.scot/digital

Engestrom, Y., & Young, M. (2001). *Expansive learning at work: Toward an activity-theoretical reconceptualisation*. London: University of London.

Gilchrist, R., Jeffs, T., & Spence, J. (Eds.). (2001). *Essays on the history of community and youth work*. Leicester: Youth Work Press.

Growing up Digital Taskforce. (2017). *Growing up digital: A report of the growing up digital taskforce*. London: Children's Commissioner for England.

Harvey, C. (2016). *Screenagers international research project: Using ICT, digital and social media in youth work*. Retrieved from http://www.youth.ie/screenagers

Helsper, E. (2016). *Slipping through the net: Are disadvantaged young people being left further behind in the digital era?* London: London School of Economics. Retrieved from https://www.princes-trust.org.uk/about-the-trust/research-policies-reports/slipping-through-the-net

Hybrid Pedagogy. (n.d.). *What is digital pedagogy?* [Online]. Retrieved August 4, 2016, from http://www.digitalpedagogylab.com/hybridped/digitalpedagogy/

Itō, M. (2009). *Living and learning with new media: Summary of findings from the digital youth project*. Cambridge, MA: MIT Press.

Jeff, T. (2001) Something to give and much to learn: Settlements and youth work in T. Jeffs, & R. Gilchrist (Eds.) *Settlements, Social Change and Community Action: Good Neighbours*. London: Jessica Kingsley.

Jisc. (2018). *Developing students' digital literacy* [Online]. Retrieved April 24, 2018, from https://www.jisc.ac.uk/guides/developing-students-digital-literacy

Kivinienmi, J., & Kriauciunas, N. (2016). Taking youth work to the digital world. *Developing Digital Youth Work*. Oulu: Finnish Agency for Education.

Leaton-Gray, S. (2017). Why we need a new digital curriculum for schools. *The BERA Blog: Research Matters*. British Education Research Association. Retrieved from https://www.bera.ac.uk/blog/why-we-need-a-new-digital-curriculum-for-schools

Loveless, A., & Williamson, B. (2013). *Learning identities in a digital age: Rethinking creativity, education & technology*. Abingdon: Routledge.

McCarthy, S., & Witmer, A. (2016). *Towards a values-driven framework for digital humanities pedagogy*. Digital Pedagogy Lab.

McClurken, J. (2008). Digital history and undergraduate digital literacy. *Techist: A blog about technology, history and teaching: Digital History and Undergraduate Digital Literacy.* Retrieved from http://mcclurken.blogspot.co.uk/2008/12/digital-history-and-undergraduate.html, blogger.co.uk

Melvin, J. (2011a). *21st century youth work and the role of the youth work curriculum* (Unpublished). University of Brighton, Brighton.

Melvin, J. (2011b). *Practice-based research.* Brighton: University of Brighton.

Melvin, J. (2012) *Using Activity Theory to Explain How Youth Workers Use Digital Media to Meet Curriculum Outcomes.* Unpublished work, University of Brighton.

Melvin, J. (2016). *Youth work in digital spaces and places: A challenge to the field from a UK youth work perspective.* Paper presented at the Second Commonwealth Conference on Youth Work, Pretoria, South Africa. The Commonwealth and Foreign Office, HM Government, London.

Melvin, J. (2018). *Digital tools, spaces and places as mediators of youth work practice* (School of Education). University of Brighton, Brighton.

Merton, B., & Wylie, T. (2002). *Towards a contemporary youth work curriculum.* Leicester: National Youth Agency.

Morris, S. M. (2013). *Decoding digital pedagogy part 1: Beyond the LMS* [Online]. Retrieved October 9, 2017, from http://www.digitalpedagogylab.com/hybridped/decoding-digital-pedagogy-pt-1-beyond-the-lms/

National Audit Office. (n.d.). *What are third sector organisations and their benefits for commissioners?* [Online]. Retrieved October 6, 2017, from https://www.nao.org.uk/successful-commissioning/introduction/what-are-civil-society-organisations-and-their-benefits-for-commissioners/

National Youth Agency NYA. (2017). *General Election 2017: Party Manifestos – Policies for young people* [Online]. Retrieved March 19, 2018, from https://www.nya.org.uk/2017/05/general-election-2017-party-manifestos-policies-young-people/

Oblinger, D. (2012). Game changers: Education and information technologies. In G. Dobbin (Ed.), *Educause.* Retrieved from http://www.educause.edu/books

Ord, J. (2016). *Youth work process, product and practice: Creating an authentic curriculum in work with young people* (Kindle ed.). Abingdon: Taylor & Francis, Ltd.

Pirsig, R. (1974). *Zen and the art of motorcycle maintenance.* London: The Bodley Head, Ltd.

Ranstorp, M. (2016). RAN issue paper: The roots of violent extremism. *European Commission radicalisation awareness network.* Retrieved from https://ec.europa.eu/home-affairs/what-we-do/networks/radicalisation_awareness_network/ran-papers_en

Rheingold, H. (2012). *Netsmart: How to thrive online.* Cambridge, MA: MIT Press.

Rorabaugh, P. (2012). *Occupy the critical: Critical and new media* [Online]. Retrieved October 9, 2017, from http://www.digitalpedagogylab.com/hybridped/occupy-the-digital-critical-pedagogy-and-new-media/

Smith, M. K. (2012). *What is pedagogy?* [Online]. Retrieved October 9, 2017, from http://infed.org/mobi/what-is-pedagogy/

Spencer, K. (2015). *What is digital fluency?* [Online]. Retrieved April 23, 2018, from http://blog.core-ed.org/blog/2015/10/what-is-digital-fluency.html

Stommel, J. (2012). *Hybridity, pt. 2: What is hybrid pedagogy?* [Online]. Retrieved November 13, 2017, from http://www.digitalpedagogylab.com/hybridped/hybridity-pt-2-what-is-hybrid-pedagogy/

Stommel, J. (2014). *Critical digital pedagogy: A definition* [Online]. Retrieved October 9, 2017, from https://news.continuingstudies.wisc.edu/critical-digital-pedagogy-a-definition/

The Prince's Trust. (2013). *The Prince's Trust digital literacy report March 2013.* Retrieved from http://princes-trust.org.uk/about_the_trust/what_we_do/research/digital_literacy_research_2013.aspx

The Tech Partnership. (2015). *Basic digital skills framework: Addressing the 5 areas of digital capability* [Online]. Retrieved July 5, 2017, from https://www.thetechpartnership.com/basic-digital-skills/basic-digital-skills-framework/

Think U Know. (n.d.). *Think u know: You and your tattoo* [Online]. Retrieved April 24, 2018, from https://www.thinkuknow.co.uk/14_plus/Need-advice/Digital-footprint/

UK Council for Child Internet Safety. (n.d.). *Education for a connected world.* Retrieved from https://www.gov.uk/government/groups/uk-council-for-child-internet-safety-ukccis

Verdegaal, M., & Haanstra, W. (2017). The role of youth work in the preventaiton of radicalisation and violent extremism. *European Commission radicalisation awareness network: Youth, families and communities working group.* Retrieved from https://ec.europa.eu/home-affairs/what-

Von Behr, I., Reading, A., Edwards, C., & Gribbon, L. (2013). Radicalisation in the digital era: The use of the internet in 15 cases of terrorism and extremism. *RAND Europe.* Retrieved from http://www.rand.org/pubs/research_reports/RR453.html

Wenger, E., White, N., & Smith, J. D. (2009). *Digital habitats: Stewarding technology for communities* (1st Kindle Version ed.). Portland, OR: CPsquare.

Wenham, A. (2015). Youth policy: Future prospects? *Youth and Policy, 114,* 1–4.

Wenmoth, D. (2013). Our digital aspiration? *Derek's Blog.* Retrieved from http://blog.core-ed.org/derek/2013/11/our-digital-aspiration.html

Whelan, M. (2015). Re-locating detached youth work'. In G. Bright (Ed.), *Youth work: Histories, policy and contexts.* London: Palgrave Macmillan.

Wylie, T. (2015). Youth work. *Youth and Policy Special Edition, 114.*

Young Minds and Ecorys. (2016). *Resilience for the digital world.* Retrieved from http://www.youngminds.org.uk/assets/0002/5852/Resilience_for_the_Digital_World.pdf

Youth Working Party. (2017). Background document on the terms of digital youth work and smart youth work to accompany the council conclusions on smart youth work. Unpublished, Council of the European Union.

CHAPTER 11

On the Future of Youth Work with Young Women

Janet Batsleer and Karen McCarthy

Introduction

Women have long taken responsibility for the practice of sustaining bonds of relationship, yet this has sometimes been at a cost to their own aspirations and development. In neoliberal times, youth work practice has strongly focussed on individuals and their development. The measurement of outcomes for young people as a result of their involvement with youth work processes has intensified and accompanied this individualisation (McGimpsey, 2017). In this chapter we discuss another way of seeing youth work practice as intergenerational and rooted in practices of connection and even community, which we argue is what will support a sustainable and alternative practice in the future.

This chapter draws on the specific context of Manchester, UK, and also on research undertaken across eight European cities as part of the *Partispace* project (www.partispace.eu). Consideration of cities and superdiversity are therefore central to the discussion here. We believe that community-based youth work occurring in small towns and villages, though it has its own specific places and challenges, will also be challenged by the themes we have identified, and that the forms of network practice which we see as the future, will need to be resourced across a wide range of different locations. Youth work practice can be inspired by the thinking of urban analysts who see in the spaces of cities an opportunity to reclaim a sense of civility and public space which could cross the borders of communities, and institute a sense of common ground lived among strangers (Gilbert, 2014). Karen McCarthy's MA Dissertation (Lived Experience of Sexualities) investigated the stories of women in LISG (Lesbian Immigration Support Group). Janet Batsleer's role in the *Partispace* project was to lead on ethnographic work concerning young people's participation in civil society and democratic life across eight European cities. Key themes emerged from both these research projects which can contribute to feminist discussion of coalition building, transversal politics and also to building sustainable practices of urban life and future-oriented thinking about Girls' Work. It is possible to seek out glimpses of new imaginations of the commons here, as spaces protected from the market where a sense of mutuality across difference and shared access to resource occurs.

© KONINKLIJKE BRILL NV, LEIDEN, 2019 | DOI:10.1163/9789004396555_011

'Community' has been a difficult word for women. It is accompanied by other loaded words such as 'family', 'belonging' and 'identity' and comes with a set of threats of punishment for those who cannot and/or will not conform to the expectations of a particular community. Whilst men may most readily be named and recognised as 'community leaders', women – and especially older women including mothers, mothers-in-law and aunts – have been the ones who have sustained community practices, and who have passed these traditions of relationship on to the next generation. Such patterns have had widespread recognition among feminists, both as activists and theorists, and it is therefore to feminist debates that we look to inform and shape arguments about youth work futures presented here. In particular, we draw on the work of Donna Haraway (2016), who, has for many years, argued for feminist practice as a networked (and now multispecies) practice which takes pleasure in the confusion of boundaries, and provokes imagination of more sustainable futures.

'Community', can be taken to refer to an ideal or dream for the future, or a past idyllic state, a state that existed once, and now has been lost. As a term, it suggests a deep togetherness and unity which is rarely experienced, except perhaps in the context of war. It is this drawing of a boundary between 'us' and 'them' combined with a reference to an imaginary and transcendental ideal – such as 'God' or 'my country' or 'the workers' – which seems to constitute the most powerful experience of community. In the case of liberal democratic and social democratic discourses of community, especially when these are aligned with the nation-state, 'community discourses' create a practice of abjection of all who are pushed to the edge. These practices of abjection – of foreigners, of radicalised Muslims, of the non-working poor are powerful and can be at times the basis of a counter-community – of all who do not belong or fit in easily: the society of outsiders. At the same time, the groups of people who are designated as outsiders and whose lives are rendered precarious and vulnerable are not naturally aligned; their experiences are fractured and separated across spaces, times and generations. Practices of community-building and coalition-building have therefore been at the centre of discussions in feminist theory about what forms feminist practices might take in a sustainable future (Young, 1990; Mohanty, 2003).

The chapter presents two challenges which we argue will be generative for Girls' Work in the future. The first is the challenge of responding in ways that sustain openness at places and times when a border between 'us' and 'them' is being drawn. It is for this reason we have chosen to draw on material concerning Lesbian Asylum Seekers, a population living with a double form of otherness/outsiderness. The Lesbian Immigration Support Group (LISG) is not a classic youth project, and by definition, works with women who are established in their adult lives. It is however closely linked with the youth group associated with The Proud Trust in Manchester, and the border-crossing practices identified in the work of LISG, are evocative for many other contexts.

The second, is the challenge of responding to the difficulty, conflict and anger that accompanies the experience of abjection without resorting to seeking to cure or rescue individuals, whilst leaving the sources of anger and frustration unexamined. Girls involved in youth work in North Manchester had significant stories of being offered anger management courses and medication from a young age, being sent to special units for behaviour management in schools, whilst being encouraged to identify their mental health problems as an inherited family pathology, as they often had parents and siblings with similar experiences. Youth work which offers only an encouragement of positivity and individual mentoring through engagement in short programmes of volunteering or confidence building, has little hope of being able to engage with these issues.

It is with these challenges to the fore, that the chapter turns to explore some aspects of the role of the youth worker as enabler and facilitator of inter-generational and peer learning in socio-cultural accompaniment. A key method of neoliberal youth work has been termed 'pedagogisation': here youth work is concerned with passing on of inherited values and skills through more or less formal programmes of youth development. We are interested in the ways in which network-based models of youth work/Girls' Work can also enable support to individuals as they establish a sense of adult identity, exploring the role of the facilitator of support groups and networks, and suggesting that youth work with girls and women can be inspired from this role. The work of the youth worker as community educator, is then, not so much to teach, as to fuel the desires to know, and connect across the divides of urban space.

Transversal organising and working (Cockburn, 1998; Yuval-Davis, 2005) requires practices which encourage the abandonment of a singular bounded identity and the recognition of complexity. When disagreement, difference and passion emerge in youth workers' practices, this is not a failure to be one and united, a failure of community; rather, these are the places from which new figurations and new practices and imaginations of community might emerge. Loyalty to such dissident practices often requires a painful disloyalty or unfaithfulness to origins; it embraces the yearning for a connection which does not obliterate difference.

Drawing on earlier discussions of coalition building and transversal politics (Batsleer et al., 2017; Soni, 2011), it is possible to identify some key aspects of this practice. These are: Border-Crossing and Border-Disrupting Practices; Re-grouping and Shifting Practices; Practices of Friendship; Creating Microspheres of Public Education and of Accompaniment.

By border-crossing and border-disrupting practices, we refer to ways in which girls and women who have had a routine experience of rejection and hostility are made welcome. This may be at the border of the jurisdiction in the form of the passport control. It may be at other places of border, such as the school lunch table (for those on free school meals), the Inclusion Unit in a school (for those with behavioural difficulties) or in the Accident and Emergency Department of a hospital when entitlement is assessed. Making welcome and giving support after such marked experiences of rejection and separation requires an active commitment to challenge the existing divisions of the entitled and not-entitled, the deserving and the undeserving.

By re-grouping and shifting practices, we refer to the ways in which complex identities and senses of belonging and capability are negotiated and re-negotiated. Here we address questions of knowledge in its broadest sense, of whose expertise is valued and recognised, and how 'being new' is also acknowledged and shared. These practices also involve finding names for, and ways of talking about experience, which do not divide up groups in established ways which reinforce abjection and inclusion. This then has implications for the ways in which identity is negotiated, and in which, inter-generational debts are acknowledged and paid.

Practices of friendship refers to the practices in which (young) women seek to give mutual support to one another. These include small acts of every day exchange through which women support each other. We are interested in how these practices are networked through contemporary communications systems. We are also interested in how other living things and inanimate objects are present and exchanged in networks of care and connection.

Practices which create microspheres of public education and accompaniment are explored in connection with the development of new public spaces and networks. We could call this Youth Work in Public: but it is a problematic space for girls and women and for all whose lives have been abjected and rubbished at the hands of the Public Authorities, whether these be the Border Agency or the school or the police. In this theme, we ask the question of how, whether and where the personal becomes political, and, what the role of facilitation and socio-cultural accompaniment might be in that process. This has been discussed elsewhere in relation to the question of assimilation of 'otherness to ourness', and yet, the question of how this 'ourness' is negotiated and comes into being needs further analysis (Batsleer et al., 2017).

It will be readily apparent that approaching the question of youth work with girls and women in this way rapidly and readily moves the discussion of youth work, and, specifically Girls' Work into a new space beyond those of mid-twentieth century, Local Authority provided support, and beyond coaching and mentoring based forms of practice. The vignettes which follow show the groundedness of this claim for the significance of a networked and collaborative practice.

Challenge One: Responding to and at the Border

Starting as an anti-deportation campaign for Florence Moses, a lesbian, and her son from Sierra Leone in January 2007, the Florence and Michael Campaign was supported by the Lesbian Community Project, but ran as an independent group. In February 2008, Florence and Michael were given leave to remain, as part of the Home Office amnesty for 'legacy' (long standing) cases. Florence said she could not have held out for her status without the support of the campaign. During this time, the campaign group became aware of other lesbian asylum seekers, so they decided to continue their work and formed the Lesbian Immigration Support Group (LISG), with the aim of providing support for lesbian and bisexual women asylum seekers and refugees. Around 80 countries in the world still criminalise consensual same sex acts among adults, with punishments including torture, imprison and death. There are some asylum issues specific to lesbian and bi-sexual women. As well as dealing with gender based violence and the position of women in their countries of origin often meaning they have little access to support, money or an independent life outside of the family, lesbian and bisexual women asylum seekers and refugees often find it difficult to be 'out', a western centric concept, often having spent most of their lives hiding their sexuality and experiencing horrific abuse if they were discovered. Members may have experienced verbal, physical, sexual and/or psychological abuse in home countries – therefore, women/lesbian only environments are important to enable a feeling of safety.

Fundraising is undertaken to provide travel expenses to meetings, Home Office interviews, and solicitors' appointments. Subsistence payments are made to those members who are literally destitute. Payments are also made for child care costs, interpreters, refreshments for meetings, social outings, mobile phone credits and miscellaneous other items of need. Asylum seeker and refugee members support each other and are also supported by a group of volunteers.

The process of establishing an adult sexual identity (so strongly associated with adolescence in Western psychological models) has often been one which is extremely complex for members of LISG, who are usually older as they arrive and negotiate their emergent identities alongside young locally-born-and-raised lesbians and bisexual women in the urban space. Arriving from contexts in which homosexuality remains criminalised, the group offers a space to explore the complexities and nuances of becoming openly lesbian, and of having the complexities of identity affirmed. This small support group offers affirmation and makes it possible for women to own complex and fluid identities, in which for example, 'Christian' or 'Muslim', 'mother' and 'lesbian' are not lived as classifications which cancel each other out. However, at the same time as encountering the possibility of living differently, LISG members also encounter the racism and homophobia of the Borders Agency, where there is a default position of disbelieving all asylum seekers' accounts, alongside stereotypes of what an 'out' lesbian or bisexual woman looks like and how they behave.

This was identified as an issue for women who, having arrived somewhere relatively safe, being able to be more open about their sexuality, having learnt to be able to talk about it: 'then having their sexuality completely trashed by the Home Office and the courts and no-one believed ... the really terrible thing as well is, it's not just about disbelieving the category, yeah, but disbelieving all of the experiences' (McCarthy, 2015). For one woman, echoing this description of how emotionally hard it is to tell the truth, and then to be disbelieved, led to a mental health crisis when she was detained: "I was like start, start crazy, it was very, very hard for me, it was very hard, very, very hard, I don't, ... I was like maybe the world the world is finished, maybe everything is finished in the world".

The welcoming space of a women's support group formed by the lesbian community has become a place where complex identifications can be acknowledged and explored, and the impact of everyday micro-violence, as well as State violence in the form of detention, can be owned. The group also supports women with their cases, some of which take years with multiple appeals, and the support of the group in exploring and celebrating sexual identity is important in this. This practice of trying out a new form of living and identification alongside having to prove oneself to the authorities is testing for the women involved in the group, and for those who accompany them. When a possible name change was discussed, the favoured alternative name was 'Border Crossing Women'. The proposed name reflected transitions of expressed sexuality, and of living in another country and culture. However, the group chose to remain with LISG as it had developed a strong reputation.

Girls' Work/youth work at the border is required to respond with affirmation to those whose lives are being routinely rubbished and subjected to the micro-violences of classification in the education system, in welfare systems as well as by The Border Agency. As well as responding by creating a welcoming space, community-based practice which seeks to turn otherness to ourness also requires a position in wider networks. In the example of LISG, the group is linked with The Proud Trust, the Community Choir and the wide network of lesbian households in the city and region. This network is the basis for establishing a practice of friendship which does not depend solely on the volunteers at LISG.

There are recurrent moments in the negotiation of a more equal practice that can become highly charged: a woman asylum seeker may be 'adopted' by a particular group or individual, and the personal dynamics can affect a group process in power-charged ways; women who have been successful in their applications to remain can quickly need to distance themselves from a group which reminds them of a painful moment in their lives. LISG is seen above all as a family, and the kind of relational practice discussed here participates in family-like dynamics, for good or ill. More often, the patterns of mutual support established in the group continue with some of those whose applications have been successful supporting those who have yet to succeed, and using strategically the power, presence and privilege of 'proper British' volunteers to support the legitimacy of claims. This alliance formation is a very significant aspect of community-based practice in which Girls' Work/youth work is situated.

In such spaces at the border, there is often a sense of breakdown and of complex and bottomless need, which is present to and among both participants and volunteers and to those who take paid roles in facilitating community learning. We will discuss what this means for the supervision and support of practitioners briefly at the end of the chapter. And it is in this context that the anger, always present at the border, forms the basis for the second challenge.

Challenge Two: Responding to Precarity, Anger and Alienation

A newly built youth centre in a part of the city that has been subject to much abjection (including the production of the 'poverty porn' series *People Like Us*) contains a Girls' Room. The allocation of a Girls' Room does indicate an awareness of how historically marginalised girls were, and, still are in open access youth club provision. This was much less so in 'community projects' in which women formed the backbone. Poverty, and its associated precarity, the abjection of people who live in poor neighbourhoods, and, the representation of such neighbourhoods as places of horror, produces a complex sense of shame which is borne by young women in specific ways.

The ethnographic research for *Partispace* brought to the fore many examples of young women who were dealing with complex issues of anger and mental health as well as ill health more broadly understood. We encountered young women who were using informal buddying and supporting one another with chronic illness, and others who were campaigning to have young people's mental and emotional wellbeing recognised as a serious issue. Sometimes these themes emerge in single sex spaces, and sometimes in open-access spaces where girls' friendship groups are strong. It is to the question of the challenge of depression and activation that we now turn.

Young women (more often than young men) experience diagnoses concerned with their mental health. Very often these are interpreted as essentially individual and family-based problems, and it is this which leads to common and fatalistic statements such as: 'I've got mental health' and 'My mum's got nerves'. Yet the extent of the distress among girls and women on social housing estates (just as among the asylum seeking women in LISG) suggests an alternative analysis. It is the stresses and forms of alienation imposed on children and families living in poverty which are being medicated. The following cameo taken from research fieldnotes encapsulates some of what the *Partispace* team encountered:

A. *Is a young woman in a creative youth work project in the city. When she starts to talk about her project, she says: 'It's about honesty'. Her project is about creative writing as a way of supporting people with 'mental health' as they all say, as in 'she's got mental health'. After discussion of a domestic violence project, we talk about the following dilemma: do you say it straight out, it's for women who want to leave violent partners, or do you go come and do pretty girly things and make it look innocuous, kind of disguise it so women can get out of the house? A. then explains her project: she is doing it because she has found a way of coping, she writes as a way of dealing with her own problems. She already has about 50 poems on YouTube. She used to self-harm. She has a lot of mental health problems, she goes to Child and Adolescent Mental Health Services, she is on medication, she has ADHD and depression. She used to go to another school, but she says there were too many bullies there. Her mum also has a lot of mental health problems and has problems with speaking/writing. Her mum didn't go to school. A explains how she herself tried to make friends by going out with a group who were drinking and smoking and going with boys. She got very drunk with them and was picked up by the police. After that, she was so ashamed of herself she began to self-harm and was isolating herself. When she started on medication, she didn't like it. 'I can't control myself so medication has to control me'. But now she likes it and is fine.*

This fieldnote points to the need for a form of Girls' Work/youth work practice which is attentive to mood and pressure. It points to the ways in which family, school and peer group pressures are all entangled, and the ways in which medication can become a stopping point or a place of no return. Nevertheless, A's experience of youth work was also enabling her to amplify her understanding though her poetry and her engagement with support workers in an enterprise-focussed project, through which she was able to promote the value of creative writing as a response to stress.

Other young women emphasised the significance of shame and stigma in the acknowledgement of mental health issues, which nevertheless regularly becomes a focus for campaigning. The campaigns have a dual focus: inward and outward. Voicing and making visible an experience that so many hide is the internal focus. One *YouTube* video, produced by the Youth Council, dramatized it by featuring a young woman's voice coming from behind the duvet: 'To the world it's hidden: where am I? Panic? Who am I? Fear? I can't breathe. I feel like something awful is about to happen. No matter where I try and hide from the pain it always seeps back in. Think. Breathe. Take control. I am here. Consumed by my fear. We get brilliant at covering it up and change starts with you'.

This internal focus about secrecy and breaking out of hiding overlaps with the external focus. There is, for example, recognition of how anxiety can stop young women engaging with others as well as of how young women's peer friendship groups can be places of risk. In A's story, her heavy drinking at a very young age was connected to issues of inclusion/exclusion in her friendship group. But the ways services fail to engage with young people is also evident in the process of going to the GP or not. Reluctance comes from a sense that the prescription of anti-depressants seems to be the first response. Or else it comes from the stigma associated with mental health, which means that even when young women know about services they will not use them 'because having weak mental health is seen in a negative light'.

A youth work led campaign can suggest the need for places to go for young people which would be somewhere where people want to go anyway; and the need for non-stigmatised venues and places for evenings and weekends, as well as for a single point of contact in every educational establishment. In order to be accessible to young women in the diverse communities of cities, these need to be gender specific spaces as well as gender various spaces in which women are strongly present and respected. They will also by definition be culturally specific and culturally various spaces too. Most importantly they will be non-hegemonic spaces, where women and girls who are routinely disbelieved and seen as problematic are supported and affirmed.

Microspheres of Public Education and Accompaniment: The Role of the Community-Based Girls' Worker

Henry Giroux (2005, 2013) has argued that educators who seek to challenge the devastating impacts of neoliberalism, including what he has termed the war on youth and the creation of the role of disposable populations, can take part in creating microspheres of public education. In the field of youth work, recognition has been given to the importance of creating 'small places close to home'. These microspheres can contribute to the reconstruction of a public and common ground as distinct from more corporate or governmental spaces. In cities this means staying with the trouble and difficulty of finding ways of being together, and finding ways of articulating the challenges which emerge, without too much recourse to bureaucracy.

Attentiveness and analysis (emotional, material, spatial, and historical) are basic to the craft of the Girls' Worker. Attention needs to be paid to the complexity of the relationship between the spaces of personal life, of home and family like spaces, and the spaces and practices of public life, including practices which institute a border, and the patterns of oppression and violence which may be experienced in both private and public. It is not enough to argue for a microsphere of public education in Girls' Work without considering the ways in which power is experienced and addressed in public spaces. Although ideas of empowerment have been successfully colonised and taken over by corporate agendas, it is possible to re-imagine an empowerment process which does not shame or judge individuals, but rather seeks to build networks and relationships.

Relational practice means developing the craft of creating networks of mutual support. Such networks become source of power and create the possibility of flourishing. These networks are often intergenerational and, in cities, they allow the possibility of movement between roles over time and place. The idea of people acting 'by proxy' in a network is powerful, with sufficient closeness to provide ongoing personal support and sufficient distance to enable a sustaining of support over time, in which individuals move in and out of the webs of support which are created. This relational practice is supported by means both ancient and modern, such as sharing in the growing and preparation of food, as well as by new communications systems and social media. A practice of friendship will at one and the same time include a Whatsapp message and a suitcase full of food. The ability to support and create networks requires a fluency in both recognising and meeting bodily and emotional needs in person, and in establishing many kinds of communication over a variety of distances. Girls' Work/youth work of the future will therefore be connected both locally and globally.

The role of the worker is one of facilitator and enabler (not a leader) who develops networks of support and enables courageous conversation as these redact may emerge over time. This depends on finding forms of network which can remain open, and, which challenge and unsettle border controlling practices, whilst recognising the impact of flows of power within the 'small places close to home'. These challenges may be most visible in work which builds networks between settled communities and refugees/asylum seekers, but are present in all community learning spaces. They involve the ways in which certain voices are privileged and credible within systems, and others not, and so develop forms of advocacy to make trouble visible and audible in wider democratic fora. This requires recognition and support. If the role of socio-cultural accompaniment is one which seeks to build social solidarity and turn 'otherness to ourness', the worker herself needs support. The borders of practice that we write of here are exhausting and joyful places. The history of non-managerial supervision in youth work, of action learning sets and 'each one teach one' methods will need to be drawn on to enable exploration of and critical reflection on practice.

Such independent and mutual supervision helps for example in the avoidance of assimilation practices, and forms of adoption and possessiveness which seem to remove agentic power from relationship, and locate it in the more socially advantaged groups in any network. The ability to facilitate dialogue is central to the future role of Girls' Workers as well as the ability to affirm but not reify difference, but rather to enable movement and fluidity, advocacy and enabling personal issues to become public troubles.

Conclusion

This chapter has presented a perspective on the future of youth work with girls and young women which highlights the grave dangers and threats posed to the wellbeing of women and girls, as well as men and boys, in the most disadvantaged and excluded communities. We suggest that life-affirming practice at borders must see youth work move away from acting as a border-control force – from practices of individualisation which place entire responsibility on young women to get active and have a life plan, and, which shame them when their plans fail – and towards practices which embrace, but do not commodify difference. Such praxes must understand the power struggles that occur when borders are drawn, and seek to address them alongside the less powerful participants in those struggles.

In doing so, we have highlighted the importance of a community and network based approach to practice. Cities are a vital source of such networks as they become home to more and more diverse communities seeking to live peacefully on common ground. However, lack of resource and the threat of strong and stable austerity means that such imagined practice could seem utopian. It is however the only sustainable alternative to a medicalised form of practice in which medication and short courses of counselling are offered as palliative analgesics for the microviolences of profoundly unjust border-controlling institutions.

References

Batsleer, J., Andersson, B., Hansson, S. L., Lütgens, J., Mengilli, Y., Pais, A., Pohl, A., & Wissö, T. (2017). Non-formal spaces of socio-cultural accompaniment: Responding to young unaccompanied refugees. Reflections from the partispace project. *PPi – European Education Research Journal, 17*(2), 305–322. doi:10.1177/1474904117716368

Cockburn, C. (1998). *The space between us: Negotiating gender and national identities in conflict*. London: Zed Books.

Gilbert, J. (2014). *Common ground: Democracy and collectivity in an age of individualism*. London: Pluto.

Giroux, H. (2005). *Border crossings: Cultural workers and the politics of education*. New York, NY: Routledge.

Giroux, H. (2013). *America's education deficit and the war on youth*. New York, NY: Monthly Review Press.

Haraway, D. (2016). *Staying with the trouble: Making Kin in the Chluctucene*. Durham: Duke University Press.

McCarthy, K. (2015). *What is the experience of lesbian asylum seekers of living their sexuality in their home countries and in the UK?* (Unpublished MA Dissertation). University of Zambia, Lusaka.

McGimpsey, I. (2017). Late neoliberalism: Delineating a policy regime. *Critical Social Policy, 37*(1), 64–84.

Mohanty, C. T. (2003). *Feminism without borders. Decolonising theory. Practicing solidarity*. Durham: Duke University Press.

Soni, S. (2011). *Working with diversity in youth and community work*. Exeter: Learning Matters.

Young, I. M. (1990). *Justice and the politics of difference*. Princeton, NJ: Princeton University Press.

Yuval-Davis, N. (2005). Racism, cosmopolitanism and the contemporary politics of belonging. *Soundings, 30*, 166–178.

CHAPTER 12

Towards New Horizons? 'Youth and Community Work' and Rhizomatic Possibilities

Graham Bright and Carole Pugh

Introduction[1]

While the future of neoliberalism is contested, its impact on youth and community work in England and beyond cannot be overstated. The hostile environment which it has created over the last 20-plus years has fundamentally (de-)sculpted the form, vitality and quality of practice. Whilst the demise of neoliberalism may be longed for, longing alone is un-pragmatic. Critical engagement with theoretical understandings supports us to 'name the world' (Freire, 1972); but naming must lead to action. This chapter considers the 'resilience'[2] of youth and community work values and pedagogical approaches in England, which, we trust also speaks to wider contexts. Drawing on analytics from plant physiology, it considers the possibilities presented by conceptualising youth and community work values and practices as 'rhizomatic'. Rhizomes are underground networks of plant roots which store starch, protein and nutrients, enabling the plant to survive in unfavourable conditions. Rhizomes have the capability to propagate asexually, producing both roots and stems, creating new plants, and supporting expansion and movement. By exploring key rhizomatic features of interconnectedness, linear interruption, threshold-border operations and reproduction/reconstitution, together with their capacity for expansion and escape (Deleuze & Guattari, 2015), we seek to highlight potential sites and sources of resistance, and trace roots/routes that can sustain.

Neoliberalism and Youth and Community Work as 'Actually Existing'

The hegemonic 'norms' of pervasively enculturated neoliberal rationalities, together with their usurpation and 'assault' of democracy (Brown, 2015), welfare (Juhilia et al., 2017) and education (Ball, 2017) by means of reductionist, positivist, managerialist and monetarist discourses are now well rehearsed (Brown, 2015; Cahill, 2015; Davies, 2017). Analyses of its effects have been comprehensively extended to youth and community work, and demonstrate how the very telos and character of practice has been transmogrified towards the narrow pursuit of different forms of capital accumulation and management (Taylor et al., 2018; de St Croix, 2016, 2017) via the assimilative forces of technicist and performative rationalities (de St Croix, 2017; Duffy, 2017a, 2017b). While youth and community work has been harnessed, assimilated and decimated by successive waves of neoliberal governmentality, it continues to survive in different forms, due to its practitioners' passionate commitment to its values and ideals (de St Croix, 2016).

Recently however, neoliberalism's future seems to have been momentarily contested. Perhaps its dominance is limited (Davies, 2017), as belief in its veneered logic, much like the cladding on London's Grenfell Tower,[3] begins to crumble, burn and fail. But despite the continuing economic and social degeneration stemming from the pursuit and acceleration of its policy approaches, the neoliberal perennial shows fundamentally little sign of abeyance. Cahill (2015) argues that this is because academics, policy makers, 'progressive' thinkers and actors, and indeed, the public at large, have misunderstood, and have been misled in thinking about, its deeply embedded and enculturated nature. Indeed, Cahill posits that there is a rupture between imagined and 'actually existing' neoliberalism as a 'durable and embedded' parasitic phenomenon capable of adaption and evolution (ibid.). Those who hope for, fight for and prophesy neoliberalism's demise, and a return to something more socio-democratic, perhaps risk being cruelly duped (Berlant, 2011). The question for youth and community work as vehicle of critical pedagogical and democratic action, is 'how should we now respond'? Perhaps the starting point in addressing this question is to examine 'actually existing' youth and community work.

Back to the Future?

The first one hundred and fifty years of youth and community work as a movement and profession, witnessed the proliferation of particular forms of physical and professional architecture – buildings designed as associative spaces for practice that reflected the mores, tastes and practice approaches of the day, discrete organisational and management structures and strong professional networks which signalled and amplified particular statuses and identities for youth and community work as something to be valued.

The erosion and decimation of these and other architectures (with few notable exceptions aside) over the last two decades is all too clear. Much youth and

FIGURE 12.1

YMCA Newcastle, Blackett
Street. Opened in 1900, it
included two halls to seat 700
and 300 people, a reception
room, reading room and library
(Sitelines, DU)

community work has been amalgamated, shifted, cajoled and contorted into
mechanisms of diffuse network governance (Birrell & Gray, 2017), designed to
steer particular cohorts of young people uncritically in the 'right' direction.
Simultaneously, through threat, fear, precarity and the realities of decimation
(Jones, 2016; Unison, 2016), many practitioners have found themselves working in ways that are contrary to their personal and professional values, and of
attempting to find spaces for subtly resistant forms of practice that maintain
both integrity and identity. Inevitably, some have been more successful than
others. Youth and community work is founded on a commitment to 'name the
world' (Freire, 1972), both as it is, and, as it could be. In justifying resistance
and its own survival, the Profession has albeit reluctantly, played the neoliberal
game, and, in doing so has inadvertently risked propagating the very system
that seeks the assimilated destruction of the democratic and collectivist ideals
it espouses. In naming *itself* therefore, youth and community work, needs to
evaluate the extent to which it has become critically acceptant of, and systemi-
cally complicit in the processes of neoliberal injustice it critiques.

   Austerity has hit youth and community work hard morally, professionally, financially and structurally. It has been dissembled (Youdell & McGimpsey, 2014); its architecture lies desolate, empty (Allan & Youdell, 2017) and

arborified[4] (Deleuze & Guattari, 2015). Yet, it strangely continues to exist in different ways. Drawing on Derrida (1994), Allan and Youdell (2017: 74) describe this as a form of ghosting, of 'actively erasing a person or thing, while creating an impression of its continued presence'. Ghostings represent an unnatural attachment to something that has died, or the eternal mourning of an entity that exists in a liminal, half-life, or zombified state. The living embody the ghost, they become its crypt and ventriloquize its speech (Derrida, 1994). Youth and community work it would appear is ghosted through particular discourses of policy and practice. It continues to appear discursively in relation to particular forms of control, crisis intervention and ideologically driven 'opportunities' like the National Citizen Service (NCS), and in the peripheral fabric of particular localised practices. It makes transmogrified appearances at moments of political expediency. But the profession is also ghosted by its own practitioners. Some speak of a return to the now 'empty architecture' (Allan and Youdell, op. cit.) of 'the good old days'. They are right, perhaps, to hope – who would deny them? But their optimism may yet prove to be a cruel distraction (Berlant, 2011).

As a profession, youth and community work must continue to draw axiologically on its past. But it must find new expressions, spaces and architectures for the reification and critical animation of its values as 'an emancipatory practice for social justice' (Coburn & Gormally, 2017: 33) that meet the needs of *today's* young people and the communities of which they are a part. In doing so, it must take account of neoliberalism's durability and its continuously pernicious ability to assimilate everything within its reach in its advancing its own hegemony, and its all-pervasive pursuit of capital accrual via 'discourse, institutional morphology and subjectivity' (McGimpsey, 2017: 67). New, responsive and mobile architectures, capable of territorialising 'smooth spaces'[5] (Skott-Myhre, 2009) of practice beyond neoliberal reach are required.

Whilst examining the realities and causes of the current predicament, Jeffs (2015) argues the necessity of remaking youth and community work for wider democratic regeneration. Drawing on history, Jeffs demonstrates how the Profession's immanent capacities for change, innovation and renewal have often been characterised by grass-roots responsiveness to local need. Structural decimation means that the passion of grass-roots practitioners (de St Croix, 2016) is once again the Profession's best hope. Youth and community work therefore needs to move from attempting to generate itself out of assumptive, pre-existing knowns (Coburn & Gormally, 2015, 2017) with the implicit burden of ghosted memories, towards *re-generation* that pays attention to values, whilst beginning to imagine how practice might begin to look in resistantly occupying new spaces and places in promoting social justice and change. This points

us towards *re*imagining and *re*claiming the Profession, not as binary, or arbore-
ally stagnant, but as rhizomatically becoming.

Exploring Rhizomes

The rhizome is an analytical device that critiques binary systems of organisation, logic and reality (Deleuze & Guattari, 2015). Rhizomatics challenge us
to think in connective multiplicities, rather than singularities; they move us
beyond what was, or is, towards a continuous focus on what *might be*. The rhizome is 'an underground root system, an open decentralized network, which
branches out to all sides, unpredictably and horizontally' (Loots et al., 2013:
111) – '... a structure that spreads under the ground in all directions at once and
connects to everything' (Skott-Myhre, 2009: 83). '[R]hizomes are acentered
multiplicities, composed of heterogenous elements that form connections and
change as they come into composition, always in a fluid state of becoming
different as they move from one threshold to another' (Strom & Martin, 2017:
6). Binary (or tree) logic is replaced by the possibilities of ceaselessly created
'ands' – of connective and generative multiplicities that produce the yet to be
imagined. Subterranean, like burrows, they offer 'shelter, supply, movement,
evasion and breakout' (Deleuze & Guattari, 2015: 5). 'These are the spaces of
the subjectum,[6] or the spaces that constantly exceed the definitions of boundaries and limits' (Skott-Myhre, 2009: 82). They are spaces of production that
are fluid and ever-changing in composition and duration. Their multiplicities
generate lines of flight that enable escape, thus subverting regimes of power.
They have infinite capacities to find ways around. Rhizomes are immanent
and liminal – self-renewing, always becoming, always between. Their liminality represents an 'intuitive sense of pure possibility' (Skott-Myhre et al.,
2016: 6), a counterforce to the abstract immanent machinery of global capitalism. They inhabit thresholds, and are capable of creating spaces and practices
that raise and express desire, yet which are beyond language, and thus capture
(Skott-Myhre, 2009; Skott-Myhre et al., 2016).

    Many historical/existing youth and community assemblages (taken
here as the spaces, localities, artefacts, histories, language, narratives, discourses, relationships, subjectivities, identities, practices, flows, architectures,
finances and forces that constitute practice) have been assimilated and dissembled by distinct and unfolding phases of neoliberal governance (Youdell &
McGimpey, 2014; McGimpsey, 2017). *Rhizomatic* assemblages however present
opportunities to go beyond the structural bindings of existing desolations, to
actively reconstitute praxes through critical *re*assemblages that reimagine the

reconstitution of the 'diverse elements ... [and] productive relations ... [with] multiple significances, potentialities and realisations' (ibid.: 119) that can shape future work. Thus, youth and community work holds the potential to reimagine and reconstitute itself once more as a 'field of immanent relations' (Skott-Myhre et al., 2016: 6) that is committed to praxes of continual becoming which seek to promote a more just society (Coburn & Gormally, 2017). Youth work reassemblages must therefore be imagined as sites of subjectum (Skott-Myhre, 2009), as critically collaborative pedagogical spaces that dialogue, understand, plan, act, resist and revolt (Skott-Myhre et al., 2016). Rhizomatic reassemblages should continually seek out new and 'smooth spaces' (Skott-Myhre, 2009) beyond the striated contours of mutating neoliberal assimilation, whilst recognising that 'each contingent assemblage of desire is fodder for social reappropriation' (Skott-Myhre, 2016: 26). '[T]he logic of rule must always frantically follow behind the burrows and rhizomes of the subjectum' (Skott-Myhre, 2009: 86). This points to the necessity of continually creating infinite mutability – of perpetually going beyond existing frames of reference that are all too easily decoded and subjugated by the matrix of capitalist logic. Such reassemblages must therefore continually remake practice, territorialise new maps and understand continually shifting topographies, rather than be stultified by tracing over what was, or is (Deleuze & Guattari, 2015). They must be committed to continual co-creative processes of dissembling and reassembling, to deteritorialising and reterritorializing, to becoming, over being, to fluidity over fixedness, and to the pursuit of critical alliances beyond silos. Critical rhizomatics thus hold the potential to become a form of 'practical anarchism' (de St Croix, 2016: 182) that continually trick, unsettle and usurp fluid relations of power.

Rhizomes occupy becoming spaces of ecotonal encounter: 'borderland places where ecologies are in tension, where the interplay of resources and nutrients contain the characteristic species of each ecological community. These overlapping communities are places of complexity and dynamism, generating rich possibilities for change' (Linds et al., 2010: xiii). Rhizomatic praxes thus reflect the border-dialogical pedagogies of youth and community work (Coburn, 2010; Giroux, 2005). They continuously territorialise smooth and possibilising spaces of encounter that afford understandings of shared experiences, differences and generative collaboration (Coburn & Gormally, 2017). They 'ceaselessly [establish] connections between semiotic chains [and] organisations of power' (Deleuze & Guattari, 2015: 6). Border-rhizomes are unfolding, and, continuously contingent sites of synergy and creative bricolage:

> By crossing borders, we come to meet, understand, and osmose others' worlds, and, in doing so, understand ourselves and our place in the world

more fully. We are enabled to critically recognise the power, intersubjec-
tivities and oppression of differing privileges and positionalities. Border
pedagogy challenges our existing, limited worldviews. It is education.
(Bright et al., 2018: 207)

Rhizomatic-border practices are not only sites of exchange, excitement, reju-
venation and flow, but of sometimes uncomfortable hybridity – contradictory
spaces that challenge our sense of perspective, fixedness/contingency, identity, telos and becoming (Anzaldúa, 2012). Yet, they enable us to continuously
reimagine issues of social (in)justice and what our critically collaborative
responses to them might be. Rhizomatic border work holds the potential to
enhance professional perspectives and practices, and, to critically enrich the
communities with which we work. As Bolt (2009: 107) argues:

> Border praxis is fundamentally concerned with metaphoric doorsteps,
> stepping from one experience, or perspective to another and often

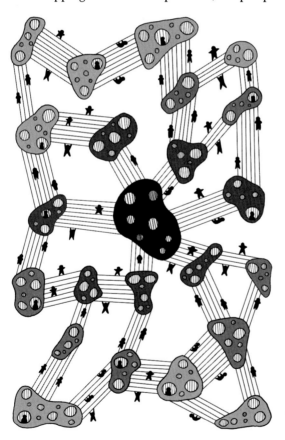

FIGURE 12.2
'Rhizomatic Lines of Flight' by
Bryony Watson, BA (Hons)
Illustration Student, York St
John University, UK (used here
with permission)

staying and creating on the limits between experiences. Border praxis is about edges, verges, margins, collisions and intersections – all thresholds into new perceptions.

Like the dialogical pedagogy of youth and community work, rhizomatic praxes interrupt assumptive limits and linearities, allowing thought, experiment and action to flow and develop in creatively unexpected directions. Rhizomatic work is therefore already central, indeed second nature, to youth and community work at the 'everyday' or micro levels of practice interactions; the challenge however is to consider how we might rhizomatically reimagine and release the development and organisation of practice on more 'macro' scales.

Rhizomatic Histories

History and discursive memory should never be cast aside in futurizing practice. They can teach us, provide continuance and sustenance, and inform identity. They can be moral compasses for our work. But they should never bind or deceive us into particular forms of constrictive action that fail to address the social, educational, spiritual and political needs and desires of today's young people as they are experienced. Youth and community work must *remain* an ethical profession, not one that discourses voids for self-justificatory and ultimately disempowering means (Seal & Harris, 2016; after Illich, 1977). The early history of youth and community work has much to teach us about rhizomatic practice. Individuals and (often small) collectives met local needs, and practice developed and spread through a growing series of connective networks (Bright, 2015) that shared broadly similar ideals. There are also some striking socio-political similarities between the Profession's early history and the landscapes which it finds itself in today – a *laissez faire* state that cares little, beyond discipline, for young people and communities, particularly those that are more disadvantaged. Similarly, there is fractured and contested professional infrastructure and architecture – yet desire continues to stir.

Later facets of the Profession's histories also mirror rhizomatic ideals. During the late nineteenth and early twentieth centuries, a range of services that crossed borders and thresholds of provision were developed in response to the needs of local communities. Many YMCAs for example provided affordable housing, ran saving schemes, housed educational and leisure facilities, promoted arts and sporting interests and even held medical dispensaries (Solly, 1867; Stanley, 1890). Early youth work training courses reflected debates regarding the threshold nature of practice, and whether it should be principally founded on educational or social work ideals (Davies, 1999). The introduction of 'emergency' full-time courses, and recognition of youth leadership as a potential full-time 'professional' career (Bradford, 2007/2008) generated a number of tensions, which required the creation of distinct (and complicated) professional training structures that recognized the interconnected network of volunteers, 'part-time' and 'full-time' staff.

Before the investment generated by the Albemarle Report, which sought to replace the dingy unsuitable premises, that around 80% of clubs were using (Sewell, 1966), rhizomatic tendencies to expand and escape were again to be found. Where no space was 'provided', youth work expanded into spaces that were left vacant. Despite a 'crippling absence of funds', youth work found and claimed unused, abandoned spaces, comprising 'derelict chapels and schools, even derelict air-raid shelters, warehouses, decayed town mansions' (Ministry of Education, 1960: 64). These had been pressed in to service through 'determined leadership and a valiant spirit of self-help' (ibid.), turning them into places where young people could meet. Investment in physical buildings was mirrored by investment in training infrastructures. An emergency national training college was established to double number of full-time youth leaders and the first recognised qualification for youth work was laid down (Davies, 1999). The formation of the Joint Negotiating Committee to oversee the qualification, required the synthesis of a range of heterogeneous elements into an alliance to agree the direction that professional training should take. The entry of the state into the delivery of much provision represented another border crossed, a new 'line of flight', but not one that was universally welcomed.

The emergence of Thatcherism, in the 1980s with its neoliberal underpinnings began to undermine youth work professionalism and resources (Bradford, 2015). Much English statutory youth work was reduced to little more than ad hoc recreational provision, lacking purpose and critical theoretical understanding, although 'bright spots' of practice remained, often in Women's or black political movements (Smith, 1988: 81). The election of New Labour in 1997 heralded a re-investment in youth work, but bought with requirements to target, monitor and demonstrate the monetary 'value' of the work; again rhizomatic roots of critical emancipatory practice retreated underground, providing the potential to sustain practice in an environment that was colonised.

Rhizomatic Futures

Rhizomatic practices have been central to youth and community work's history and development. Given current conditions, we argue their centrality for its future(s). Rhizomatic thought calls us to reimagine youth and community work, not as singular, but as a polyvalent multiplicity of innovatively interconnected structures and praxes that share the same axiological commitment to critical and emancipatory thinking and action (Morciano & Mercio, 2017).[7]

Rhizomatic assemblages are synergistic fusions of critically creative force: '[w]asp and orchid, as heterogeneous elements, form a rhizome ... the rhizome is alliance, uniquely alliance' (Deleuze & Guattari, 2015: 9/26). These words demand that we continue to cross borders, to generate critical syntheses: firstly, that we continually cross the borders of young people's lives in order that we might understand their worlds as *they* live them, rather than as we imagine them to be. Secondly, that we cross borders in order to (re-)build networks and political alliances. And thirdly, that we cross professional borders in order to rebuild generative alliances with those who may hold similar values. As one English youth worker put it in a recent research interview:

> The Profession is a custodian of timeless values ... youth work doesn't own these values, it might bring them together in a unique way, but they are going on elsewhere. Youth workers have no monopoly on compassion, or emancipatory education. They can happen anywhere.

These dialogues between youth and community workers and young people and communities, between practitioners and other professionals, between practitioners and politicians and amongst the profession itself, are all potential lines of flight, generative trajectories of flow, and (re-)assemblages of creative, critical force (Youdell & McGimpsey, 2014).

> Becomings are created through alliances, as bodies, ideas, forces and other elements come into composition in assemblages, and produce something new, different. (Strom & Martin, 2017: 8)

Rhizomatic praxes thus dare us to imagine, think and act beyond known borders and existing spaces in developing heterogeneous lines of flight (Skott-Myhre, 2009) in the pursuit of social justice. They demand that we allow desire to flow, and that we challenge our own constructed staticity (Bolt, 2009), in order to address internal and external forms of discursive, professional and psychic resistance in enabling new imaginaries and frontiers of practice to be developed.

This is a rhizomatic moment – a moment of desire that offers hope of eudemonic renewal in the face of apparent devastation:

> A rhizome may be broken, shattered at a given spot, but it will start up
> again on one of its old lines, or on new lines. (Deleuze & Guattari, 2015: 8)

Ironically, neoliberalism has unwittingly induced particular lines of professional flight that represent rich rhizomatic possibilities. The decimation of traditional forms of practice has resulted in many youth and community workers
crossing borders of practice to work in a variety of different settings. Graduate destination data (see for example Ord, n.d.; Lake et al., n.d.) suggest there
remains a demand for youth and community practitioners in different arenas
including community engagement, housing, health, targeted and early intervention work, pupil engagement, sports development and child protection.
Whilst arguably this might be seen as harvesting youth and community work
skills for other agendas, or as a siphoning of skills from the traditional values
and principles of practice, it also presents opportunities for the rhizomatic
proliferation of praxis beyond existing borders. Such work holds the potential
to speak truth to systems and architectures of power where young people are,
and affords the potential to think and act collaboratively in transforming them
(Coburn & Gormally, 2017). Yet, as with any line of flight, it is essential to remain
alive to capitalism's creeping territorialisation, and to continue to move, flow
and territorialise the new and smooth spaces that are always beyond.

Conclusion

This chapter should not be read as an abandonment of youth and community
work's traditional values and practices. We believe in the potency and trans-
formational potential of relational informal education with young people that
embraces the core principle of voluntary association. We remain rhizomatically committed to this AND to the extension of these principles in the borders
beyond existing and traditional domains of practice, and thus argue for the
reclamation AND advancement of spaces in which youth and community
work is practiced. Such reclamation however cannot merely be a tracing; it
must be a new cartography. However, we concur with de St Croix (2016: 187)
who maps excellent suggestions regarding the generation of alternative practices – including:
– starting a youth work 'business' that questions and rejects market-orientated
  values and supports young people in campaigning;
– opening up a youth centre to young people as often as possible, rather than
  only at standard times;

- forming a non-hierarchical youth workers' cooperative based on principles of critical youth work and cooperation; and
- claiming spaces for open access, anti-oppressive and critical work with young people.

Clearly, the reconfiguration of practice must take account of, and, fictively think beyond, the realities of present conditions. We have argued in this chapter that this can be achieved through the development of locally responsive networks that are committed to thinking and acting rhizomatically in extending practice beyond the limits of its own borders. We contend that youth and community work is fundamentally rhizomatic in nature, but that more needs to be done to conceptualise and consciously enact it in this way. These responses may be practical and structural and involve close and honest self-examination. The challenge is to maintain values, whilst remaining open to establishing connections without restrictive preconditions in enabling practice to move beyond familiar borders. This however raises particular questions regarding the futures of the Profession – not least what such futures might mean for youth and community work in occupying the spaces 'in between', for professional youth and community work education, and indeed, for 'youth and community work' as a title for such a creatively diverse set of practices.[8] What is clear however is the continuing need for practices that continuously reimagine and embody the civil sphere, and, which work *with* people *where they are* to promote collaborative learning, and raise critical consciousness in the pursuit of more just societies.

Notes

1   This chapter can be read in its own right, but can also be viewed as complementary to, and as a development of, our thinking in Chapter 3 of this text. Our work here is indebted to Hans Skott-Myhre, and in particular his treatment of rhizomatic ideas in *Youth and Subculture as Creative Force*.

2   A word that has been assimilated in so many different ways, which we seek to reclaim here.

3   Grenfell outwardly implied improving conditions for all, but shrouded a system of privatised interest, outsourced management, competitive cost cutting and austere starvation of state resources which highlighted the disregard paid to the concerns, and ultimately the lives, of those for whom the building was home.

4   Arborified – to be, or become like a tree. Deleuze and Guattari differentiated between the 'either-or' binaries and categorisations of 'tree logic' that can be seen in many social and organisational hierarchies, and rhizomatic processes which

enable creative fusion and escape from forces of encroachment. In our view, neo-liberalism has resulted in arborified professional structures and practices.

5   Spaces which have not yet been territorialized by capitalist forces.

6   Collaborative subjects of creative critical force, which exist outside and beyond different forms of limitation and oppression.

7   Morciano and Mercio (2017: 43) describe youth work as a 'polyvalent and multifaceted educational and social practice', and argue that examining and celebrating the diversity of its practices and locations is more fruitful than attempting to fixedly define its characteristics. This chimes with Duffy (2017a: 37) who argues that youth work 'defies a bounded definition'.

References

Allan, J., & Youdell, D. (2017). Ghostings, materialisations and flows in Britain's special educational needs and disability assemblage. *Discourse: Studies in the Cultural Politics of Education, 38*(1), 70–82.

Anzaldúa, G. (2012). *Borderlands* (4th ed.). San Francisco, CA: Aunt Lute Books.

Ball, S. (2017). *The great education debate* (3rd ed.). Bristol: Policy Press.

Berlant, L. (2011). *Cruel optimism.* London: Duke University Press.

Birrell, D., & Gray, A. M. (2017). *Delivering social welfare.* Bristol: Policy Press.

Bolt, J. (2009). *Border pedagogy for democratic practice.* Saarbrücken: Dr. Muller Aktiengesllshcaft & Co.

Bradford, S. (2007/2008). Practices, policies and professionals: Emerging discourses of expertise in English youth work, 1939–1951. *Youth and Policy, 97/98*, 13–28.

Bright, G. (2015). The early history of youth work practice. In G. Bright (Ed.), *Youth work: Histories, policy and contexts.* London: Palgrave Macmillan.

Bright, G., Thompson, N., Hart, P., & Hayden, B. (2018). Faith-based youth work: Education, engagement and ethics. In P. Alldred, F. Cullen, K. Edwards, & D. Fusco (Eds.), *The Sage handbook of youth work practice.* London: Sage Publishers.

Brown, W. (2015). *Undoing the demos.* New York, NY: Zone Books.

Cahill, D. (2015). *The end of laissez-faire: On the durability of embedded neoliberalism.* Cheltenham: Edward Elgar Press.

Coburn, A. (2010). Youth work as border pedagogy. In J. Batsleer & B. Davies (Eds.), *What is youth work?* Exeter: Learning Matters.

Coburn, A., & Gormally, S. (2015). Youth work in schools. In G. Bright (Ed.), *Youth work: Histories, policy and contexts.* London: Palgrave Macmillan.

Coburn, A., & Gormally, S. (2017). *Communities for social change.* New York, NY: Peter Lang Publishing.

Davies, B. (1999). *A history of the youth service in England Volume 1: 1939–1979 from voluntarism to welfare state*. Leicester: National Youth Agency.

Davies, W. (2017). *The limits of neoliberalism*. London: Sage Publications.

Deleuze, G., & Guattari, F. (2015). *A thousand plateaus*. London: Bloomsbury.

Derrida, J. (1994). *Specters of Marx: The state of debt, the work of mourning, & the new international* (P. Kamuf, Trans.). London: Routledge.

de St Croix, T. (2016). *Grassroots youth work: Policy, passion and resistance in practice*. Bristol: Policy Press.

de St Croix, T. (2017). Youth work, performativity and the new youth impact agenda: Getting paid for numbers? *Journal of Education Policy, 33*(3), 414–438. Retrieved from http://dx.doi.org/10.1080/02680939.2017.1372637

Duffy, D. M. (2017a). *Evaluation and governing in the 21st century*. London: Palgrave Macmillan.

Duffy, D. M. (2017b). Scientism, governance and evaluation: Challenging the 'good science' of the UK evaluation agenda for youth work. *Youth and Policy, 116*, 45–61.

Freire, P. (1972). *Pedagogy of the oppressed*. London: Penguin.

Giroux, H. A. (2005). *Border crossings: Cultural workers and the politics of education* (2nd ed.). Abingdon: Routledge.

Illich, I. (1977). *Disabling professions*. Abingdon: RoutledgeFarmer.

Jeffs, T. (2015). Innovation and youth work. *Youth and Policy, 114*, 75–95.

Jones, H. (2016). Youth work in England: An uncertain future? In M. Heathfield & D. Fusco (Eds.), *Youth and inequality in education: Global actions in youth work*. Abingdon: Routledge.

Juhila, K., Raitakari, S., & Hall, C. (Eds.). (2017). *Responsibilisation at the margins of welfare services*. Abingdon: Routledge.

Lake, J., Stockham, K., & Smith, C. (n.d.). *Where are they now? Tracing destinations of youth and community work graduates*. Retrieved December 11, 2017, from http://www.tagpalycw.org/tagnews/where-are-they-now-tracing-destinations-youth-community-work-graduates

Linds, W., Gorlett, L., & Sammel, A. (2010). Introduction. In W. Linds, L. Gorlett, & A. Sammel (Eds.), *Emancipatory practices: Adult/youth engagement for social and environmental justice*. Rotterdam, The Netherlands: Sense Publishers.

Loots, G., Coppens, K., & Serminj, J. (2013). Practising a rhizomatic perspective in narrative research. In M. Andrews, C. Squire, & M. Tamboukou (Eds.), *Doing narrative research*. London: Sage Publications.

McGimpsey, I. (2017). Late neoliberalism: Delineating a policy regime. *Critical Social Policy, 37*(1), 64–84.

Morciano, D., & Mercio, M. (2017). Critical youth work for youth-driven innovation: A theoretical framework. In S. Bastien & H. B. Holmarsdottir (Eds.), *Youth as architects of social change*. London: Palgrave Macmillan.

Ord, J. (n.d.). *Copy of youth and community work jobs*. Retrieved December 11, 2017, from https://prezi.com/bzk_vs-rvc3m/copy-of-youth-community-work-jobs/

Seal, M., & Harris, P. (2016). *Responding to youth violence through youth work*. Bristol: Policy Press.

Skott-Myhre, H. (2016). Shizoanalysing the encounters of young people and adults: The question of desire. In H. Skott-Myhre, V. Pacini-Ketchabaw, & K. S. G. Skott-Myhre (Eds.), *Youth work, early education, and psychology: Liminal encounters*. London: Palgrave Macmillan.

Skott-Myhre, H., Pacini-Ketchabaw, V., & Skott-Myhre, K. S. G. (2016). Introduction. In H. Skott-Myhre, V. Pacini-Ketchabaw, & K. S. G. Skott-Myhre (Eds.), *Youth work, early education, and psychology: Liminal encounters*. London: Palgrave Macmillan.

Skott-Myhre, H. A. (2009). *Youth and subculture as creative force*. Toronto: University of Toronto Press.

Smith, M. (1988). *Developing youth work. Informal education, mutual aid and popular practice*. Milton Keynes: Open University Press.

Strom, K. J., & Martin, A. D. (2017). *Becoming-teacher*. Rotterdam, The Netherlands: Sense Publishers.

Taylor, T., Connaughton, P., de St Croix, T., Davies, B., & Grace, P. (2018). The impact of neoliberalism upon the character and purpose of English youth work and beyond. In P. Alldred, F. Cullen, K. Edwards, & D. Fusco (Eds.), *The Sage handbook of youth work practice*. London: Sage Publications.

Unison. (2016). *A future at risk – Cuts in youth services*. Retrieved October 24, 2016, from https://www.unison.org.uk/content/uploads/2016/08/23996.pdf

Youdell, D., & McGimpsey, I. (2014). Assembling, disassembling and reassembling 'youth services' in Austerity Britain. *Critical Studies in Education, 2014*, 1–15.

Index